Robert Owen, and His Social Philosophy

William Lucas Sargant

THE MAKING OF ENGLAND.

Time was when elementary education meant simply the three R's. But the day is rapidly approaching, if, indeed, in some Council Schools it has not already arrived, when the training and care given to children of the working-class will not lag far behind the essentials—though it will always lack the amenities—of those provided for the children of wealthy parents in expensive private schools. The latest step in this advance is indicated in a new syllabus issued by the Board of Education on the physical training of school children. In it reference is made to the unhealthy conditions of town life, and to the need of organised bodily exercises calculated to promote a harmonious physical development. But the syllabus does not only prescribe a formal drill, it advocates games. It even condescends to name such well-established favourites as "Fox and Geese," "London Bridge," and "Leap Frog." We are at a loss, however—perhaps it is our insular prejudice—to understand why French "Blind Man's Buff" should be preferred to the English variety. Perhaps some one will ask a question in Parliament about this. Dancing, too, is to be recognised as a branch of physical culture, but only in the case of morris dances and reels. There is no educational value, it appears, in either the Kitchen Lancers or the Cake Walk. Some will remember that dancing was a very important item in the school for factory children established by Robert Owen, who was the father not only of the Factory Laws and the co-operative movement, but also of modern education.

It is interesting to note, by the way, that two of these reforms, as we are accustomed to consider them, are being attacked by Professor Karl Pearson. In a pamphlet, "The problem of Practical Eugenics," he declares that our elaborate education laws and our refusal to

birth-rate. The child, who used to be a "pecuniary asset," as in the days of Defoe, who reported joyfully that in a certain district there was "not a thing of four years but earned its living by its hands." Now, says Professor Pearson, children are only a source of expense to parents, sometimes (as when working by expectant mothers is forbidden) actually a cause of loss of income. There is no doubt that Professor Pearson calls attention here to a very serious question. Mr. Rowntree has already pointed out the insufficiency of a working-man's income before his children begin to make money, and this point—the actual need of the children's earnings—must not be forgotten in plans for raising the school age. But there can be no turning back from the path of education and factory legislation. This wealthy country must not depend on the labour of children. But social reform will turn its attention later to the problem of relief.

9.3

16/6

H∖
6%o
.01
5≃

∶ ↳ .

ROBERT OWEN,

AND

HIS SOCIAL PHILOSOPHY.

BY

WILLIAM LUCAS SARGANT,

AUTHOR OF " SOCIAL INNOVATORS," ETC.

LONDON:

SMITH, ELDER AND CO., 65, CORNHILL.

———

M.DCCC.LX.

1860

PREFACE.

WHEN I published a volume on *Social Innovators*, about a year ago, I was asked why I left Robert Owen out of my list. My answer was, that while I was writing and even printing that work, Owen was living and was engaged upon his autobiography.

He died in November 1858; having appointed as his literary executors, his eldest son, Mr. Pare of Dublin, and Dr. Travis of London. Soon afterwards, I determined upon the present volume, and began to collect materials for it, to complete those I already possessed.

I wrote to Mr. Pare, with whom I had an acquaintance of long standing, to request his assistance. He kindly offered me a number of books to which I had no other access, furnished me with private information, and volunteered to read over what I should write. I accordingly sent my manuscript chapter by chapter; and I have to offer Mr. Pare my cordial thanks for having performed the wearisome task which he spontaneously undertook, and for having thus given to my book a nearer approach to completeness and authenticity than I could have otherwise claimed for it.

It must not be supposed, however, that Mr. Pare agrees with me in the opinions I have expressed, or in the estimate I have formed of the value of Owen's doctrine and achievements. These have not even been, to any extent, a subject of discussion between us. Mr. Pare's attention has been confined to the bare supervision of the facts I have related.

CONTENTS.

CHAPTER I.

CHAPTER II.

CHAPTER III.

CHAPTER IV.

CHAPTER V.

CHAPTER VI.

CHAPTER VII.

CHAPTER VIII.

CHAPTER IX.

CHAPTER X.

CHAPTER XI.

CHAPTER XII.

CHAPTER XIII.

CHAPTER XIV.

CHAPTER XV.

CHAPTER XVI.

CHAPTER XVII.

CHAPTER XVIII.

CHAPTER XIX.

CHAPTER XX.

CHAPTER XXI.

CHAPTER XXII.

CHAPTER XXX.

PART II.

CHAPTER XXXI.

CHAPTER XXXII.

CHAPTER XXXIII.

CHAPTER XXXIV.

INTRODUCTION.

THE present generation is ignorant of the important position which Robert Owen once held. Young men, and even those of middle age, think of him as the founder of an obscure political sect among the uneducated classes; as an heresiarch, whose publications are unknown in polite society, and are not even to be seen on the counters of respectable newsvendors; as one whose writings have long been proscribed for their downright infidelity, and for their ambiguous teaching, as reported by his enemies, on the topic of marriage.

We have all of us indeed, heard of New Lanark, and of the extraordinary success achieved in improving the condition of its people; but if the untravelled among us were asked to fix its position on the map, many, I fear, would hesitate between England and Scotland, and some might confound the place with New Harmony in the United States.

Owen lived so long, that the remembrance of the good he accomplished was interred even before his bones. His proceedings during the last thirty or forty years, had been so entirely apart from the ordinary current of affairs, that the man himself was forgotten. In 1857, at the great Educational Conference in London, when a feeble, white-haired man, took an irregular place on the platform, and tried to get a hearing for notions apparently quite beside, or perhaps above, the questions at issue; many persons, hearing the name of the intruder, pronounced that he must be the son of the notorious Robert Owen of their childhood.

Yet there were men present at that Educational Conference, who were familiar with the wrinkled face and attenuated frame of the utopian; and who, in their deep respect for what the old man had once accomplished, and in their reverential pity for his obscure old age, unwillingly lent themselves to the necessary refusal to hear the last dull droppings of his sense. Lord Brougham and the Marquis of Lansdowne had not forgotten the time, when the name of Owen, and even his person, were well known and highly respected by all classes of society.

Those who are well acquainted with our domestic history for the twenty years which succeeded the peace of 1815, though they may differ as to Robert Owen's merits, will all acknowledge that he played an important part upon our stage, and left a deep impression upon the nation that was his audience. It would be a most false judgment to estimate him by his exit, after he had outstayed his time and worn out the patience of the spectators.

His youth was contemporaneous with the sudden and vast extension of the cotton manufacture which began at the close of the last century. He was one of the most vigorous offshoots of that trade; and the history of his growth and of his characteristics, seems to me eminently worthy of our attention. Wanting a liberal education, and early entangled in the perplexities of religious controversy, he thought out in a childish fashion a moral philosophy of his own; which he prudently nursed while he was rising in life, but which the warmth of prosperity developed into a surprising monster: into something which was not merely heterodoxy, not merely scepticism, not merely a disbelief of all known religion. He publicly declared that there was no such thing as moral responsibility: he said that man was the creature of circumstances; that his character was formed for him, partly by nature at his birth, and then by the external influences to which he was exposed.

If he had been merely a rich manufacturer, who, like a hundred others, had through skill and industry and frugality risen from the ranks, this auda-

cious assertion of his own untutored thoughts, against
the matured opinions of reflective minds of all ages of
the world, would have been simply ridiculous. Owen
however, was a man of much sympathy with the working
classes, and one who was little disposed to let his notions
remain barren. He had indeed, no nostrum to recommend by which to cure the original vice of men's nature;
but he proclaimed aloud that it was the duty of governments, and of all influential persons, to provide desirable "surroundings" for those under their care. The
inference was much happier than the doctrine. Nothing
can be truer than the assertions, that it is better to prevent crime than to punish it; and that as far as possible, neither child nor man ought to be exposed to
temptation stronger than he can resist. The experiment at New Lanark happily illustrated these maxims,
though it failed to prove the truth of the exaggerated
dogmas of its conductor.

From this root of superficial philosophy, sprang
Owen's peremptory denial of the truth of the theologies
of the world. Every religion with which he was acquainted, addressed men as beings capable of making
a choice between right and wrong; as deserving of
punishment for offences and of reward for good deeds.
In his view, the doctrine was not only false, but eminently injurious; as tending to divert the attention from
the one thing needful, the improvement of the "sur-

roundings" of men.   His condemnation of religion was
not the result of libertine excesses, nor of a philosophical conceit, but followed honestly from the shallow
theory he had adopted.

The present generation however, does not think of
Owen as a moral philosopher, nor even as a reformer of
the factory system ; but as the father of co-operative societies, as the founder of equitable labour exchanges, as
the promoter of communistic arrangements, as the great
leader of English Socialism.   Nor would he himself
have complained of having had this reputation.   Yet
co-operation and communism were not the dreams of
his early life, but took possession of him as a middle-
aged man, after he had amassed his fortune, and had
attained a high renown as a social reformer.   They
resulted from a desire to extend to the world at large,
the benefits he had undoubtedly conferred on the people
of New Lanark.   The issue of these later efforts was
singularly unfortunate for his reputation.

Those however, who think of the old man with a
contemptuous pity, have need to be reminded how important was the position he once occupied, and how
great was the good he effected.   As a young man he
was the munificent supporter of Lancaster and of Bell
in their early efforts, and the liberal friend of Fulton
in his various mechanical projects.   It was Owen's
publications which recommended to the Prussian Go-

vernment its scheme of national education, and a
system of pauper management to the Dutch. The
establishment of infant schools is his work, and followed inevitably from his studious care to place the
people in circumstances favourable to their development. By his persevering efforts, first at Manchester
and then at New Lanark, he showed in practice that
much might be done to improve the condition and the
character of factory workers: and the various plans
since carried out for that purpose are traceable to him
as their originator. The first Sir Robert Peel had the
honour of being the prime mover in Parliament, of the
measures for restraining by law the abuses of the
factory system; but it was at the instigation of Owen
that the movement of 1819 commenced.

It is a matter of surprise too, to persons unacquainted
with the facts, to find what personal influence in the
highest quarters Owen once possessed. He had frequent access to the Earl of Liverpool when he was
premier; and the old man related with much satisfaction, how in one of his visits he was received, and
treated with obeisance, by young Mr. Peel, the private
secretary, then fresh from Oxford, but afterwards a far
greater minister than ever was Lord Liverpool. If we
may trust Owen's memory, he was at one time the
object of considerable apprehension to the ministry as
a popular leader. He was unquestionably greatly liked

and respected by the Duke of Kent, who dared to continue his patronage long after the public and wild condemnation of all religion: and the Duke at the time of his sudden death, was under an engagement to carry the future Queen and her mother on a private visit to New Lanark. Owen had also much friendly correspondence with the ministers of the great European sovereigns.

Men's posthumous fame depends greatly on the moment of their death. Sydney Smith thought that Horner lived long enough for his reputation. Sir Robert Peel's decease at the time when it occurred, secured to him a perpetuity of popularity, by the statues which the great towns erected to his memory as a free-trader, and which his death at any other period would not have produced. Owen was in this respect less fortunate. If he had died in middle life, before he had earned the antipathy of society by the loud proclamation of his ill-considered moral philosophy, before he had unsuccessfully laboured to reconstruct society, before he had bestowed infinite efforts and a large fortune on projects of communism or socialism, his memory would have been revered, as that of a man who had evinced a profound sympathy with the working classes, and who had invented and perseveringly carried out important plans for their advantage.

We should be guilty of great injustice, if we allowed the misdirected efforts of the latter half of a life, to blot out the recollection of the benevolent achievements of the first half. Nothing that occurred, threw a shade of doubt over the purity of his motives. The Bishop of Exeter himself, when attacking the English socialists, had no severity of condemnation for the character of their leader. After such a tacit testimony, who shall be an accuser? And if we compare Owen's career with that of other great manufacturers, we can scarcely fail to assign him a high position in moral worth. Among the respectable Arkwrights and Boultons and Marshalls and Strutts, we could not pitch upon one who made such sacrifices and who accomplished such good.

To make this sketch complete, I must mention one circumstance little known out of the immediate circle of Owen's friends and readers. In his old age he became a believer in spiritual manifestations. He was favoured with visits by his parents long departed, by the Duke of Kent his patron forty years before, by Franklin, Tom Paine, and Byron, and above all by a celestial being whom he calls a crowned angel. Those who had shuddered at his former disbelief, had now their revenge, and might well exult at these strange hallucinations. His friends may fairly reply, that a man of eighty years and upwards, must be excused the aberrations of a failing intellect: though his publications up to a very late period, if they have even more than his original deviousness of manner, yet certainly mark nothing that can be called dotage.

On the whole, Owen's private career was remarkably free from anything like romantic incident. He rose by his own skill and prudence, from a very humble place to that of a wealthy and influential manufacturer. He married young and happily, and frequently expressed his satisfaction in the family which grew up around him. Had he been intent on mere worldly greatness, his shrewdness and capacity for affairs might have made him a millionnaire, a member of Parliament, the founder of a family. But the peculiarities of his understanding and of his sympathies, led him into a public course of life, in which he exhibited startling contrasts. His success in all his undertakings as a boy and a young man, his social influence and great popularity in middle life, were in curious opposition to his subsequent failure in all his projects, to the antipathy felt towards him by the world, and to the obscurity of his old age. The manly and well-directed vigour of the first half of his life, were in direct antagonism to the useless activity and hopeless ill-success of the latter half: the unbelief of his nonage and ripe manhood, show strangely by the foolish credulity of his old age. And from first to last there is a remarkable inconsistency, between his vehement denial of moral responsibility, and on the other hand, his kindness of disposition, his regular conduct, his universal benevolence, his contempt of riches and luxury, and his unwearied and munificent support of projects of philanthropy.

———————————

ROBERT OWEN.

CHAPTER I.

Birth and Parentage—Delicate Health—Childish Activity and Diligence — Miscellaneous Reading — Effect Produced — Religion—
Scepticism—Popularity—Degree of Precocity—Obstinacy—Love
of Nature—First Employment—Leaves Home—Situation at Stamford—Literature and Religion—Imperfect Judgment — Situation
in London—At Manchester—Character.

ROBERT OWEN was born on the 14th of May, 1771,
at Newtown, Montgomeryshire. His father kept a
shop, was postmaster, and had a predominant influence in the affairs of his parish. His mother's maiden
name was Williams, and her kindred were respectable
farmers in the same neighbourhood. His father believed
that he had lost an estate of 500*l.* a year, through the
villany of his lawyer in selling himself, for a bribe,
to his antagonist.

Robert was the youngest but one of a family of
seven children. His health was delicate, in consequence, as he believed, of having while very young,
swallowed some flummery that was scalding hot. But
even before this painful accident there seems to have
been a fragility of constitution; since he was one day

1

found in a fainting fit caused by the pain of twisting
one of his fingers in a keyhole. But from whatever
cause, he suffered much from a disordered stomach;
and he says that this led him early to close observation
of the effects produced on him by different kinds of
food. Apparently, his abstemiousness and temperance
in after-life were much owing to this tenderness of
constitution. We must all have noticed that a man
who can eat a heavy supper and muddle himself with
drink, and yet rise with a clear head the next morning,
is in great danger of indulging in the coarser pleasures
of the table; while another man of more delicate health
is constrained to a higher course of life.

Owen's weakness of digestion did not impair his
activity as a child. At four to five years old he was
sent to school, and was generally the first to arrive
there and the first to reach home again. By the age
of seven he had received all the instruction required
in that primitive time and place : reading, writing, and
the four first rules of arithmetic. His master then
agreed with his father that he should become " assistant
master and usher," or what we should call monitor;
and this arrangement continued till he was nine years
old. But during this period he had a passion for reading, and was able to indulge it by access to the libraries
of the clergyman, the physician, and the lawyer.
The books were sufficiently miscellaneous; comprising
Robinson Crusoe, *Shakspeare*, *Quarle*, *Paradise Lost*,
Hervey's Meditations, *Young's Night Thoughts*, all the
standard novels, including Richardson's, many voyages

and travels, Rollin's history, and infinite biographies.
He read at the rate of a volume a day, and had the
delight of believing every word to be true. Adam
and Eve, Pamela and Crœsus, were equally historical
to his simple faith. All the poets and romancers, however, do not seem to have excited his imagination so
much as they stimulated his understanding. Accepting
as genuine history all the wonders he read, he was led
at last to inquire whether these could indeed all be
true; and thence to ask himself over and over again,
whether it were possible to discover any criterion of
truth. At last, says he (writing however in old age),
it occurred to me that "truth must always be consistent with itself, and in accordance with all facts."
If he indeed got so far as this, he was almost fit to
be introduced to the *Method of Descartes.*

His parents were of the communion of the Established Church; but two Methodist ladies who became
intimate with the family, took a fancy to him, lent
him their books, and tried to convert him to their
persuasion. At this time he was of a serious cast of
mind, reflected gravely in his puerile way, on theological topics, and perplexed his immature understanding with polemical mysteries. He wrote three sermons,
and acquired the name of the young parson. In his
old age he related with grave simplicity, that he kept
the sermons until he became acquainted with Sterne's
works: that he found among these, three discourses
so much like his own "in idea and turn of mind,"
that fearing to be regarded as a plagiarist he destroyed

his own. Impartial critics will not easily believe that
the Welsh child was a formidable rival of the pithy
Irishman.

This desultory and thorny course of reading led to
the natural result. The child was first surprised to
find what antagonism existed between different sects
of Christians: then he was startled at the deadly mutual
hatred of Jews, Christians, Mahomedans, and Hindoos:
the study (or what he thought such) of the contending
faiths, raised doubts within him of the truth of all.
By the age of ten, he had a strong conviction that
there was something fundamentally wrong in all known
creeds.

It does not appear that he communicated his doubts;
and he seems to have been a general favourite. He
was a lively, frail, precocious child; and injudicious
people took a pleasure in calling forth and exhibiting
the trifling superiority he possessed. One example of
this made a deep and salutary impression on him.
Some one made a bet that Robert could write better
than his brother, who was two years older; and Robert's
backer won. John's affection for his brother never
quite recovered from the shock given by this rivalry.
I agree in the opinion that parents should deeply
ponder this little incident. When natural affection
is soured, a deadly poison is apt to be formed.

That Owen, then, was a precocious child is certain;
but I am happy, on his behalf, to believe that there was
nothing marvellous in his attainments. Indeed he says
that a cousin who was a year younger than himself,

excelled him in everything. There was, however, an unusual forwardness of understanding. Children of nine or ten do not commonly perplex themselves with doubts as to the authenticity of the Bible; nor do they ransack a library for treatises on the Athanasian Creed. We are told, also, that before Owen was ten years old, his parents had a habit of consulting him about their affairs. If they did this gravely, they must have felt, one would think, that they were receiving the responses of an oracle, rather than the opinions of an infant.

Owen during the whole of his life showed an exaggerated firmness, in retaining opinions once conceived, and in pursuing any course on which he had entered. One incident shows that as a child he was of an obstinate disposition. Through a mere misapprehension of some remark, his mother reported him to his father as having disobeyed her; and then came a flogging with a whip often used on the other children, but which he had never tasted before. After refusing submission several times, each refusal being followed by a lash, he concluded with saying, "You may kill me, but I will not do it:" and so the contest ended. He was never chastised afterwards.

He mentions that when he was eight or nine years old, he contracted a love of natural scenery, by forming an acquaintance with an Oxford student, ten years older than himself, with whom he rambled about the beautiful woods and lanes and rising grounds around Newtown. This sensibility to the beauties of nature, he says, never deserted him, but even increased with his years.

At about nine years old he finally left the school where he had of late acted as monitor; and went regularly to serve in a shop, apparently without wages, yet continued to live at home. But the knowledge he had acquired, or the promptings of a natural ambition, made him desirous of going to London as a wider sphere. He hints also, that his extreme temperance did not accord with the habits in Newtown. His parents unwillingly yielded to his importunity, and promised that, favourite as he was, he should go at ten years old.

This promise was kept, and he was consigned to the care of a brother who had adopted his late master's widow and business as a saddler, in Holborn. At the end of six weeks a situation was found with a Mr. McGuffog at Stamford, on the borders of Lincolnshire.

Owen was very fortunate in this choice. His master who had commenced with half a crown as a hawker, and had saved money, is described as a thoroughly honest, methodical, liberal, and kind-hearted man. Owen was treated as one of the family, and was carefully instructed in the business, to his great benefit in after-life. He remained here four years, very happy in the kind treatment of both master and mistress.

During this period he had sufficient leisure to allow him five hours a day for reading; and in fine weather he took his book early in the morning into the noble avenues of Burleigh Park. Circumstances concurred to foster the doubts about religion which had tormented him as a child: for his master and mistress, being of different persuasions, went alternately to the church and the kirk; and controversial sermons were common in both places. But he had not yet cast off the reverence for Sunday. And seeing the day much desecrated by his neighbours, he wrote a letter about it to Mr. Pitt, then lately appointed Prime Minister. The draper and his wife were privy to the boyish effusion; and were delighted a few days afterwards, to see in a London paper, what they regarded as an answer, in the form of a royal proclamation recommending a more strict observance of Sunday. Owen afterwards had sufficient acquaintance with ministers, to convince him that the apparent reply was only a casual coincidence.

A comment of his on a trifling incident that occurred, seems to me to illustrate the obliquity of judgment which corrupted a great part of his well-intentioned efforts through life. His master had a female customer of more money than wit. Being shown some Irish linen at 8s. a yard, she refused it as not good enough. Another piece of the same quality was produced, and the price of 10s. was asked : this she pronounced to be just what she wanted. The bill, however, was made out at only 8s., and it was explained to her that 8s. linen was the best which was made. She was hurt, and never came again. Owen's injudicious comment is, "so much for honest dealing in a tradesman." My comment would be, "in dealing with fools, better be a rogue than a practical jester."

At the age of fourteen, Owen, happy as he had been at Stamford, refused to remain there, being set on obtaining more knowledge and a wider field for his

abilities.   The McGuffogs pressed him to stay, but failing in that, did their best to speed him on his way, by
strong recommendations to a friend.   After a visit to his
relatives in Wales, he entered a shop on the Borough
side of old London Bridge.   Here he boarded and
lodged in the house, with a salary of 25*l.* a year: a
handsome remuneration for a boy's services.   He was
required to work hard for his money; commencing
business at eight in the morning, and during the
season, not being in bed before one or two o'clock.
He understood that this was the first shop established
to sell at a low profit for ready money ; and there seems
to have been a constant crowd of customers.   The
assistants were required to appear with all the dignity
of gentlemen;   and   even   little   Owen   was   required
every morning to submit to powder and pomatum,
two large curls on each side of the head, and stiff
pigtail.

He thought the work more than he could bear; but
when a quieter season followed he found himself very
happy, and as was his way, made a friend among his
companions.   However, a desirable situation was offered
him in Manchester at an advance of 15*l.* a year on his
London salary ; and he rather unwillingly accepted it.
Here again he was well treated and was quite happy:
feeling himself abounding in wealth with 40*l.* a year for
clothes and pocket-money, without any taste for drinking or other expensive pleasures.   He remained in this
shop till he was eighteen.

It appears then, that up to eighteen Owen was quiet,

regular, well-conducted : secure of success by his industry and unusual temperance. He must also have been amiable, since he made friends everywhere; and of a happy disposition to which nothing came amiss. Ambitious as he was, there can have been no undue love of display; for during the eight years from the time he left Wales he maintained himself without aid from home. We have seen that his mind was not fanciful or imaginative, but thoughtful and inquiring; led into early scepticism by the theological perplexities he encountered, in the absence of regular educational training, and without the advantages of the friendship of cultivated persons.

CHAPTER II.

THIS was the heroic age of the cotton trade, during
which men of enterprise and steadiness could easily do
great things. A mechanic named Jones, whom Owen
saw constantly, stirred his ambition by proposing to join
in setting up a little manufactory for making the new
machinery. Jones had no money, but he would give
half the profits to a partner who could advance 100*l.*
Owen borrowed this sum from his London brother, left
his situation, and began with Jones to make *mules* for
spinning. Forty men were soon set to work on wood,
iron, and brass, bought upon credit. Jones proved to
be an ignorant mechanic, without a notion about super-
intending workmen or conducting a considerable business: but Owen undertook to manage the finances and
keep the accounts; and attending assiduously from
morning to night, covered his ignorance of the processes
by wise looks and vigilant attention. He was very

apprehensive, however, of the result, and at the end of a few months, jumped at an offer made by a capitalist to buy him out.

At this time, Owen, being about nineteen, received from his old master at Stamford the liberal offer of a partnership with half the profits of his business, and the promise of the whole of it in a few years. He believed that if he had accepted this, he would have ended by marrying the niece of McGuffog, whose property, in that case, he and his wife would have inherited.

But the youth's aspirations would not allow him to settle down for life as a linendraper at Stamford. He chose rather again to incur the anxieties of manufacturing, but this time without a partner. He took a large new factory (then a recent name) in Ancoats Lane, Manchester; and letting off the greater part of it so as to sit rent free, he commenced spinning with three mules which he had received in part payment from Jones and his new partner; and found himself earning 6l. a week. The concern he had left soon broke up without paying the remainder of Owen's capital: but it is quite possible that if he had continued manager it would have become profitable.

From disappointment at his loss, or from other motives not mentioned, Owen in a short time abandoned this fair prospect. The manner of the change was characteristic. Going to his little factory on Monday morning, he was told that a Mr. Drinkwater had advertised for a manager. This gentleman, a rich merchant, had lately erected a mill for the finer sorts of spinning, and was filling it with machinery; having a scientific man, Mr. George Lee, for a superintendent. Mr. Lee was enticed away by the offer of a partnership, leaving Mr. Drinkwater, who was ignorant of the business, in a very awkward position. As soon as Owen heard of the advertisement, he put on his hat, and without further reflection applied for the situation.

He was only twenty, and his rosy cheeks made him look still less. " You are too young," said Mr. Drinkwater.—" Four or five years ago I should have thought so." " How often in the week do you get drunk?" (the ordinary vice then of Lancashire, and indeed of every shire). " I was never drunk in my life," replied Owen, blushing. The answer and the ingenuous manner, made an impression. " What salary do you ask?" —" Three hundred a year." The questioner was astounded; for he had received many applicants that morning, and their aggregate demands scarcely amounted to 300l. a year. Owen declined to take less, and stated that he was making that income by his own business. Mr. Drinkwater asked for proof of this, and receiving it, he made the necessary inquiries as to character, which of course met with such replies from McGuffog and others, as got Owen the situation. The three mules were taken at cost price, and his services were at once transferred to the new mill.

When he entered on the situation, and found what he had undertaken, he was astonished at his own presumption. There were five hundred people, of various

ages and both sexes, at work in the mill: the previous
manager had gone away the day before, leaving, indeed, drawings and calculations of the machinery: Mr.
Drinkwater furnished no instructions, and did not even
introduce his new manager: the mill itself was an
experiment, being the first that had been put up for
spinning fine cotton by machinery: Owen's experience
was of a limited sort, not having extended beyond
serving in retail shops, or the control for a short period
of thirty men; and he himself had hitherto been a
sensitive youth of retired habits, hardly able to address
one of the other sex without blushing. Yet he was
now required to take the entire management of this
considerable factory; to purchase the raw material, to
construct the machinery still wanting, to spin the cotton
into yarn, to pay the wages, sell the produce, and keep
the accounts. We cannot wonder at what he afterwards heard: that the gossips predicted disappointment
and failure, and declared that Mr. Drinkwater had lost
his senses.

But the result proved that that gentleman had either
singular penetration or singular good fortune. The
situation was one which would have been the ruin of
a fool or of a sluggard, but which was just fitted for
the industrious, temperate, capable, Owen. He had
been thoroughly trained to regular industry; and he
now daily entered the factory with the workpeople in
the morning, and himself locked the doors at night.
He looked grave, made good use of his eyes, answered
in monosyllables to all questions asked him, anxiously

studied the documents the late manager had left; and
at the end of six weeks, found the primeval chaos falling into order.

His experience acquired at Stamford proved of in-
estimable value in this crisis. McGuffog's customers
were many of them the gentry of the neighbourhood;
and for them he had kept a stock of goods of the finest
quality. Owen had thus acquired a familiarity with
fabrics of the highest excellence, and his skill now stood
him in good stead. The article he was required to
produce was yarn of unusual fineness, and it was
thought a triumph for his predecessor that he had made
what was technically known as 120 hanks to the pound.
The quality of this, however, was not very good; and
Owen soon saw that there were certain defects in the
processes, and imperfections in some parts of the
machinery. By his unremitting care he effected such
improvements in the quality of the yarn as to make
the customers prefer the new to the old stock.

Mr. Drinkwater lived in the town during the winter,
but as this was summer-time, he was in the country,
and was only to be seen at his counting-house twice
a week. He was fully aware of the improvement that
had taken place in the yarns, and heard from other
quarters that the work-people were at once well-
disciplined and contented. From week to week
he was more satisfied with his boy-manager, and
with the lie given to the malicious prophecies of the
quidnuncs.

He was wise enough to know that uncommon services were deserving of a proportionate remuneration; and probably his liberality was quickened by his recent loss of a useful manager. What if some one should again allure his superintendent to quit him! Owen was invited to pay a visit to the country house, without any intimation of what was intended. He went with misgivings; for he had never been even in his employer's town house; and he was still an awkward, blushing youth, embarrassed by his want of education and his ungrammatical Welsh idiom, with the consciousness that he had within him notions which he could not express. The visit proved satisfactory on both sides. Mr. Drinkwater got a signed agreement for service, and Owen received an accession of salary, which was to be 400*l.* for the second year and 500*l.* for the third.

But what was of far higher importance for the future, at the end of the third year, when Owen would be only twenty-two, he was to enter into partnership in the factory with Mr. Drinkwater and his two sons, and was to have a fourth share of the profits. In consequence of this permanent engagement, Owen was allowed to put his name on the goods manufactured, in order to distinguish them from those which were made under the old *régime.* It may be guessed that under these circumstances he did not relax his exertions: and in fact, he soon so far improved the quality of the yarns, that they easily fetched ten per cent. higher prices than could be got for those first spun. Two years later he had carried the manufacture to a

far higher point. Instead of remaining satisfied with
the fineness of 120 hanks to the pound, he reached
250 hanks, and afterwards even 300. This yarn too
was so good, that it sold for half as much again as the
ordinary list price.

Owen at this period had formed an acquaintance with
Dalton, afterwards the celebrated chemist, who was
already feeling his way to his atomic theory. Dalton
and Mr. Winstanley were assistants under Dr. Baines,
in the Manchester Unitarian College, afterwards removed to York under the learned Mr. Wellbeloved.
The three friends often met in the evening and discussed theology, moral philosophy, and science. Coleridge, then an undergraduate at Cambridge, begged to
be admitted to the party. Owen now made no secret of
his opinions; and he maintains that though Coleridge
had all the learning and eloquence on his side, and
though his fluency and high-sounding sentences made
far the greater show, yet his own few words pat to the
point, commonly, in the opinion of the other friends,
carried the greatest weight of argument.

Owen was also made a member of the " Literary and
Philosophical Society." For some time he continued a
silent member, without even the desire to speak; but
being called on by name one day, he stammered out a
few sentences, and subsequently took a more forward
part. He was also elected into a committee, or club, of
the more thoughtful members, including the eminent
Dr. Ferriar and Mr. Henry the chemist. His tastes
were above those of the manufacturers, who were gene-

rally plodding men of business without love of literature or science; the merchants being only a shade
better.

About this time also, that is, in 1794, Owen was
lodging in the same house with the celebrated Robert
Fulton, and formed an intimacy with him. Fulton's
mind was teeming with mechanical inventions, many
of which he tried without success to carry into effect,
before he applied himself to that one which has immortalized him. The particular scheme in 1794 was
one for an improved mode of excavating the bed of
canals: and as he had exhausted his means and credit,
in obtaining his patent, he offered Owen half the profits
if he would help him with funds. Nothing came of this.
Next there was a project for superseding locks on canals,
and this proved a failure. Then there was an improvement in the art of tanning, of which we hear little.
But before this last invention, Owen had backed out of
the partnership, Fulton undertaking to repay the advances with interest, an agreement that he partially
fulfilled. Owen, like a truly liberal man, never regretted the money he lost; but rejoiced that he had
done something towards helping on the precarious
career, which ended in the happy application of steam
to navigation, for the world's great benefit. The last
sum which Fulton received, enabled him to visit
Glasgow, where he saw Bell's imperfect attempt, on
which was founded the successful invention of the
paddle steamer.

Owen was of course well known to the manufacturing

2

world of Manchester; and the reputation which he had
gained of being the first spinner of fine cotton in the
world, was an unfailing source of fortune to him. At
the end of his third year of management at Mr. Drinkwater's mill, he was entitled to a quarter share of the
profits. That gentleman, however, desired to make an
alteration in the terms of the agreement. The hand of
his daughter was solicited by a manufacturer of high
standing and reputed wealth, who urged that the partnership should if possible be annulled. Owen had
heard that something was afoot, and being sent for to
his principal's country house, put the agreement in his
pocket. Mr. Drinkwater candidly explained the circumstances, and asked whether he would be content to
surrender the partnership, naming for himself whatever salary he pleased. Owen at once produced his
agreement and thrust it into the fire, saying that he
would never force himself on an unwilling partner;
but as to continuing a manager, that was not to be
thought of. He consented, however, to remain until he
could find a substitute, and with much difficulty, at the
end of a few months, he accomplished this. The result
to Mr. Drinkwater was disastrous; for the intended
son-in-law proved less wealthy than was supposed, and
the match was broken off; the new manager was not
an Owen, and so the business fell into confusion and
the factory was sold.

Owen did not afterwards approve of his own
hasty decision to break off his partnership; but
attributed it to "feeling, not judgment," caused by

his "constitution and the previous circumstances in which he had been placed." It was not himself, but his destiny, that was in fault. If he had turned out a sluggard, a drunkard, a profligate, the same apology would have been equally applicable. The truth seems to be, that his natural ambition had been a little inflated by his rapid advancement while still a youth, from the calling of a draper's assistant, to the situation of a highly successful manufacturer, who could command any salary he chose to ask, or make his own terms for a lucrative partnership.

The same undue pride led him to decline a valuable offer, which was made him as soon as it was known that he was at liberty. A Mr. Samuel Marsland had joined some other gentlemen in buying the Chorlton estate, near Manchester, as a building speculation: and intending to erect mills there, he offered Owen a third of the profits as a partner. Owen's pride led him to refuse anything less than half the profits, a folly he afterwards laid to the door of his destiny.

He was thus driven by "nature and surroundings," to join two young men, who had capital but no experience, in a project to build some mills, on the terms of an equal division of profits. While the mills were rising, however, another arrangement was made with some wealthy people, by which the "Chorlton Twist Company" was established, with Owen and a Mr. Atkinson for managers. Two to three years elapsed before the Company was fairly at work.

It would have been natural enough if Owen had

indulged some resentment against his principal, and had commenced business in opposition to him. It is much to the credit of destiny that he acted in a manner the reverse of this. He felt that Mr. Drinkwater had behaved towards him with kindness and liberality, and that a want of firmness was the only fault he had committed. The new factory, therefore, was constructed for making yarns of a sort quite different from those very fine ones by which Owen's reputation had been established. A man of different "nature and surroundings" would not have so unreservedly written his gratitude in marble and his resentments in sand.

During all these transactions Owen remained a bachelor. But when he was five or six and twenty, and found himself a partner with some of the most respectable people in his neighbourhood, he began to think of marrying, and no doubt he was regarded as a desirable *parti*. There is, however, a little simple vanity in the way he speaks of the matter in his old age. He had a family of high standing living not far from him, with some daughters; the eldest of whom Owen had often seen in public. This young lady, of great beauty and refinement, called one day in company with a chaperone, to ask permission to go over the old Chorlton Hall and grounds where the bachelor was keeping house. Owen himself acted as cicerone; but was prevented by his bashfulness from entering into conversation or establishing an acquaintance. He was afterwards told that the young lady had pre-

viously been prepossessed in his favour; and he speaks
with a regret, that his wife would scarcely have
approved, of his stupidity in letting such an occasion
slip. His destiny, however, was soon to be accomplished.

CHAPTER III.

OWEN, among other duties, had that of visiting his
customers in the north of England: and not very long
after the new mills got to work, he consented to extend
one of his journeys as far as Scotland. Mail coaches
had not been established; and it took two days' and
three nights' unbroken travelling by post carriages, to
go from Manchester to Glasgow. Owen and a companion reached Glasgow early in the morning; and
taking a walk at once round the green, they were a
little scandalized at witnessing the peculiar mode of
washing, by women publicly tramping in tubs, which
was afterwards rather over-graphically described by
Professor Wilson, in an early number of *Blackwood*, to
the distress of some of his more strait-laced readers.
Owen's comment to his companions was, that early habit
is everything.

Having an accidental opportunity of going to New
Lanark with his fellow traveller, he embraced it and
made the visit. The place then consisted of a primitive
manufacturing Scotch village with four water-mills for
cotton-spinning. The manufacture had been com-

menced in 1784 by a Mr. Dale, in conjunction with Sir Richard Arkwright,* and was one of the earliest establishments of that kind in Scotland. New Lanark was placed on the falls of the Clyde for the sake of the water-power; and was about a mile from Old Lanark, and thirty miles by the road from Glasgow. Owen was pleased with the scenery around and with the situation of the mills: and as he stood in front of the buildings, he said to his companion, "Of all places I have yet seen, I should prefer this in which to try an experiment I have long contemplated, and have wished to have an opportunity to put in practice." At that time he had no reason to anticipate that his wish would be gratified, though in a short time such proved to be the case.

Mr. Dale, the proprietor of New Lanark, was a rather extraordinary person. He was a merchant, a manufacturer with various large concerns, a magistrate of his town, and what is more unusual, a zealous lay preacher: being at the head of a sect of Independents, with some control over forty churches, one of which in Glasgow he served every Sunday. He was kind hearted, munificent in his benefactions, and hospitable to all his poor brethren. But to crown all, his religious zeal did not outrun his charity. Owen in after days was constantly in his company, and did not conceal from him the peculiar notions he cherished. Frequent discussions arose, in which Owen put forth his opinions: that belief or disbelief was not in the power of man; and that all

* *New Existence,* v. xlvii.

religions being founded on the reverse supposition, were
mere emanations of disordered or mistaken minds.   Mr.
Dale listened patiently, and would say, " Thou needest
be very right, for thou art very positive : " but not a
single harsh expression or unkind word ever followed.
Such amicable discussions were equally creditable to
both disputants.

Mr. Dale had long been a widower, without any son ;
and with five daughters, the eldest of whom had, from
the age of twelve, had the care of the house and of her
sisters.   Owen had a casual introduction to Miss Dale
on his first visit to Glasgow, and it was to her that he
owed his access to her father's mills.   Before his return
to Manchester, not having as yet seen Mr. Dale, he
called on the young lady to acknowledge her kindness,
and she politely expressed a wish that he should repeat
his visit when he again came into the north.   His
acquaintance had been formed through a Miss Spear of
Manchester, who seems to have set her heart on uniting
her two friends in the closest of all intimacies.   In a
subsequent journey Owen was entrusted with letters
between the friends ; and this led, during his stay in
Glasgow, to morning walks with Miss Dale : though
diffidence and a cool complexion might have prevented
any further progress, but for the interposition of a third
person.   Miss Spear, after a time, revealed to Owen
under the seal of secrecy, that Miss Dale was strongly
prepossessed in his favour ; and had even said, after the
first introduction, that if ever she married, he should be
her husband.

It would have been strange if on this hint Benedick had not spoken. He felt, indeed, that there were great obstacles in the father's wealth, his comparatively high position, and the prevailing piety of his character. But he was a second time entrusted with letter and message; and he again found himself taking frequent walks with Miss Dale. The way in which his attentions were received emboldened him to ask her whether her affections were otherwise engaged. She replied that they were not; but that she could scarcely believe in the probability of Mr. Dale's consenting to receive Owen as a son-in-law. If this difficulty were overcome, she should make no objection; but she would under no circumstances marry without her excellent father's consent.

The burden of removing the obstacle was thrown entirely upon Owen, and he was sorely perplexed, besides being now heartily in love. He was not even acquainted with the father, who was constantly carried from home by his various avocations; but an innocent stratagem occurred to him. He had heard that Mr. Dale was desirous of contracting his affairs; and he made this an excuse for calling, and asked whether it was a true report that the New Lanark mills were in the market. Owen's reception was cold, and, as he fancifully thought, suspicious; and when he asked about the mills he received for reply, that so young a man could not want to buy them. He answered that he was in partnership with older and richer men, and was already extensively engaged in cotton-spinning. Mr.

Dale now took up the matter seriously; asked if Owen
had seen New Lanark; advised him to go again and
make a more exact inspection; and told him that if his
partners wished to treat for the purchase, they might
do so.

This negotiation had been begun as a ruse, but was
now carried on in good earnest. Owen on his return reported to his partners the conversation which
had passed; omitting, we may presume, the motives
which led to it; and feeling anything but sanguine as
to a favourable reception of the scheme. The partners,
however, took the matter up gravely, and proposed that
two of them should at once proceed to Scotland with
Owen. This plan was carried out: the party visited
New Lanark; and the impression created being satisfactory, a treaty for purchase was set on foot. Owen's
previous visit to the counting-house had been so abrupt
and unexpected, that Mr. Dale's suspicions had been
aroused, and he had not expected to hear anything
further about a negotiation. He was agreeably surprised when the three gentlemen called upon him; and
after a day for reflection and inquiry, he expressed himself willing to treat for the sale of the land, village, and
mills, at New Lanark, just as they stood. But who was
to set a value on the property? Mr. Dale must have
been really, what Owen says he had the reputation of
being, a man of an honest simplicity. He confessed his
own ignorance, and said, "Mr. Owen knows better than
I do the value of such property at this period; and I
wish he would name what he would consider a fair

price between honest buyers and sellers." An awkward proposition for one of the intending buyers! Owen felt it to be such; but spite of his embarrassment, he mentioned three thousand a year for twenty years as what he thought a fair price. Mr. Dale at once acceded to the terms, and the two partners could do no less: and so the property passed from Mr. Dale and was vested in the "New Lanark Twist Company." This was in 1799, when Owen was about twenty-eight.

In the meantime, Owen had informed Miss Dale of the first visit he had made to the counting-house; and she had communicated to her father the conversation which had taken place with herself. But, as she had expected, he was very unfavourable to their wishes. Owen, he said, was a stranger, a land-louper (adventurer) who had called on him under the pretence of making a purchase which he had no means of completing: and he would like an honest Scotchman for his successor, a man with whom he was acquainted, and whom he could trust. Miss Dale informed her lover of this decided opposition, and advised him to give up all thoughts of her. The father's objections, however, were weakened by the sale of the property, or he took his measures very ill: for he allowed his daughter, with her sisters, to spend the summer at New Lanark, while Owen was in the same neighbourhood, arranging the transfer of the property: and so the courtship went on; and Miss Dale on her return to Glasgow appears to have told her father, that if the match were broken off, she would die a maid. The old gentleman was of a

kindly, affectionate temper: and the quiet interposition
of friends and further intercourse with the English *land-
louper*, smoothed down his prejudices, and secured his
consent.   On the 30th September, 1799, the marriage
took place.   Owen was astonished at the brevity of the
ceremony.   The interested parties assembled in the
drawing-room: the Rev. Mr. Balfour, a minister of the
established Scottish Church, desired the lady and gentleman to stand up; and asked them separately whether
each of them was willing to receive the other as husband
or wife: when after a nod of assent from each, they
were declared to be married.

Owen's property at this time was about 3,000*l.*; a
smaller sum than might have been supposed from his
great success, and a far smaller sum than he might have
realized if he had been an avaricious man.   But we
have seen in Fulton's case that he was quite ready to
support a friend in any project; and the constant
changes in his own business arrangements had invited
the fate attributed by the proverb to the rolling stone.
Besides this, he had already exhibited that munificent
disposition which always distinguished him: having
subscribed no less than 1,000*l.* towards Lancaster's
educational schemes, and 500*l.* towards Dr. Bell's, with
an offer of another 500*l.* on certain conditions, which,
however, were not fulfilled.   A third of his entire
savings applied to the promotion of education, was a
noble earnest of his future philanthropical sacrifices.

Mr. Dale's many mills had not been under his own
immediate superintendence, but had been committed to

the care of agents; and New Lanark was for some time
after the purchase left under the previous managers, one
of whom was a half-brother of Mr. Dale. The Manchester firm, however, were not satisfied with these
gentlemen; finding that they did not work together
cordially, and that they were altogether unequal to their
task. It was now agreed that Owen should give up the
direction of the Chorlton mill, and should remove to
Lanark. Thus, in three months after his marriage he
returned to Scotland, where he received a cordial welcome from his father-in-law; and immediately found
himself at the head of the mills on the Clyde. He says
himself that he entered upon the government of New
Lanark, on the 1st of January, 1800: and that he uses
the word government, rather than management, ad-
visedly; because in undertaking this task, he did not
merely intend to conduct a commercial speculation, but
proposed to himself to introduce plans founded on the
principles by which he had guided himself as manager
of Mr. Drinkwater's factory; and hoped to be able to
alter many arrangements which had obviously a most injurious influence on the Scotch workpeople. He rejoiced
that by an unexpected course of events, he was now in
a situation to try an experiment he had long contemplated; and on the very spot which he had pointed out
on his first visit to Scotland, as the one his wishes would
have selected. In Manchester no doubt, he must often
have been controlled by the joint management; but in
the secluded place now confided to him, he would have
a freer scope for action.

CHAPTER IV.

History of New Lanark—The Hands—Condition of the Children—Of the Adults—Owen's Resolve—Difficulties—Caution—Change of Agents—Paupers discontinued—Thieving, &c., corrected—Improved Shops — Self-government — Punishments — The Silent Monitor.

In the previous chapter I have related the circumstances under which Owen became connected with New Lanark: and I have done this with more detail than I should otherwise have allowed myself, because New Lanark is, in the eyes of most men, the crown of Owen's glory. Before 1800 his efforts as a philanthropist were obscure, and were hampered by the control of other persons: in the latter part of his life, with the greatest latitude for action, his projects were unsuccessful; because, as I think, he aimed at the unattainable. But at New Lanark he proposed to himself an object that was within his reach: he looked far forward: he was contented to wait and to work with patience: he steadily and placidly lived down the prejudices of his neighbours: he resided among his workpeople like a prince among his subjects: he managed the property under his care advantageously for himself and his partners and with infinite benefit for his people: and his long-continued exertions were rewarded with national fame and influence. This period of his life is therefore well worthy of our careful study.

I have already stated that the manufactory at New Lanark was commenced by Sir Richard Arkwright and Mr. Dale in 1784, when cotton spinning was first introduced into Scotland. The advantage of water power at the Falls of the Clyde, was the inducement to fix upon that site; which was otherwise an undesirable one: the country around being uncultivated, the inhabitants few and poor, and the roads so bad as effectually to exclude tourists if they had been disposed to visit the Falls. Hands had to be found to work in the mills: no easy task, because the long hours and the confinement were disgustful to the peasantry. Recourse was had to charitable establishments for a supply of children. As many as five hundred of these were ultimately working together, most of whom had been sent from Edinburgh. They were fed, clothed, and educated, in a large house built for the purpose; and Mr. Dale's benevolence was tasked to secure the due performance of his contract. To obtain a supply of adult labourers, a village was built round the works, and the houses were let at a low rent; but the business was so unpopular that few except the bad, the unemployed, and the destitute, would settle there. Even of such ragged labourers the numbers were insufficient; and these, when they had learned their trade and become valuable, were self-willed and insubordinate.

The provision made for maintaining the children,

was everything that could be desired. The rooms
were spacious, clean, and well ventilated: the food
was abundant and excellent; and the clothes neat and
well chosen. Medical attendance was provided: there
were competent teachers and careful superintendents.
But there were serious drawbacks. The pauper authorities insisted that the children, if sent at all, should
be received ás early as six years old. It was found,
or thought, necessary, that these little creatures should
work with the other people from six in the morning
till seven in the evening; and it was only after this
task was over that instruction began. The inevitable
results followed. The poor children hated their slavery:
many absconded: some were stunted and even dwarfed
in stature: at thirteen to fifteen years old, when their
apprenticeship expired, they commonly went off to
Glasgow and Edinburgh, with no natural guardians,
ignorant of the world beyond their village, and altogether admirably trained for swelling the mass of vice
and misery in the towns. Owen entirely exonerates
Mr. Dale from all blame in the matter; contending
that the authorities ought to have deferred the apprenticeship of the children till they were educated and
fit for labour. But he says with justice: if such
miseries followed under the best of masters, what
must have been the result under the worst?

The condition of the families who had immigrated to
the village was also very lamentable.* The people lived

* I take these statements on Mr. Owen's authority. See his *Autobiography*, I. xxvi. 57, 61, 62, 276. I have no doubt of their accu-

almost without control, in habits of vice, idleness, poverty, debt, and destitution. The brother of one of the managers habitually went out on a *spree*, when he left his business for weeks together, and was drunk the whole time. Thieving was general, and went to such a ruinous extent that Mr. Dale's property appeared to be treated on a regular communistic principle. Owen's disgust was of course exceedingly aggravated, by finding a film of religious profession spread over these abominations. He says that there was a strict attention to the forms of religion: that the people were of various sects, much opposed to each other, each person being quite sure of the correctness of his own creed: and that unhappily, though from the best of motives, Mr. Dale had aggravated this evil, by showing a decided preference to one set of opinions, and treating the professors of them as privileged persons. There was also a considerable drawback from the comfort of the people, in the high price, and bad quality, of the commodities supplied in the village.

Owen had now had ten years' experience in the management of factories: had struggled successfully through difficulties; and was warranted in feeling an entire reliance on his own powers of administration. He was resolved to carry out a thorough reform: and he considered the disordered colony with the same satisfaction, which animates a physician at the sight of a diseased patient whom he is confident of curing.

racy. It is not very easy to collect the facts from a book written in old age, and in a discursive, not to say a rambling style.

He frankly told his intimate friends, that he was about to inaugurate a new system of management, on the principles of justice and kindness; and that he meant gradually to discontinue the use of punishment. They of course laughed at him; but in the long run he got the jest on his side.

No doubt, he had great obstacles to overcome: ignorance, improvidence, immorality, a religion divorced from good works, excessive tasks, exorbitant prices of commodities; and to crown all, a strong prejudice against himself as an Englishman, speaking a dialect far different from that both of the Highlanders and the Lowlanders among them. Besides this, the other partners were commercial men, fairly intent on making an income out of their purchase; and reasonably expecting that as Owen shared the gains made at Chorlton by their means, they should also partake in the advantages of his exertions. Even now, and much more in those days, a young and unmoneyed man would excite great surprise, if he proposed to pay his partners with philanthropic aspirations instead of net profits. Nor is it probable that Owen himself, whose fortune was then but small, was indifferent to pecuniary success. He was a prudent man, not at all deficient in the art of making money, and quite shrewd enough to take care of himself in a bargain.* The workpeople imagined, reasonably enough, that Owen's main object was to increase his gains; and that the alterations he made, or proposed, however speciously

* William Allen, quoted by Holyoake at p. 19 of *Owen's Last Days.*

disguised, were really intended to swell the annual profits of the business. We cannot wonder, therefore, that during two tedious years little progress was made. Owen, writing when the whole affair was fresh in his mind, said that he was opposed by every means which ingenuity could devise; and that a systematic defence was made of that stronghold of prejudices and malpractices, which it was his fixed resolution to subdue.

But Owen was too prudent to attempt a conquest by violent means. He saw that the alterations required, in order to make the business profitable, and to carry out his peculiar views, were numerous; and as he examined one department after another, he began to think that it was not reform which was needed, but reconstruction. He communicated his wishes to the various superintendents, hoping for their assistance: but these persons were wedded to old plans and to the notions which had grown up with themselves; and no doubt regarded their new employer as a troublesome visionary. They would rather leave than lend themselves to impracticable schemes; and new men had to be sought.

Owen determined to receive no more pauper children; and as the parish agreements made by Mr. Dale expired, he renewed none of them. It was of course necessary to put an end to the constant and extensive depredations which were taking place; and this might have been done more or less successfully, by detecting the thieves, imprisoning some, transporting others, and hanging the most audacious. But this

would have kept up a chronic state of irritation and
illwill, quite inconsistent with the projects on hand:
besides that, Owen regarded these offenders as the
creatures of circumstances, committing crime as the
result of the evil influences to which they had been
exposed. At the present day, a great many persons
will go very far in the direction of this opinion, without accompanying its author absolutely to the conclusion he arrived at: most thoughtful persons will assent
to the proposition that punishment should be resorted
to only in the last extremity: and all will feel it to
have been a matter of legitimate pride, that the habit
of thieving was corrected without recourse in a single
instance to a legal tribunal. Checks were adopted to
render detection easy; and all possible means of pre-
vention were made use of: as, for example, in one
department, in which pilfering had gone on to a ruinous extent, and was easily performed because a hundred
thousand portable articles passed every day through
four different sets of hands, a plan was devised which
dispensed with counting and yet noted the actual thief
of even a single article. Every facility was also given
for obtaining profitable employment, so as to make
honest industry more gainful than illicit practices.
Drunkenness, in a similar manner, was rather under-
mined than openly attacked. It was systematically
discountenanced; its pernicious effects were dwelt upon;
taverns were not at once pulled down or shut up, but
were step by step removed to greater distances.

One of the first alterations immediately beneficial to

the people was that of the shops. The provisions and clothing hitherto sold in the village, had been bad in quality and high priced, as is commonly the case in small places, and as is always the case when the buyers are improvident persons who insist on getting credit. Owen arranged superior shops, bought all the commodities on the best terms, and had them retailed at cost price, without any reserve of profit. This was going very near an infringement of the old laws against trucking; though it does not appear from the account we have, that the articles were actually paid over as part wages. The men saved one-fourth of previous prices, besides getting better articles than before.

An attempt was also made to interest the people in the schemes proposed, by giving them a part to play in the government of the village.* A number of adjoining houses were to be classed together and called neighbour divisions : and the heads of the families were to meet once a year to elect one of themselves as principal. The whole village being thus mapped out, and each division having made its selection, the various principals were to have an early meeting, for the purpose of balloting for twelve of their number, who were to be called jurymen. These jurymen were to meet the resident partner, or head manager, once a week, in order to act as a board of examination, and to give a verdict of guilty or not guilty upon cases of misconduct brought before them. This scheme, however, is so

---

* See *The New Existence*, Part 5, Appendix ix., 1854. At the same place are to be seen the rules laid down to the householders.

little referred to in Owen's ordinary lucubrations, and is so far from assuming any prominence in the accounts of New Lanark given by other persons, that I suppose it turned out of little value. Owen's notions of government generally were anything but democratic, and had rather a paternal leaning: to such an extent indeed, as to cause him to be denounced by the Radical party as an obstructive.

Owen, in his old age, wrote as though at New Lanark he had entirely discontinued the use of punishments.[*] But this was far from being strictly true. He said that the weapons with which crimes should be attacked are "real knowledge, charity, and love;" and that these "when wisely applied, will never fail to eradicate the cause of crime, and to make men and women rational in mind and conduct, and without exception, ultimately, from birth, good, wise, and happy." At New Lanark, however, he did not succeed in dispensing with punishment: as, for instance, any irregular familiarities between the sexes were fined:[†] and at quite a late period of his management, making an effort to break through the long established practice of drinking in the New Year, he offered a day's pay to all who abstained from it, and stopped a day's pay from all who persisted.

The most characteristic means of influence, however, was the *Silent Monitor*. This consisted of a four-sided piece of wood, about two inches long and one broad ; with the sides painted respectively, black, white, yel-

[*] *Autobiog.* Introd. xxvii.　　　　　[†] Ibid. 281.

low, and blue: one of these instruments being hung up near every person employed. The 2,500 toys had their positions arranged every day, according to the conduct of each worker during the preceding day: white indicating superexcellence; yellow, moderate goodness; blue, a neutral condition of morals; and black, exceeding naughtiness. A register was kept of each day's colours, and this furnished a statistical account of the behaviour of every person employed. This scheme savours strongly of the ingenious devices of Lancaster for maintaining discipline: of fool's-caps and tin crowns and pinafores turned inside out. But I can hardly think without laughing of its introduction among full-grown men and women: and I suspect that those who were behind the scenes, extracted abundant amusement out of the whim of their excellent *gaffer*. The Paraguay Indians might have gravely accepted such a scheme from their Jesuit masters. Owen, however, had the gratification of being fooled to the top of his bent. In his daily progresses through his dominions, he noted anxiously the prevalence of the good or bad colours in the moral atmosphere: and he was delighted to find, that though at first there was a predominance of black, with some blue, a little yellow, and scarcely any white, yet gradually the white increased, blended with more blue and less of the demoniacal black.

CHAPTER V.

Six years' Prejudice—How overcome—Pecuniary Sacrifice—Was Owen right?—Mr. Dale's Death—Infant School—Difficulties—Partners are alarmed—Visits New Lanark—Second Visit—Dissolve the Partnership—New Partners.

FROM 1800 to 1806, while Owen was sedulously perfecting his spinning machinery, was carefully improving his fortune, was patiently amending the condition of his subjects, and was preparing the way for still greater ameliorations, the workpeople continued to regard his proceedings with sulky obduracy; refusing to believe that he meant anything but his own good. In 1806, however, there occurred an opportunity of exhibiting, on an imposing scale, the sympathy he felt with their wants.

The manufacturing interest suffered a calamity, the recollection of which has been a copious source of alarm ever since. When Owen was Mr. Drinkwater's manager, most of the cotton-wool worked up in England came from the West Indies; and the first sample of American Sea-island cotton was entrusted to Owen, and pronounced by him, after trial, to be of an excellent quality. But fifteen years had accomplished a great change: in 1806 a large portion of our cotton was supplied by the United States: and their government, in consequence of some diplomatic disagreement with us, laid an embargo on the exportation. Prices went up suddenly to a great height: manufacturers hesitated to buy what to-morrow might not be worth half the money it had cost: some found courage to do this, while the majority stopped their mills and discharged their hands. But Owen adopted a scheme of his own.

He did not venture to buy cotton at the artificial price it had reached: he thought it cruel and unjust to expose the people to destitution and beggary by turning them adrift: and he felt, no doubt, that if he did this, he should have to begin his ameliorating process over again. - He therefore resolved to stop the mills, but to retain the people and to pay them full wages, requiring nothing from them but to keep the machinery clean. From day to day, from week to week, and from month to month, this unprofitable arrangement was carried on: until at the end of four months, when the embargo was removed, the workpeople had received no less than seven thousand pounds. This munificent proceeding "won the confidence and the hearts of the whole population;" and henceforward there were no more internal obstructions to the reforms proposed.

This transaction, on the face of it, and with the very meagre explanation given of it fifty years afterwards, appears to me of rather an ambiguous complexion. It was certainly a noble thing to maintain during four months, five hundred families, who would have been exposed to the horrors of destitution, without much previous opportunity of saving from the low wages they

had been receiving, and in a country where no public
provision is made for able-bodied persons out of work.
But the 7,000*l.* did not come out of the giver's pocket;
for the terms on which Owen went to New Lanark
were, a salary of 1,000*l.* a year and one-ninth of the
profits. His salary would be paid in the embargo year
just as at any other time; and therefore only one-ninth
of the 7,000*l.* was furnished by Owen, and the remaining 6,200*l.* by his partners. It may be contended that
manufacturers are bound, in the absence of a public
provision, to maintain their own poor. But it does not
appear to me that it is competent for any one partner to
commit his brethren to the application of such a principle, without first consulting them: and if they had
been consulted, I can hardly believe that they would
have agreed to pay full wages; since most persons
would have thought a much smaller allowance to be all
that could be required. It may be, after all, that Owen's
conviction at the time was, that the pecuniary interests
of the company would be promoted by the course
adopted: believing that a corps of trained workpeople
was as important as good machinery. He knew also,
that the concern was a profitable one, and that his services were of such value to his partners, that they would
not scan his conduct very closely.

About this time Owen lost his father-in-law. In
despite of differences as to religion, the two had lived
together most amicably; each respecting the conscientious convictions of the other: a rare example! In
Mr. Dale's last illness, he was unhappy if Owen was

absent, and was even unwilling to take his medicines from any one else. When hope was at an end, Mr. Dale consulted his son-in-law as to the pecuniary arrangements he should make: and Owen, supposing the property to be larger than it really was, strongly urged some considerable legacies to collateral relations: but Mr. Dale resisted these importunities, fearing probably, that such bequests would be felt as too great a reduction of his moderate means. At last he consented to leave Owen the power to act as he pleased in the matter; a safe compliment to his liberality. Mr. Dale appears to have been regarded by every one with respect and affection: the Glasgow people closed their places of business during his funeral: and Owen himself was greatly distressed by his loss. He says: " There was a peculiarly attractive and winning benevolence in his manner, that won the hearts of all who were known to him; but especially of those who were admitted to his familiarity. To me, who had his full confidence in all his affairs for the last six years of his life, and to whom he was most affectionately kind, his loss, as a parent and confidential friend, to whom I was attached in a manner only known and felt by myself, was as though I had been deprived of a large part of myself. The morning after his death the world appeared a blank to me; and his death was a heavy loss to and severely felt by every member of his family." A biography of Owen, which should omit this statement, would be wanting in one element for a due estimate of his character: for his permanent separation from his family when he was only ten years old,

the considerable distance to which he removed, the want
of a habit of letter-writing at a time when postage was
an expensive luxury, and the paucity of his recorded
visits to his relations, might arouse in our minds a suspicion, that in his case, as in that of many amiable and
benevolent men, the domestic affections were feeble. His
cordial attachment to Mr. Dale, may correct our doubts.

In revolving the condition of workpeople, and the
means of amending it, a happy thought crossed Owen's
mind. His fundamental notion was, as we have seen,
that we are all of us creatures of circumstances; and
that with some allowance for variety of nature, we are
what our "surroundings" have made us. But looking
at the homes of the poor, he thought he saw there one
great cause of the imperfections of the class, in the very
imperfect arrangements for rearing the young children.
If in the pliant age of infancy, good impressions could
be made in the mind, and good habits could be formed,
a step of great value would be gained.

But Owen liked to work in everything, on a grand
scale. He was not contented with a scheme for merely
assembling the young children for a few hours a day, a
proceeding which would have cost but little: he approved the Spartan plan of making the entire education
of the children a public concern; and to do this would
have required a first outlay of 5,000l., and a large
annual expense afterwards. Besides, there were the
natural dislike of the parents to parting with their
young ones, and an equally natural prepossession of the
parish minister, against entrusting infant education to

one who was an alien from all known creeds. For the present then, the plan could not be carried into practice; and various circumstances still to be related, postponed even its partial accomplishment seven years longer.

After 1806, when an apparent sacrifice of 7,000*l.* purchased the confidence of the people, three years passed on smoothly: and the partners in London and Manchester seem to have been contented with the results. But in 1809, the success which had been attained, led Owen to desire an extension of the concern, as well as a further development of his benevolent projects; particularly that of the infant school. He communicated these views to his partners; who, he says, " were all good commercial men, and looked to the main chance, as they termed it—which was a good return for their capital." They had, as far as we see, taken quietly the outlay of 7,000*l.* in 1806, perhaps being ignorant of the fact, and being contented with the average profits realized. But the projects now suggested, alarmed them.

The leading partners therefore, made a journey to Scotland, stayed several days at Owen's residence of Braxfield, near the mills, inspected all the arrangements, and listened to the enthusiastic projects for the future. They expressed themselves highly pleased with the progress that had been made, and with the actual condition of affairs; but thought it necessary to hold a consultation with the absent partners as to the feasibility of the proposed plans; and in a short time gave promise of assent by sending Owen a large silver salver with a flattering inscription. But timidity intervened, and after some months' hesitation another visit was made to New Lanark for the sake of more detailed statements.

The projected measures were again explained step by step, and Owen was patiently heard; when at last, he was equally surprised and amused at the answer of the spokesman of the party:—"Each of your propositions is true individually: but as they lead to conclusions contrary to our education, habits, and practices, they must in the aggregate be erroneous; and we cannot proceed on such new principles for governing and extending this already very large establishment." This reply does not seem to me ridiculous, although it does not abound in logic. It is just that answer which men generally give in real affairs: it is just the answer of Diogenes to the philosopher, who proved that motion was impossible; he put out his leg. A man of experience, having to do, or to forbear, a certain action, does not reduce his notions into syllogisms, or put a chain of reasoning into words: he contents himself with satisfying his mind as to which is the wiser course. To these plain men of business Owen may have appeared a philosopher, and it was no part of their scheme of affairs to spin cotton by the light of psychology: he may have appeared a fanatic, and they may have thought that his fanaticism would make him a very uncomfortable partner.

However, they seemed to hesitate what course to take, knowing as they did, that Owen, so long as he continued managing partner, would follow that course which he thought most beneficial for the business. Owen then made them an offer: that he would set a value on the works; and that at the price he named, they should take the works, or let him take them. The proposition was declared liberal: what was his valuation? Eighty-four thousand pounds (24,000*l*. more than the purchase-money in 1800; but the terms of payment do not appear). After some consultation, Owen was declared to be the buyer. The profits of the business since 1800, had been on an average, six thousand a year, besides five per cent. interest on the capital advanced.

Owen was not possessed of sufficient property to enable him to pay this considerable purchase-money, and to find the additional free capital that was necessary: but he had previously had an offer of partnership, if an opportunity should arise, from two Glasgow merchants, relatives of the Dales, and sons-in-law of Mr. Campbell of Zura. As soon as these gentlemen heard of what had taken place, they eagerly claimed a share in New Lanark, but one of the old partners was allowed to remain. The profits were to be divided into five unequal shares, of which Owen was to have the largest, besides his 1,000*l*. a year for management.

CHAPTER VI.

MATTERS went on smoothly for a short time; the business was prosperous; the new schools were rising from the foundation: but the Glasgow partners raised unexpected obstacles. Mr. Campbell of Zura, their father-in-law, had some time before, deposited with Owen on interest, the sum of 20,000*l.*, the existence of which he was unwilling to have known. The secret was unhappily divulged: and this led to feelings on the part of the sons-in-law, of dissatisfaction with Owen, warming gradually into dislike, hatred, revenge, and a resolve to compass his ruin. At first they objected to building the schools: (why should they act differently from other manufacturers?) and then they put their veto on all further measures for improving the people. They carped at the scale of wages, and were for cutting down the salaries of the managers, which on policy as well as principle were fixed at a liberal rate. Partners living only thirty miles off, were found far more inconvenient checks, than their predecessors in another kingdom.

With all Owen's amiability of disposition, there was a restless haste about his proceedings, partly caused, probably, by the early success he met with; and which a longer struggle with difficulties in youth might have corrected. Greater experience would have suggested to him that it was better to rub on with his old partners, who had treated him with singular confidence, and that it was wiser to make further alterations with the same caution which he had exercised in his early management, than it was to subject himself to the possible caprices of new men, and to enter wildly on great projects. However, he had now no choice, and he took his usual independent course; carrying on the works as usual, until he received formal notice not to proceed with the school-building. Upon this, he at once said that he would resign the management and surrender the 1,000l. a year salary. He was taken at his word: the partners took possession of the books; had all the funds into their own keeping, and acted in so vindictive a spirit as to withhold from him even the means of housekeeping, forcing him to become a borrower for his daily bread.

It was agreed that the partnership should be dissolved: and Owen was desirous of again naming a sum to be either given or taken at their option; but this proposition they refused, and insisted on a public auction. According to Owen's account, written after an interval of forty years should have calmed his anger, and written

too by one whose estimate of his opponents was generally remarkable for its candour, the resentful partners
had recourse to unjustifiable means for gaining their
ends.   They circulated reports tending to deteriorate
the saleable value of the property: they threw obstacles
in the way of Owen's finding a partner, by commenting
freely on the visionary and monstrous schemes he
nourished : they declared that though they had given
84,000*l.* for the property, they should think themselves
fortunate to get 40,000*l.* back again.

About this time, Owen had occasion to go to London,
to arrange for the publication of some essays he had
written: and the partners imagined that he was intent
on this business, and on forwarding the plans of Lancaster and Bell.   This was in 1813, when the education
and improvement of the working classes were beginning
to attract public attention.   The partners, however,
were ignorant, or had forgotten, how shrewd and
capable a man they had as an opponent.   Owen, also,
had now realized what he regarded as an abundant
fortune, and he could afford to indulge the dislike
which he felt, of being connected with men who thought
of nothing but "buying cheap and selling dear."   He
conceived the bold scheme of putting New Lanark on
an entirely new foundation: of abandoning it as a commercial speculation; of carrying it on for philanthropical purposes alone, with the view of teaching the
world what great things might be done by an earnest
desire to benefit the working classes.

But money was necessary, and a very large sum, to

purchase the property and furnish capital for the business: where was this to be found? Owen wrote a pamphlet and gave it a private circulation: setting forth what he had done and what he desired to do; showing that after a reasonable remuneration for capital and management, there would remain the means of doing much good among the workpeople; and calling on those who were at once wealthy and benevolent, to join him in this grand project. The appeal was successful and the right men were not wanting.

The most celebrated of the new partners was the publicist, Jeremy Bentham; and Owen gives an amusing account of his own interview with him. He had already heard of the nervousness of the recluse philosopher, at having to be introduced to a stranger; and he was greatly entertained with the preliminary formalities. First, there were some communications with the intimate associates, James Mill and Francis Place; then some letters between Owen and Bentham himself; and at last it was agreed that at a particular hour Owen should visit Bentham's " hermit-like retreat," and that the two should meet half-way up the stairs. Hajji Baba and his master could scarcely have made more careful stipulations as to the reception of the Great King's embassy. The instructions were carefully observed, the auspicious point was reached by both gentlemen at the same moment. Bentham, in great apparent trepidation, took his guest's hand, and said in an excited manner, " Well, well, it is all over. We are introduced." They went into the study, and sat down,

4—2

much relieved by the performance of the arduous feat.
Bentham took one-thirteenth share of the concern; and
it is said that during his whole life, this was his only
successful adventure. It will be easily believed that a
man of such a precarious nervous system never visited
New Lanark.

We may learn a good deal about Owen's character,
by noting the estimate he formed of his distinguished
partner. It would have been wonderful if the two men
had duly appreciated each other: since they differed as
much as two innovators, both unbelievers, and both of
unflinching boldness, could well differ. The one lived
in his study, devoted through a long course of years to
the investigation of lofty problems; the other had
passed his time in mills and factories, intent on carrying into practice a few ill-considered but clearly-defined
notions: the one laboured to explore the whole range
of moral and political philosophy; the other confined
his attention to a narrow field, which he worked over
and over till he fairly worked it out: the one investigated the laws by which mankind ought to govern
themselves; the other patiently and strenuously endeavoured to exercise a paternal administration over those
under his influence: the one, finally, was a recluse
who shrank from contact with a stranger; the other
was a man of genial temperament, whose original diffidence, much intercourse with the world, and great
success, had corrected. I am not surprised then, to
find Owen saying, that Bentham " spent a long life in
an endeavour to amend laws, all based on a funda-

mental error, without discovering this error; and therefore was his life, although a life of incessant well-intended industry, occupied in showing and attempting to remedy the evils of individual laws, but never attempting to dive to the foundation of all laws, and thus ascertain the cause of the errors and evils of them." In short, Bentham, according to Owen's opinion, was utterly wrong in every step he took, because he did not believe the dogma that man is an irresponsible being; and because he therefore thought it worth his while, to investigate the theory of those foolish things called rewards and punishments.

Of the other associates, the one who, I suppose, was best known to the public, was William Allen, of Plough Court, Lombard Street: a chemist by vocation, and a lecturer at one of the hospitals. He was a leading member of the Society of Friends; but like Mrs. Fry and many others of that sect, insisted little on the original theological peculiarities of Penn and George Fox, and came very near in sentiments, to the Evangelical Church and the Trinitarian dissenters. He was persuaded by his friends to join in this undertaking; but it was not very long before his strict notions were scandalized by the extravagant unbelief of his partner. Many bickerings followed: and we cannot wonder that Owen should characterize him with some little bitterness, as " active, bustling, ambitious, most desirous of doing good in his own way (as a large majority of the Quakers are);" with " kind feelings and

high aspirations; but easily impressible, and therefore
much more unsteady in mind and feeling than his other
partners."

Joseph Foster, another partner, was also a Quaker:
and of him Owen speaks in the most pleasing terms,
a man "without guile, possessed with the genuine as
spirit of charity and kindness; and who had one of the
most expanded, liberal, and well-informed minds," of
any among the Society of Friends.

But of all Owen's new allies, none was so much after
his heart as John Walker of Arno's Grove, Southgate,
and of Bedford Square. He had inherited a large
fortune, and was by birth a Quaker. But his parents,
with great liberality, set him free from the trammels of
the sect, by sending him with a superior tutor to Rome,
when he was twelve years old, and allowing him to
remain there several years. "He was a most disinterested, benevolent man, highly educated, possessing
great taste in the arts, himself a superior amateur artist,
well versed in the sciences, and a perfect gentleman, in
mind, manner and conduct, throughout his life." He
spent much in improving his country house, and in the
cultivation of exotic plants, and had a very choice
collection of specimens in natural history. He was
regarded as one of the Quakers, though he had dropped
their peculiarities of dress and language, and was remarkable for the neatness and correctness of everything
about him.

So far, no one will quarrel with Owen's estimate of
his friend; but we may dispute his opinion on another

point. He says that of all men he ever knew, either
in this or any other country, Mr. Walker had been the
least injured by the "present false system of forming
character and of constructing society." He attributes
this exemption from common human frailties, partly to
the fact of Mr. Walker's never having had his character
deteriorated by being in any business. Is it true, then,
that the best way to form a perfect man, is to send him
away from his country as a boy, and to train him afterwards to a life of idleness? Is Rome with a private
tutor, a better school for a youth, than Eton or Rugby?
Is continental dawdling more beneficial to manhood,
than a course of reading, or even of boating and hunt-
ing, at Oxford or Cambridge? Is a life passed in
playing with an easel, in purchasing exotics, and in
collecting a museum, more fitted to train a man to
athletic virtue, than the pursuit of politics, of an
honourable profession, or even of an honestly conducted
business? Owen might have afterwards suspected his
own accuracy: for thinking that if any one could be
called happy, his friend was that man, he questioned
him; and received for reply, that Mr. Walker felt a
grievous deficiency in life: he wanted a pursuit. He was

"Stretched on the rack of a too easy chair."

The number of partners, including Owen, was seven:
and the two I have not as yet mentioned, were Joseph
Fox, who was a dentist; and Michael Gibbs, afterwards
Lord Mayor of London, and known at a much later
day, for some very energetic proceedings as a metropo-
litan churchwarden.

These seven gentlemen, then, resolved to enter on their new career of benevolence, if they could succeed in buying New Lanark; a contingency which had to be determined by a public auction. The capital proposed to be raised was 130,000*l.*, in thirteen shares of 10,000*l.* each: and of these shares, Owen claimed five. But the peculiarity of the arrangement was this; that the factory was not to be carried on as an ordinary business, for the mere profit of the principals; nor as it had been carried on a dozen years, for the joint advantage of principals and workpeople: but the profits, after setting aside from them five per cent. interest on capital, were to be applied wholly to education and philanthropic schemes. This was certainly a very noble undertaking. It may appear that if the capitalists got five per cent. for their money, they practised a cheap benevolence. But to me, five per cent. seems a very poor remuneration for the risks involved in any commercial enterprise; and the more so because the place of business was far distant from London, the residence of the new partners; and because the management was to be in the hands of one almost a stranger. Whether the arrangement was, legally speaking, a partnership, does not appear. It would seem, that as Mr. Walker and his friends were to receive only the legal rate of interest for their money, their capital may have been lent to Owen on interest, with an undertaking on his part, express or implied, that he would apply the profits in the way described. Even if the lawyers gave this form to the transaction, Owen might still fairly speak of it as a partnership: and in truth, the arrangement would have been a dangerous one for him, since in case of loss he would have been debarred from any legal claim on his partners. It appears from a letter of William Allen,* of 7th January, 1814, that some conversation had passed, as to the desirability of securing a charter for the new concern; probably with a view of protecting the partners from unlimited liability: and on the 14th January, John Walker writes,† that the notion of a charter had been very favourably received, especially by Lord Sidmouth; adding that if it should be granted, it would attract the attention of the public, thus rendering New Lanark more widely known and therefore more useful. I presume that the projected charter was not obtained; though I should not imagine that any failure was owing to a want of friendliness on the part of the ministers; who, as we shall afterward see, gave a cordial and patient attention to Owen's schemes.

While Owen was in London, printing his essays, and secretly arranging his new project, the hostile partners imagined that he was dreaming away his time in utopian schemes. The property was advertised for several months; and there appeared nothing to prevent the conspirators from buying it at their own price. When the time of selling drew near, Owen quietly returned to Glasgow, accompanied by Allen, Foster, and Gibbs, who put up incognito at an hotel.

The old partners were so completely deceived as to their prospects, that they invited a party of friends

* *New Existence*, lxvi. 1854.   † Ibid. lxix.

to dine with them after the auction, to commemorate
their expected purchase. They had resolved to have
the property put up at 40,000*l.*; and supposing that no
one would rise on that price, they thought it would at
once be knocked down to themselves. Owen did not
meet them till the morning of the sale; but he then
questioned them about the upset price. They named
40,000*l.*—Will you take 60,000*l.* for the property?
—We will not.—Then I claim 60,000*l.* as the upset
price.—They were obliged to submit. There had been
a discussion in London as to the price to which Owen
and his friends would go: it was agreed that they
would venture even to 120,000*l.*; a rise of nearly
40,000*l.* on the sale of three or four years before.
Owen authorized a solicitor to act for him; and to
bid from time to time an advance of 100*l.*, the lowest
sum fixed by the conditions: and if the biddings rose
to 120,000*l.*, a further consultation was to take place.
The hostile partners were there to do their own work,
and they entered the sale room with a great appearance
of confidence. The auction, Owen says, had excited
much interest in Glasgow, from the popularity which
he had acquired, as well as from a notion which had got
abroad, that he was to be crushed by the superior
wealth of his opponents.

The property was put up at 60,000*l.*: the solicitor
advanced 100*l.*: the clan advanced 1,000*l.*: another
hundred and another thousand followed again and
again, until the offer reached 84,000*l.* Then a pause
was asked that the Campbells might have a private

consultation; the result of which was, that their next advance was 500*l.* : and immediately the mortifying 100*l.* followed. The biddings rose to 100,000*l.*, when another pause and private consultation. The confident Galwegians were crest-fallen, pale, and agitated. They returned to the charge however, advancing only 100*l.* at a time, till they got to 110,000*l.*, when the solicitor again stepped in with 110,100*l.* Owen had planted himself in a quiet corner, to watch the drama, like an uninterested spectator: but at this point a brother-in-law of the Scotch partners advised him to desist: the interference was decidedly disclaimed. Mr. Kirkman Finlay, a leading man of business, and a friend of both sides, now left the room, saying in a stage whisper, " the little one will have it." This stimulated the clan to another effort: but after rising to 114,000*l.*, the solicitor's reiterated 100*l.* broke their spirits, and the property was knocked down to the new partners at 114,100*l.* The dinner that had been ordered, came off gloomily. One of the guests, Colonel Hunter, a newspaper proprietor, was cruel enough to propose an ironical toast, " success to the men who had sold for 114,000*l.*, what they had valued that morning at 40,000*l.*" There remained one hope: that the purchasers would not prove wealthy enough to give the required security: but when the names were disclosed, that vision was at end. To crown the vexation of the whole affair, it was announced the day after the sale, that the people of New Lanark, on hearing of the result, had illuminated their windows for joy.

The accounts of the late partnership were now made
up, and the result was surprising.   During the five
years, the net profit was 160,000*l.*, besides five per cent.
on the capital employed.   It is true that the successful
sale of the works for 30,000*l.* more than they had been
bought for, accounts for a portion of this large sum;
though after all, part of this excess may have represented money laid out in improvements during the four
years.   If however, we deduct the whole advance, there
will still be left nearly 32,000*l.* a year clear profit,
besides an interest of five per cent. on capital.   Such a
business ought not to have gone a begging : but the
Scotch partners were wealthy and angry; and Owen
could afford to indulge a higher taste than that for
money-getting, his share of the property at New Lanark
turning out to be worth more than 70,000*l.*

The three London partners who had come to Scotland,
showed themselves as soon as the auction had passed
over; and they remained in Glasgow a short time, for
the execution of the transfer.   In the meantime, the
inhabitants of New Lanark impatiently expected the
return of their benevolent governor (as he loved to
think himself); and having learned the day he intended
to visit them, they made preparations for his reception.
When he and his partners got near to the old burgh,
which was not far distant from the works, the shouts of
a multitude of people surprised Owen, and rather
alarmed his Quaker companions.   The postilions were
stopped, the traces unhooked, and the carriage dragged
in triumph all the way to New Lanark.   The new part-

ners were at last delighted with this proof of Owen's popularity; and he himself, though he fairly disclaims all undue love of tumultuous applause, was deeply gratified by this unsought testimony of the love of his voluntary subjects. Thus was Owen again in possession of the uncontrolled management of his people: thus by the disinterested sacrifice of a great income, had he attained to the position he had nobly sought, of the head of a great manufacturing establishment carried on for the benefit of the working classes.

CHAPTER VII.

Domestic Establishment—Promotion of Lancaster's Plans—Presides at a Dinner in 1812—His Speech on Education—Quotation from it—Noticed by Persons of high rank: the Archbishop of Canterbury—Absence of Offence—Becomes an Author: Four Essays—Earl of Liverpool—Lord Sidmouth—Other Persons—Contents of Essays—The New Lanark Experiment—Denounces certain Laws—Those that foster Drunkenness—State Lotteries—Poor Law—Church Tests—Recommendations :· Education—Employment—Conclusion of Essays.

IN the present chapter, I propose to mention some circumstances which have no particular relation to the management of New Lanark, but which are necessary to the full understanding of Owen's career.

When he first went to New Lanark, and for some years afterwards, he resided entirely in a house close to the works. But Mr. Dale's unmarried daughters after their father's death, came to live with their sister; and this led to Owen's taking as a summer residence, the neighbouring mansion of Braxfield. It was this place which gave the title to Macqueen, Lord Braxfield, one of the judges of the Supreme Court of Scotland; a man noted for the coarseness of his observations on the bench, and particularly for his brutal remark, addressed to a former companion at chess, *on condemning him to death :·*

that he had checkmated him at last. Lord Braxfield had died in 1800. He had been a good neighbour to Mr. Dale; and had been shrewd enough to see the advantage to his own property of having works in its neighbourhood. About 1808, Mr. Macqueen, the son, on whom the property was entailed, let the house to Owen. Here then, the Miss Dales lived with their brother-in-law : a carriage and horses being kept for the family, and another for the young ladies. Owen was much attached to his sisters-in-law: took them to travel both in England and on the Continent; and for some years sent them to the best schools he could find in London. One of them died unmarried, and two married English clergymen, whose religious convictions gradually caused a separation between the relations.

I have already related how Owen, when he was far from having achieved a competency, bestowed no less than 1,500*l.* for promoting the Lancaster and Bell schemes of education. In the twenty years that followed these munificent donations, Lancaster had become a man of note; and Owen, seeing the evil results that the manufacturing system was causing in Scotland, and believing that an improved plan of education was the most hopeful corrective, encouraged Lancaster to visit Glasgow. It was proposed that a public dinner should be given to welcome his arrival. Lancaster, as a Quaker and a stranger, declined this honour, unless his old friend, whom he supposed to be well acquainted with Scotch customs, would act as chairman. Owen declined this task, feeling himself unequal to it from want of experience in public life, but gave way when Lancaster refused to come on any other condition.

Owen at this time had not made enemies by any wild expression of his opinions: he had warm friends among the professors at Edinburgh and Glasgow: and at this banquet Professors Jardine and Mylne supported him on either hand; while Mr. Wardlaw, a highly popular preacher, acted as croupier. Owen seized this public occasion of bringing forward his doctrine, that man is the creature of circumstances; and that it depends on our social arrangements, whether the children who are growing up shall be the blessings or the scourges of the world. The speech was pithy, and so short that it can hardly have taken a quarter of an hour to deliver. But Owen says, that the hearers were so much taken by surprise that they seemed electrified: that the professors were highly delighted: and that the enthusiastic applause bestowed upon him at the close of his remarks, exceeded anything he elsewhere witnessed in a Scotch assembly. Any suspicion that this agreeable reception was accidental, was allayed by a very complimentary letter from Mr. Kirkman Finlay, who was casually absent.

The speech is fortunately preserved in the appendix to Owen's autobiography: and it appears to me to be an excellent essay, expressing in very few words, sentiments as to education, exactly in unison with our present opinions, and certainly much in advance of the ordinary convictions of that day. Even now, I find many people expressing alarm lest the working classes should be taught too much, so as to unfit them for their station: and fifty years ago, such fears were far more common. Owen was convinced of the groundlessness of these alarms. Then again, he anticipated the doctrine, that education must be taken to mean, not merely the instruction given in school, but also all those impressions "which we receive from our earliest infancy, until our characters are generally fixed and established." He forcibly illustrated the importance of education, taken in this wide sense.

" From whence do these general bodily and mental differences proceed? Are they inherent in our nature, or do they arise from the respective soils on which we are born?

"Evidently from neither. They are wholly and solely the effects of that education which I have described. Man becomes a wild ferocious savage, a cannibal, or a highly civilized and benevolent being, according to the circumstances in which he may be placed from his birth.

" It is an important point then, for us to consider, whether we have any influence over these circumstances; if we can command any of them; and if we can, to what extent.

" Let us then, suppose that wishing to try the experiment, we were to convey a number of infants so soon as they were born, from this country into distant regions; deliver them to the natives of those countries, and allow them to remain among them. Can we suppose the result to be uncertain? No; they would become, one and all, like unto those natives, whatever their characters might be.

"In the same manner, were an exchange of any given number of children to be made at their birth, between the Society of Friends, of which our worthy guest, Joseph Lancaster, is a member, and the loose fraternity which inhabit St. Giles' in London, the children of the former would grow up like the members of the latter, prepared for every degree of crime, while those of the latter would become the same temperate good moral characters as the former."

All this is excellently put, and is without the offensive inference commonly drawn in after years. Owen did not go on to say: " Shall then, the barbarian be held accountable for his savagery? Shall the man-eater be held accountable for his cannibalism? Shall the Scotch murderer be held accountable for his brutality? Heaven forbid! In my opinion, they are not responsible to God or to man." This is what he delighted in reiterating when he was an older man: but at the Glasgow dinner he confined himself to a much sounder, and far more important inference: " Let us then, take every means in our power, to interest all those who have any weight or influence in the city, to enter heartily into the support and extension of the Lancasterian system of education for the poor, until every child of that class shall find a place in one of the schools."

The applause which attended this public effort, stimulated Owen to further exertions. It appeared to him worth while to circulate more widely, and in a more permanent form, those sentiments which had commanded the warm approbation of his Glasgow friends. He therefore wrote a pamphlet, explaining at rather greater length, but still very shortly, the views contained in his speech. This constituted the first of the four treatises which he afterwards called, *A New View of Society: or, Essays on the Principle of the Formation of the Human Character.* The first was written in 1812 and printed in 1813: the second, third, and fourth were written and printed about the end of 1813. They were not published however, at that time; * but were distributed very widely among the "principal political, literary, and religious characters in this country and on the Continent; as well as among the governments of Europe, America, and British India." They were not published for sale until 1816: they afterwards went through many editions. The private edition was dedicated to Mr. Wilberforce: the others, successively, to "The British public," to the "Superintendents of Manufactories," and to the "Prince Regent."

These essays on the formation of character, are frequently mentioned in notices of the period just before the close of the war. But Owen, even before he had written all of them, had attracted the attention of the leading men of the day. He had sent a copy of the

---

* *Autobiography*, 256. At pp. 265 to 271 will be found the first essay. But it must have been altered after the first printing, since at p. 268, Napoleon is spoken of as the *late* ruler of France.

two first essays to the Archbishop of Canterbury, and had been introduced to him. Meeting his Grace afterwards, he told him of his having a third and fourth in manuscript, and was asked for a sight of them at Lambeth. Owen went to the palace the next day, and having read out the third essay, was pressed by the Archbishop to go on reading the fourth, and found a ready and attentive listener. A correspondence was afterwards carried on between the manufacturer and the great Churchman. Several members of the Cabinet, with English and Irish bishops, also exhibited an interest quite inconsistent with that bigoted dislike to improvement, which it was the fashion with the radicals of the day, to impute to them. Owen was acceptable to them, because he aimed at a social, and not at a political reform.

Copies of the essays having been sent to the Earl of Liverpool, and an interview requested, the very next day was fixed on by his lordship. At his private house, the place appointed, Owen was shown into the drawing-room; where he found the premier with Lady Liverpool, to whom he was introduced, and whom he found deeply interested in his views. Among other things, she communicated to him that her husband had just taken as private secretary, " a very promising young man," who had lately left Oxford, where he had obtained high honours: this was young Peel, afterwards the great minister. At this interview, very little of importance seems to have occurred, beyond the expression on Lord Liverpool's part, of general agree-

ment with Owen's views. It was encouraging however, to be received on friendly terms by the first
dignitary and by the first statesman of the day.

I do not profess to understand the motives by which
Owen was actuated, in enlisting the Government on
his side. But not satisfied with the premier's approbation, he communicated the essays formally to the
Government; who found in them nothing to object to.
Lord Sidmouth, the Home Secretary, asked what it
was proposed to do further with them. Owen replied,
with affected diffidence, that as the views he advocated
were much opposed to existing prejudices, and as the
changes he proposed were of high importance, he should
like every means to be used for the detection of possible
error: and that he would willingly have two hundred
copies bound up with alternate blank leaves, in the
hope that the Ministry would circulate these among the
governments of Europe and America, and the European universities, with the request that apparent objections should be written on the blank leaves. It is
rather surprising to find that this course was adopted:
that many of the vagrant pamphlets found their way
back again; and that their author was summoned to
share the task of perusing the commentaries. Nothing
seems to have come of this elaborate invitation of
criticism. The pamphlets were afterwards published;
and Lord Sidmouth asked to have so many copies
sent him that he might furnish one to each of the
bishops.

Owen called one day, by desire of the Home Secretary, upon the Archbishop of Armagh, who was in London; and there he met with Mr. Edgeworth, who said of him, " I have read that man's works, and he has been in my brains, and has stolen all my ideas." John Quincey Adams also, then minister in London, asked for a number of copies, and sent one to the governor of every state in the Union. A copy found its way to Elba, and Owen believed that Napoleon had read it with great attention; and that perhaps, this was the cause of the pacific policy which he promised to pursue, if his enemies would allow him the quiet enjoyment of the French throne.

I have said that Owen's first essay was not much more than an elaboration of his Lancaster speech. But as he went on, the approbation he received, and which possibly, he assimilated rather readily, together it may be, with an improved facility of writing,* led him to a bolder flight than he had begun with. The four essays fill nearly seventy octavo pages; and the spinner of the finest yarn would require a good quantity of material to occupy so considerable a space. The gold of the first speech was not so pure as to bear without addition to be spread to this intolerable extent.

In the second essay, an account was given of what had been done at New Lanark: and after detailing

* In a subsequent chapter, I shall have to mention that in writing these essays Owen received the assistance of Bentham's friend, Francis Place. His Glasgow speech, also, as I have given it, probably received many finishing touches from another hand.

the original condition of the place, the difficulties to be encountered, and the prejudices to be smoothed down, Owen states what he regards as the results actually effected at the time he was writing: that is, at about the period the benevolent partnership began. He says that the society was certainly much improved: that with the infliction of *scarcely* one legal punishment, the worst habits had disappeared, with a fair prospect that the minor ones would be rooted out: that an application for parish relief was almost unknown: that drunkenness was not seen in the streets: that the children were educated without resort to punishment: and that the community of more than two thousand persons, exhibited an appearance "of industry, temperance, comfort, health, and happiness."

In the fourth essay, after denouncing "*that greatest of all errors, the notion that individuals form their own characters*," he declaims against certain national laws which he regards as growing out of that doctrine.

First, those which encourage drinking, by fostering and extending taverns and gin-shops. Total abstinence had not been thought of in Owen's day: and temperate as he was, he had registered no vow to deny himself spirituous liquors. But the teetotallers may claim him as a brother in his declamations against houses for drinking. The remedies he proposed however, would be highly unpalatable to that very dogmatical race of social reformers: for while he would have reduced the number of pothouses, and would have screwed up the tax on ardent spirits, so as to put them out of the

reach of the people generally; he would at the same
time have reduced the price of beer, in order that the
poorest might have it at command.

Next to this, he recommends the discontinuance of
the state lottery. He declares that "the law which
creates this measure, is neither more nor less than a
law to legalize gambling, entrap the unwary, and rob
the ignorant." I have no doubt that Lords Liverpool
and Sidmouth, Mr. Canning and Lord Castlereagh,
fully assented to the denunciation of this legalized
gambling, in which not even a pretence of skill, or of
industry, was called into action; and which did not,
like horse-racing, produce any secondary results of
importance. But the Chancellor of the Exchequer
stood in the way of a change: and the period was one
when the national revenue was strained to the utmost.
Owen thought truly enough, that the amount of the
national revenue depends mainly on the number of the
population, and their strength, industry, and capacity
(supposing land and capital to remain unchanged):
and that any tax, or any law, which deteriorates the
character of the population, will certainly lessen their
industry, and reduce the national revenue. But this
is true only in the long run: and there are periods in
the history of a nation, when some future advantage
must be sacrificed to present necessities. The close of
the war of a quarter of a century, of a war carried on
against the greatest genius of modern times, command-
ing the resources of a large part of Europe, was
eminently such a period. It was reserved for more

halcyon days, a dozen years later, to abandon for ever that authorized gambling, which for a hundred and fifty years had disgraced the state.

Owen next attacked the poor laws; and in doing this he merely echoed the cry of Arthur Young, of Malthus, of the French economists, and of a hundred others. At first he only says that those laws require revisal; a proposition few would dispute. The long wars with Napoleon had led to great abuses in administration. Before 1793, the expenditure on parish relief was not outrageously large: and the administration had been so far from erring on the side of compassion, that a system of farming the workhouses had been generally introduced; and it requires no elaborate proof to convince us, that a governor who boarded the paupers at so much a head, would be very unlikely to coddle his peevish guests. But the commencement of the great war, developed a new feature in our history. During all previous European wars, Great Britain had habitually exported grain to the Continent; and then, the breaking out of hostilities had thrown obstacles in the way of transporting the grain, and had thus caused such a plenty at home as easily furnished any demand for our army and navy. But about the date of the revolt of the American colonies, our manufactures had increased so much, that we not only consumed all our own corn, but became dependent on a foreign supply. And when the French revolutionary war broke out, the immense risk and expense of bringing corn from abroad, added to its high price there, reduced us to a condition

of dearth, or something like famine.* To keep the
labourers from destitution, a large increase of wages
would have been required. But the farmers, as it
appears from Arthur Young's *Annals*, dreaded to give
this rise, because they thought that the high rate would
become traditional and permanent; and they much
preferred that the wants of the labourers should be
supplied from the poor-rate: a most unfair arrangement to many rate-payers, and a disastrous one to the
labourers. A revisal of the laws was therefore, as
Owen says, much needed. But when he adds that by
these laws, the industrious, temperate, and comparatively virtuous, are compelled to support the ignorant,
the idle, and the vicious; and that greater encouragement is held out to idleness and extravagance, than to
industry and frugality; he indulges in some extravagance of declamation, and represents only one side of
the question. He forgets the claims of the numerous
class of sick, of widows, and of orphans.

These denunciations of drunkenness, of state lotteries,
and of poor-laws, would pass current among his ministerial friends; but not so his next: that of religious

---

* Evelyn says, early in 1703, in the heat of the war of the succession, " Corn and provisions so cheap that the farmers are unable
to pay their rents." But in April to May, 1859, the mere declaration
of war between France and Austria, caused the quartern loaf to rise
from 4½d. to 6½d.: an increase of price which indicates something
like a rise of 20s. a quarter in wheat. Consult also, A. Smith, A.
Young, or Maculloch, for the comparative prices in 1735 to 1745; and
in 1750 to 1765: the former period including the years of the Spanish
war; the latter that of the seven years' war: and neither of them
exhibiting any trace of what we now call war prices.

tests.   He is moderate enough not to wish to overthrow the Church, because he thinks it might be made a useful instrument of reform.   He would however, "withdraw" from it certain tenets (he does not specify what) "which constitute its weakness and create its danger." He would also "withdraw all declarations of belief in which all persons cannot conscientiously join:" and he asserts that this course would give stability to Church and State, and would put an end to "all the theological differences which now confound the intellects of men and disseminate universal discord."   I fear that Owen's episcopal friends would look askance at this very latitudinarian declaration.

Among the measures he recommends, are of course, some for promoting education.   He insists on the absurdity of the fact, that the British Government had no national system, but allowed the minds of its subjects to be formed at random.   He urged that there should be a department of the ministry, specially devoted to the purpose of systematic instruction.   He also saw clearly that little could be done without a provision of skilful teachers; and he advised the formation of training schools.   Would that this had been done in the last generation instead of the present: for now we should be reaping the full advantage of it.

His opinions as to furnishing employment for those who want it, appeared extravagant then, and would not meet with much better acceptance now.   His first plan, that of obtaining statistical returns throughout every section of the kingdom, of the respective wages paid, of the number of labourers, with their occupations, and of the proportion out of employ, has been since adopted to a great extent, by means of the decennial census, with some late additions by the Board of Trade. But Owen's views extended much beyond the mere supply of information to the public: he would have had the Government itself undertake to furnish occupation to the unemployed, by setting them to work on roads, canals, harbours, and even ship-building. We have seen two great attempts in this direction, during the last dozen years : the first in Ireland during the famine; the second in France after the revolution of '48: the results were not encouraging. In times of commercial distress, when the workhouse test must be superseded, hard labour, such as stone-breaking, is a useful substitute; but no means have yet been devised, by which results of any great money value are obtained. The work is done unwillingly, lazily, sulkily. And what is effected very imperfectly now by a local board of guardians, whose own pockets are interested, is not likely to be accomplished satisfactorily by the salaried agents of a Government.

Owen concludes his fourth and last essay, by dimly indicating the possession of a philosophy which would regenerate society, if men's minds were prepared to receive it. With a Pythagorean reticence, he reserves to himself and his initiated, an *esoteric* doctrine of which the world is unworthy. The *exoteric* doctrine is expressed by the proposed measures I have mentioned; which however, "are only a compromise with the errors of the present systems." The interior and sacred doctrine cannot at present be revealed with safety. But " as soon as the public mind shall be sufficiently prepared to receive it, the practical detail of this system shall be fully developed." It would have been happy for the enthusiastic author of these supposed novelties, if the period of revelation had never arrived. He would then have escaped the public odium which crushed all the persevering efforts of the latter half of his long life.

CHAPTER VIII.

New Lanark: Infant Schools—Elder Schools—Means of living—
Regularity of the System—Statistics—Happiness—Celebrity—
Jacobi—Esterhazy—Nicholas—Makes an Offer—Particulars of it
—Remarks upon—Other Visitors—New Difficulties.

As soon as Owen had arranged his partnership with
Jeremy Bentham, Walker, Allen, and their associates,
and found himself the uncontrolled head of New Lanark,
he went earnestly to work to carry out the further improvements he had devised.   He was able now to complete the institution, designed in 1809, for the formation
of the character of the children.   The infants even,
were admitted as soon as they could walk, with the
hope of teaching them something by signs and familiar
conversation.   The parents soon overcame their first
prejudices; and willingly paid the school fee of three
shillings a year.   The average expense of the pupils of
all ages, was about 2*l.* a year.   The children, Owen
says, were trained and educated without punishment or
any fear of it; and were, while in school, by far the
happiest human beings he had ever seen.   Besides instruction by objects, models, and paintings, dancing and
singing were taught daily to all the pupils of two years

old and upwards: but these profane accomplishments afterwards alarmed the sectarian zeal of William Allen.

There were other schools for elder children under twelve years, that being the age under which no one was admitted to work. The pupils were taken in preference to other children, not only as spinners, but as carpenters, turners, and engineers: the outlay in repairs alone, being at that time 8,000*l.* a year. These elder children were taught not only the ordinary branches of instruction, but singing and dancing as the infants were; and besides these things, were regularly trained in military evolutions.

The arrangements were now completed for supplying all the necessaries of life at cost prices, on cash terms instead of credit. Some of the larger families, with all the members working, could earn 2*l.* a week; and it was estimated that the saving they effected by the new shops, was 10*s.* a week: no improbable sum, when we remember the excessive improvidence of buying habitually on credit.

All the houses in the village, with a hundred and fifty acres of land around, as well as the mills and works, belonged to the partnership; and this gave an opportunity for perfection of administration, such as cannot be effected in a large town. Owen tells us, that Mr. Hase, a competent judge, as having been many years cashier of the Bank of England, besides having been deeply concerned in its reorganization, paid him a high compliment on the clockwork regularity of his machine: desiring to know, after repeated inspection, how many generations it had taken to attain such accuracy.   Owen's experience as a manager, and his assiduity at Mr. Drinkwater's factory, where he regularly began with the workpeople in the morning, and locked the gates at night, must have given him a command over the forces under his control, such as one originally a principal could scarcely attain.

The population seems to have reached 2,500.   It is casually mentioned in a pamphlet* written in 1854, that in the year 1816 the profits were about 15,000*l.*: and from the context I conclude that this was besides 5 per cent. interest on capital.

I see no reason to doubt the assertion of Owen, in a letter to William Allen,† that at New Lanark, "the comfort, the morals, and the happiness of the people, *far*, very far indeed, exceed those of any other cotton manufacturing establishment in the kingdom—I might with safety say in the world."   And the picture which is given of the school-children, has a geniality and heartiness about it, which at any rate illustrate the goodness of heart of the painter.   "Being always treated with kindness and confidence, and altogether without fear, even of a harsh word from any of their numerous teachers, they exhibited an unaffected grace and natural politeness, which surprised and fascinated strangers; and which new character and conduct were to most of them so unaccountable, that they knew not how to express themselves, or how to hide their wonder and amazement.

* *New Existence*, App. iii.   † Ibid. App. ii.

"These children standing up, seventy couples at a time, in the dancing-room, and often surrounded with many strangers, would with the utmost ease and natural grace go through all the dances of Europe, with so little direction from their master, that the strangers would be unconscious that there was a dancing-master in the room.

"In their singing lessons, one hundred and fifty would sing at the same time—their voices being trained to harmonize; and it was delightful to hear them sing the old popular Scotch songs; which were great favourites with most strangers, from the unaffected simplicity and hearty feeling with which these songs were sung by the children, whose natures had been naturally and rationally cultivated."

The expense and labour which Owen had bestowed on the circulation of his pamphlets, the patronage which he had won from the ministry; together, as I suppose, with the proximity of New Lanark to the falls of the Clyde, and the practice of travelling into Scotland which Scott's poems are said to have caused; led to a constant succession of visitors at the mills. Owen himself had become quite a celebrity; and during his frequent stays in London was visited by many persons of distinction.

Among these were several foreign ambassadors; and special mention is made of Baron Jacobi, the Prussian ambassador, through whom the four essays had been sent to his royal master. Jacobi himself professed great approbation of Owen's views. The King of Prussia also, esteemed them so highly, that he wrote with his own hand a letter of thanks; and added that he had given instructions to his minister of the interior, to carry out the system of education recommended, as far as circumstances would permit. This, says Owen, was the origin of the celebrated system of Prussian national education, which to this day is carried on.

Prince Esterhazy, the Austrian ambassador, was introduced by Jacobi on another occasion. Owen, not catching the name mentioned, and regarding his guest merely as a foreigner of distinction, had, for that reason, the freer and more interesting conversation with him. The misapprehension must have made an impression on him, as he mentions it forty years afterwards: though it is notorious that incidents plant themselves in our memory, not according to the importance we attach to them, but in consequence of some casual circumstance, or state of mind, that we cannot afterwards account for. No doubt Owen behaved with due politeness, for at no period of his life was he troubled with envy of rank and outward greatness, or actuated by a hatred of the powers that be. Esterhazy appeared struck with a reply he received. When he asked what was proposed by the New Views, Owen said: "To make full-formed men and women, physically and mentally, who would always think and act consistently and rationally." Notwithstanding the absence of formality in the reception, the Prince was well pleased; and showed in after years that he was so, by rendering Owen valuable services.

One of the most distinguished of the visitors at New

Lanark, was the late Czar, then the Grand Duke Nicholas; who came attended by a suite, including Sir Alexander Crighton, his confidential physician. The whole party remained at Owen's house a couple of days; and Nicholas repaid the civilities he received, by the flattering notice he took of his host's two younger sons, whom he insisted on having constantly as his companions. Owen had not to make any complaints such as those which were wrung from the refined Evelyn, when Peter the Great occupied Sayes Court at Deptford. Braxfield and its grounds suffered no pollution or dilapidation from the polished Russians. A hundred years had revolutionized the Court of Muscovy: railroads and the present Alexander's noble but perilous efforts to emancipate the serfs, may in another century issue in as great an improvement of the people at large.

Nicholas must have been favourably impressed with what he saw; for before he left New Lanark he made an attempt to induce Owen to follow him to Russia. The offer as reported, savours of romance. Alexander was then the Czar and likely to continue such: the resources at the command of Nicholas must therefore have been limited: the funds of the Russian empire had been severely taxed by the Napoleon wars. Yet Nicholas is represented as proposing a scheme, which would have required at least twenty millions sterling to carry out.

At this period, the long war, followed by the changes resulting from the peace, had caused fearful distress

in Great Britain. The doctrine of Malthus had got
possession of men's minds : and the destitution and disorder which had been the natural consequences of the
alternation of war and peace, were attributed to over-
population and deficiency of food.   Nicholas, with these
ideas in his mind, asked his host what was to be done
with his two sons; and hearing that they were to be
brought up as cotton-manufacturers, he offered to take
them under his protection.   He also made this princely
proposal : that Owen himself should emigrate to Russia,
and bring *two millions* of the surplus British population
with him.   The offer was respectfully declined.   One
cannot help regretting this refusal.   Owen now touched
upon the zenith of his greatness: he had almost reached
that point of time after which he met with insuperable
obstacles to his schemes, and with a series of almost
unmixed disappointments.   But in Russia he might
have been eminently useful.   There was nothing in the
paternal government of that country, at all abhorrent to
his political notions: for, as I have before remarked,
he was no partisan of the radical, or democratic, movement.   The sincere desire both of Alexander, and of
his brother Nicholas, to improve the condition of their
subjects, would have tolerably well satisfied his conception of the duties of princes: and the genial and
sociable tempers of the peasants, accustomed to the
harsh superintendence of German agents, would have
welcomed the benevolent treatment of the English philanthropist.   Owen, not many years later, went to the
west instead of the east; and found among the back-

woodsmen, a race far more intractable than the trained bondsmen of Muscovy.

Besides the visitors I have mentioned, Owen had many others; and I find the following in a list of them.* Lord Stowell, Sir Samuel Romilly, Joseph Hume, Dr. Bowring, Henry Brougham, Vansittart, Canning, Cobbett, Wilberforce, Godwin, Carlile, Clarkson, Zachary Macaulay (father of Lord Macaulay), the first Sir R. Peel, Malthus, James Mill, Southey, Ricardo, Sir James Mackintosh, Colonel Torrens, Francis Place, Edward Baines. The author of this list, a devoted follower, has arranged it after a fashion of his own; and does not say absolutely, that every one of these was a visitor. I mention this qualification merely for accuracy, and not because I doubt that Owen was in communication with the rank and the real greatness of the nation. I should add that the Dukes of York and of Sussex had some intercourse with him, and that the Duke of Kent, until he died, exhibited an earnest interest in his proceedings. On the whole, it is stated† that during ten years, New Lanark received two thousand visitors each year.

Owen however, even at this time, was not without his difficulties, caused by the antagonism of his notions to those of some of his partners. The children, as we have seen, were admitted into the schools as soon as they could walk. At two years old they began to learn to dance: at four years old they practised singing; and at a suitable age, both boys and girls were regularly

* Holyoake: *Last Days*, 4.   † *Autobiog.* 114.

drilled, and went through their military exercises in divisions led by young drummers and fifers. Now three of the partners were Quakers; and one of these, William Allen, was an active, managing person, who had engrafted a Puritan asceticism on the original tenets of George Fox. It may be conceived that he looked suspiciously at the worldly amusements of dancing and singing, and with something of horror at the needless training of the pupils for warlike purposes. However, for several years no schism broke out: and so far was Allen from intermeddling, that he, and his estimable partner Foster, were often to be seen, during their visits to New Lanark, looking placidly on while the children were going through their profane lessons. Yet the storm was slowly gathering.

CHAPTER IX.

Enlarged Aspirations—Owen's Doctrine: partly correct—Real Position—Exaggerated Estimate—Particular Error—Owen's State of Mind—The World's Obstinacy—First Example: Glasgow Meeting.

OWEN's career had been hitherto singularly prosperous. As a child, as a boy, as a youthful manager, as a master manufacturer, as a social innovator, as the head of a vast philanthropic establishment, he had met with obstacles just great enough to task his energies and stimulate his ingenuity, but not such as to cause failure or hesitation. He had earned wealth, position, renown: besides that satisfaction which attends success; and, I doubt not, the agreeable consciousness of being a benefactor of his race. It was natural, and almost inevitable, that he should desire to extend his operations over a wider field: and to this course, his activity, his ambition, and his benevolence, alike pointed. He had reformed a village which he had found sunk in want, immorality, and misery: had at first raised it to comparative prosperity and moral excellence, and was now (at a great pecuniary sacrifice it is true), in a fair way to restore the golden age on the Falls of the Clyde. Why should he not do for the world at large, what he had actually accomplished in a remote corner?

Why should he not inaugurate the reign of universal peace and prosperity?

According to the notions which Owen entertained, these aspirations were legitimate and not unreasonable. He conceived that he had discovered a vital truth which before his time had been hidden from the world : he imagined that in demonstrating, as he conceived himself to have demonstrated, that men are the creatures of cir-cumstances, and that their characters are formed for them and are not formed by themselves, he had put into the hands of governments, the means of removing at once and for ever, the improvidence, the immorality, and the destitution of their subjects. Now I will not stay here to combat Owen's exaggeration, in saying that a man has nothing to do with the formation of his own charac-ter, though the error seems to me a very pernicious one. I waive for the present, my right of battle on this field, because for the purpose immediately in hand, it appears to me unimportant. We are now concerned, not with individuals but with classes : and however dangerous I may feel it, to say to any one person, " circumstances have made you what you are, and you are not respon-sible for your character or for your actions," I willingly concede that, comparing a class of persons of one place and time, with a class of persons of another place and time, the difference between these classes is mainly the result of external circumstances, for which the persons themselves are not accountable.

Owen, of course, ran into a palpable error, when he assumed to himself the merit of originating this truth, as to-

the influence of circumstances on the characters of classes
of men. If he had been at all acquainted with the ordinary history of philosophy, it would never have entered
his head to set up such a claim for himself. What he
would have said, and said truly, was, that he had
brought this truth into bold relief; that he had pressed
it on the attention of mankind, and especially of the
influential classes; that he had fairly drawn from it the
inference of the overwhelming importance of education,
taken in the widest sense; and that he had himself
patiently and laboriously striven to enforce both the
truth and the inference deduced from it, within the
sphere of his own influence.

But this would have appeared to him a miserably
tame and cold acccount of his exploits. Moving, as he
did, until middle life, in a rather narrow circle, generally among persons of moderate cultivation, himself far
better acquainted with science than with philosophy, his
mind inflamed by familiarity with the wonderful recent
triumphs of mechanical art, and more accustomed to
command subordinates than to strive with his equals,
he had contracted a confirmed habit of exaggerated
self-reliance, and an excessively high estimate of his
own powers. He fancied himself in possession of the
lever (not without the fulcrum) which should move
the world: he had the elixir which should cure all the
physical, and all the moral ills of his fellow-men. He
was doomed to disappointment.

Besides the general mental inflation by which Owen
was misled, there was a distinct error in his reasoning

on his favourite topic. He had said to himself, I have discovered a new and grand truth by which the world may be regenerated: I will seek an opportunity of verifying it by applying it to practice. Men are creatures of circumstances: that is my truth. If I can get the uncontrolled management of a body of men, I will change their circumstances, and their character will be seen to change: that shall be my verification. The entire reasoning was unsound. The assertion that bodies of men are greatly influenced by circumstances, was nothing new; and no one could have been found to dispute the proposition, that if Owen would devote himself to the physical and moral improvement of his village, highly valuable results would follow. The experiment at New Lanark was noble in conception and highly valuable in execution: but regarded as a verification of a new doctrine it appears to me as simply valueless.

We can conceive then, what was Owen's state of mind, after he had formed his benevolent partnership, and while he was labouring to carry out his philanthropic schemes. He was become an enthusiast, ready to make any sacrifice, if only he might attain his Utopia. I will quote his own words. "By my own experience and reflection, I had ascertained that human nature is radically good, and is capable of being trained, educated, and placed from birth in such a manner, that all ultimately (that is as soon as the gross errors and corruptions of the present false and wicked system are overcome and destroyed), must become united, good, wise, healthy, and happy. And I felt that to attain this glorious result, the sacrifice of the character, fortune, and life of an individual, was not deserving a moment's consideration. And my decision was made: to overcome all opposition, and *to succeed or to die in the attempt.*"

To a man in this exalted state of mind, the ordinary course of events appears tedious and intolerably slow. Owen had formerly been remarkable for his habit of looking forward, for his care in breaking up his ground and sowing his seed, and for his patience in watching and tending his moral harvest. But now he was restless, and wanted to reap his crop in springtide. He allowed himself to fancy "that the simple, plain, honest enunciation of the truth," would secure the co-operation of the world; and that the reformation he proposed would not be a difficult task. He chose to forget the obstacles and the prejudices which in his own experiment he had had to overcome; and he strangely assumed that ten millions of people would be more easily managed, than two thousand had been. He found however, that the long-formed habits, the inveterate prejudices, and what he regarded as the engrained superstitions, of mankind, were not easily eradicated. He took to complaining of the obstinacy of the world.

The first proof he met with of his own impotency in opposing the prepossessions of men, was in 1815, not very long after the formation of his last partnership. On his own responsibility he had convened at Glasgow

a meeting of the Scotch manufacturers, for two purposes. The first of these was to petition Lord Liverpool's ministry to remit the heavy duty then levied
on imported cotton. The meeting was numerously
attended by the Glasgow manufacturers, and the Lord
Provost presided: the petition for a remission of the
duty was proposed and was carried by acclamation.
Unless the Chancellor of the Exchequer had been
present, who should say a word against it? But the
second proposition met with less success. The former
had been carried by acclamation: this with equal
unanimity was rejected. The manufacturers listened
to it with disgust: for it consisted of a string of resolutions, praying the Government to take into their
consideration the condition of the people employed in
the textile mills, with a view to shortening their hours
of labour. What body of manufacturers ever heard
patiently, a proposal to bring the Government between
themselves and their people? From that day, Owen,
no doubt, was the most unpopular of men, in manufacturing Glasgow. This was the first step in his
downward career.

CHAPTER X.

Results of the Peace: 1816—Meeting at City of London Tavern—A Committee, including Owen—Owen speaks—His Speech—Excellence and Faults—Increase of Mechanical Power—More exact Calculation—Paper of Suggestions—Presented to House of Commons' Committee.

In the following year, 1816, Owen made his first public appearance in London. The lifelong war was at an end: the fears of an invasion had quite passed away: there were no more rejoicings and illuminations, and no more bloody tokens of victory: the French prisoners had departed: the private mournings for the deadly field of Waterloo were mostly over: the oppressive income-tax had been surrendered. Men breathed again; and prepared after the long strife, to enjoy peace and prosperity. The event disappointed their hopes: for though they had peace, they had not prosperity. "Barns and farmyards," says Owen, "were full, and warehouses were weighed down with all manner of productions, and prices fell much below the cost at which the articles could be produced." The farmers, it is said, dismissed many of their labourers, and manufacturers either worked short time, or stopped their mills. Masters and men, town and country, were equally distressed.

The destitution was so great and so general, that influential people became frightened; and a great meeting was called in London. It was held in the City of London Tavern; was presided over by the Duke of York; and was attended by crowds of the upper classes, and by many prominent persons. Owen was present; and he was entrusted with a commission which surprised many people. At this time he was on friendly terms with several members of the Episcopal bench: particularly with Sutton, Archbishop of Canterbury, Burgess, Bishop of St. David's, Barrington, Bishop of Durham, and Bathurst, Bishop of Norwich. The last of these had invited him to breakfast on the morning of the meeting, and being unable to attend at the London Tavern, sent through him an apology and a donation of 10*l*.

Many speeches were made, and much perplexity was expressed as to the cause of the general distress, at a time when renewed prosperity had been hoped for. Large sums were subscribed for the mitigation of pressing wants. A committee was also appointed with the Archbishop of Canterbury as chairman, and Owen found himself nominated a member. On the day of the first meeting of the committee, Owen attended in company with the philanthropic Mr. Mortlock of Oxford Street, to whom at breakfast-time he had explained his views as to the existing distress. He went to the committee, expecting a great accession of wisdom from the instruction of the distinguished men who were there; but he was much disappointed, as he listened to speech after speech, to find nothing but what seemed to him mere verbiage, leaving the question at issue just as perplexed as it had been at first. Mr. Mortlock shared this unpleasant surprise, and urged Owen to tell the committee the substance of their morning conversation.

Owen was conscious of his defects of education; and this feeling, together with his want of experience, caused a dislike and almost horror of thrusting himself on the attention of persons of such distinction as those who were present: but Mr. Mortlock's importunities attracted the notice of the right reverend chairman, and he called upon Owen to give the committee the benefit of that experience and ability which he had exhibited in his essays. Owen upon this rose; though with the painful reflection, that a private breakfast table and a distinguished committee room, were arenas of a very different character.

The speech which he made, seems to me to have contained much sound sense, and certain truths with which we are now familiar, but to anticipate which did great credit to Owen's sagacity. The distress he thought, was manifestly attributable to the extraordinary changes which had occurred during the long war, with its continued waste, and unusual demand for men and commodities. War prices had arisen, and had continued so long, that to the actual generation they appeared natural, and had become the basis of all estimates. The lavish military expenditure, and the deficiency of men and materials to supply the consequent demand, had given a great stimulus to mechanical invention and chemical discovery; and these had superseded a vast amount of manual labour. "The war was a great and most extravagant customer to farmers, manufacturers, and other producers of wealth, and many during this period became very wealthy. The expenditure of the last year of the war for this country alone, was one hundred and thirty millions sterling, or an excess of eighty million pounds sterling over the peace expenditure. And on the day on which peace was signed, *this great customer of the producers died*, and prices fell as the demand diminished, until the prime cost of the articles required for war could not be obtained."

All this seems excellently expressed: and though the truths enunciated are obvious enough to us, they did not lie on the surface for that generation. The causes of the distress were, an extensive alteration in the channels of trade and a great disturbance of prices. These evils were, in their very nature, temporary; and in effect, a few years saw them all corrected. The problem therefore, was, how to help the destitute classes over the gulf of the transition state from war to peace, from inflated prices to natural prices. But Owen did not so read the problem: he regarded the ill as deeper and more permanent. He said that the increase of machinery and of chemical processes, all superseding labour, was continually lessening the demand for workpeople, and reducing the rate of wages: that this operation would continue and would effect great changes throughout society. I will not stop to argue the question of the effects of machinery. It is now well understood that the first result of a new invention is in most cases, to throw workpeople out of employment: but that in the long run the quantity of labour employed is not lessened, and that the means of living are cheapened. Some bad consequences may follow indirectly; such as the crowding people together in towns, and the substitution of unskilled for skilled labourers. But it is hard to believe in an inevitable reduction of wages, in face of the fact that comparing the present day, with the period before steam-engines and spinning machinery existed, labourers both in town and country obtain higher real wages now than they did then : that is, that they enjoy now the greater command of all the necessaries of life.

One of the committee was Mr. Colquhoun, a London magistrate, who had lately published his well-known *Resources of the British Empire.* He was struck with what he heard about the increase of machinery, and desired to have more specific information. Finding Owen unprepared as to figures, and unwilling to hazard a guess on so important a matter, he pressed and cross-questioned him until he squeezed out a conjecture, that the mechanical and chemical powers at work in 1816, must have equalled the labour of all the men, women, and children employed; or of four to five million pair of hands. Mr. Colquhoun and other members expressed astonishment and incredulity: but Owen reiterated his assertion; and added that at New Lanark, the

7

quantity of work done by two thousand persons, young
and old, with the aid of machinery, was as much as
was formerly accomplished by the whole labouring
population of Scotland. The statement was new and
startling, but quite within the competency of Owen, as
an experienced manufacturer, to make.   When he went
on to say that this increase of production was the cause
of the national distress, he entered on a domain just as
open to the other members of the committee as to himself. It must have occurred to some of them on calm
reflection, that the increase of mechanical power had
not been the work of one or two years, but had gone
on steadily during the previous thirty or forty years:
whereas the distress at present under consideration had
been felt only since the peace.   They might reasonably
decline to accept two causes for one phenomenon; and
might take their stand on Owen's striking position:
war, our great customer, is dead.

Owen was of course desirous of verifying the remarkable estimate he had made, and he happened to have
the means at hand. At this time, Sir Robert Peel's
Factory Bill was before a committee of the House of
Commons: a measure, as we shall see hereafter, really
originated at New Lanark. Owen was in daily attendance on this committee, and found there the
means of testing his conjecture: for the manufacturers
who opposed Sir R. Peel, had got together from
every corner of the kingdom, an account of the
number of spindles at work. It appeared that Owen
had been far indeed from an excessive estimate. He

had conjectured that the mechanical and chemical powers employed, were equal to the labour of five million persons: it turned out that the mechanical powers used in cotton-spinning alone, were in 1816 equal to the labour of sixteen times five million persons: and he now framed an estimate, that taking into account the woollen, flax, and silk manufactures, he ought, instead of five millions, to have said two hundred millions. When Mr. Colquhoun was made acquainted with these results, his astonishment of the former day, rose to a still higher pitch; and he expressed his regret that he had not been acquainted with these facts when he wrote his book. He afterwards stated them publicly, and they passed into the writings of other statists.

At the committee meeting, when Owen had made his remarkable statement, the archbishop, from the chair, complimented him upon it, and asked whether any remedy could be found. He replied, that in his opinion for every artificial evil a remedy might be found: that one had suggested itself to his mind; but that as he had come intending to be only a listener, he had no scheme prepared. He undertook however, on the unanimous request of chairman and committee, to have a paper ready for the next meeting. The evil proved to be far more patent than the cure. What were the exact contents of the memorandum which Owen presented to the committee at its next meeting, I do not know. Apparently, there was a tirade against the late war, " which a little common sense might have prevented:" something about Bank of England notes being made a legal

tender : a pretty sharp attack upon the Whig political
economists : and of course, an epitome of the four
essays, with a sketch of New Lanark as it had been and
as it was. But of anything like a remedy for immediate application, or a recommendation of means to
allay present discontents, I presume there was no trace :
for when the document had been read, perplexity was
on every face; and after some consultation, the archbishop said that the committee was not prepared to consider a report "so extensive in its recommendations,
so new in principle and practice, and involving great
national changes." He added that it seemed fit to be
laid before Mr. Sturges Bourne's Committee of the
House of Commons, then sitting upon the question of
the Poor Laws.

Owen, in pursuance of this suggestion, gave notice
through Mr. Brougham, to Sturges Bourne's Committee, that he had a report to present, and that he was
willing to be examined upon it. A day was appointed :
Owen entered the room at the hour fixed, and found
the forty members formally arranged in their places.
He opened his papers and plans, and set himself down
to endure a severe cross-examination. But several
members were engaged in an inaudible conversation;
probably about the contents of Owen's budget, which
were pretty well known to them through the ministerial
members of the archbishop's committee : and after a
time the chairman requested him to withdraw, in order
to allow a private discussion. In the adjoining room he
found writing materials, with which he occupied himself

hour after hour, until the bell summoned the members to the House. Mr. Brougham then came, and told him that the question whether he should be examined was not yet decided, but that he must attend the next morning at ten o'clock. At that hour Owen was again in his place as he had been ordered; again passed a long morning in company with his pen and paper, and on the ringing of the bell, heard with astonishment that the Committee had decided by a small majority, not to examine him. To revenge himself, he published in the daily papers a fictitious examination, such as he imagined would have taken place if he had been heard. We cannot be surprised to find that he was much incensed at the treatment he had received: though most of us would be far from agreeing with his assertion, that if we had a report of the debates about admitting him, "it would be a valuable document to prove a conspiracy of the upper, against the natural and legal rights of the lower, classes."

CHAPTER XI.

I HAVE already stated shortly, the measures adopted
at New Lanark, for the instruction of the young children; and I propose now to describe the management
more at large, as well as the circumstances under which
other persons followed the example thus set.

It will be remembered that as early as 1809, Owen
had in contemplation, arrangements for removing the
infants from the ill training they received at home; but
that the considerable cost necessary for carrying out his
plans, having induced him to consult his original partners, they, after consultation, presented him with a
token of their esteem, and withdrew from the business.
Then came the Scotch partnership: bickerings and
hatred: large profits: the withdrawal of Owen from
the management: a purchase by auction, shrewdly
effected: and a philanthropic alliance with Bentham
and others. Thus it was not till the first of January,
1816, that the " Institution for the formation of charac-

ter" was opened at New Lanark.   The children were
at first taken at two years old; but the parents, when
their prejudices were overcome, begged to send them still
earlier; and ultimately, the age was lowered to one year.

Owen himself at first, devoted much time to the carrying out his new plan.   The minister of the parish
regarded the attempt as vain and useless: the master
who had taught the previous school, who was under his
minister's influence, looked with aversion, like an obstinate dominie, on the new-fangled proceedings.   Owen
unwillingly, dismissed him, and looked round for a man
who was patient with children and of a tractable temper.
He found this treasure in a poor hand-weaver named
James Buchanan, who appears to have owed part of his
docility to the discipline of a shrewish wife.   The man
could scarcely read and write; but his gentleness and
his love of children, made up for this defect.   A young
woman from the mills, was employed as a nurse for the
younger pupils.

Owen himself tells us that he had won the hearts
of all the children in New Lanark, and through the
children, the hearts of the parents: a statement I
implicitly believe.   He was a man of a placid and
gentle nature, whose true benevolence was never im-
pugned even by his bitterest enemies.   He had selected
two superintendents whose hearts, as he believed, beat
in unison with his own; and kindness was the basis of
all the instructions he gave them.   " They were on no
account ever to beat any one of the children, nor to
threaten them in any manner in word or action, nor to

use abusive terms; but were always to speak to them
with a pleasant countenance, and in a kind manner and
tone of voice." We are told that these instructions
were faithfully observed: but if they were so, I will
pronounce James Buchanan and Molly Young to have
been, not man and woman, but spirits from heaven. If
their tempers were so perfect, their angelic natures cannot have been susceptible of toothache or indigestion.
Another part of their duty was not so importunate:
they were to tell the infants and young children (from
one to six years old) that each one was to study to make
his companions happy. A lofty room was provided for
play in bad weather.

Owen was entirely free from the folly of wishing to
produce prodigies of knowledge: his aim was to train
the children to good habits, and not to cram their heads
with facts; and this is the more creditable to him, because the danger of premature education was not then
recognized, and the children of the middle classes were
many of them being forced into precocity. In managing
these little creatures, under six years old, amusement
was to be the sole aim, with such instruction as they
spontaneously chose to acquire. The ordinary means
of exciting curiosity were resorted to: maps, paintings,
flowers, were hung on the walls; and the teachers were
incited to learn for themselves, that they might be able
to answer the questions that were asked. No books
were used: and Owen runs as usual into exaggeration,
when he expresses a doubt, whether in a rational state of
society, children under ten years old would be taught to

read. I have mentioned before, as a cause of dissatisfaction on the part of the Quaker partners, that while
books were excluded, music, dancing, and military exercises, were sedulously taught.

This was certainly, an important experiment of
Owen's; and the success of it seems to have rewarded
his efforts. No part of his great establishment yielded
him higher pleasure, and no part attracted more of the
attention of other people. Among the frequent visitors
at New Lanark, were Mr. Brougham (Lord Brougham),
Mr. John Smith the banker and M.P., and Mr. Henry
Hase of the Bank of England. These gentlemen were
so impressed with the order, intelligence, and happiness,
of these young children, that they were desirous of
adopting the system elsewhere; and with the co-operation of the Marquis of Lansdowne, Mr. Benjamin
Smith, M.P., and perhaps the able James Mill, they
tried the experiment.

They asked for James Buchanan as their master: he
was sent: and Owen thought that the instruction he
had received would enable him to proceed successfully.
The school was started, and it was some time before
Owen saw it, because he was detained at home by the
necessity of training a new master. When he next
visited London, he was disappointed to find that
Buchanan, though a good servant, and a docile pupil,
was quite unfit for the head of a school.

Owen had forgotten that the poor man had a wife:
but he was reminded of the fact when he unexpectedly
entered the new school, and to his surprise and disgust,

found the virago brandishing a whip over the children, while the husband cowered in a corner. Mrs. Buchanan tried to hide the whip, but the countenances of the children betrayed the harshness of the discipline; and it was clear that the marrow of the plan was wanting, and that this school differed from any ordinary one, only in the childishness of the pupils.

The proceedings at New Lanark were well known to the Society of Friends, through the three members of their body who were partners there. The infant school particularly attracted their attention, notwithstanding the profane excrescences which disfigured it: and as the public press confirmed the accounts privately given, a resolution was come to that the experiment should be tried in Spitalfields.

The first and most important step was to find a master, and this was happily accomplished. William Wilderspin, whom some persons regard as the founder of infant schools, was really only their apostle: he did not invent the system, but disseminated the knowledge of it. He had frequently visited James Buchanan and his termagant wife at Westminster; and the Quakers were induced on this account to make him their new master at Spitalfields. Owen went to see him at work; told him of the gross faults in the Westminster school; indoctrinated him into the principle of ruling the infants with kindness alone; at his request, visited him time after time; and found the instruction thankfully received and faithfully put into practice. He did not however, make any attempt to convert Wilderspin to his peculiar views of society, or to lead him to adopt any practices which might be disgustful to his patrons.

When Wilderspin became a proficient in his vocation, he published a work calling the attention of the public to the new experiment. In his first edition he fully acknowledged the services Owen had rendered him, by his advice and repeated instructions. But it is stated that in the later of his many editions, he was less honest; a dereliction which Owen attributes to the undue influence of men who were righteous overmuch. Doubtless there were men in the last generation, and worthy men in the main, who shuddered at the very name of the benevolent founder of New Lanark; and who were weak enough to believe that in dealing with a public enemy, they were absolved from the obligations of justice.

The infant school system was an inevitable consequence of Owen's doctrine, as to the vital importance of surrounding human beings with circumstances favourable to their development. It has been said that the plan was previously carried out on the Continent. That may be true. It has also been said that the experiment was suggested in a conversation between Owen and a lady. Both statements may be true, and yet Owen's claim to the invention remain unimpeached. As to the latter objection, I should say of such a scheme as this, what the law says as to a mechanical invention: that the right to it belongs, not to the person who had thought of such a thing and asserted its possibility, but to the person who successfully carries the idea into

practice.   An invention is a notion fixed and realized
in a substantial form (not meaning by that term what
the schoolmen understood by it).   Owen's glory is not
that he sent for a Swiss instructor, not that he went
about craving the advice and aid of any one : but that
he threw his own energy into the work, and with the
feeble instruments at his command, commenced and
completed his long projected task.

CHAPTER XII.

Owen's great Experience—Desire to improve the Factory Hands
generally—Factory People compared with Slaves—Cruel Treatment of Children—Owen's Testimony—Extent of the Evil—
Owen's First Proceeding—Tries to get a Bill—Sir R. Peel intro-
duces one—Delays—Objections raised—Detraction and Scandal—
Particulars of—Reported to Lord Sidmouth—Owen as a Witness
—Wearied out—Bill passed.

OWEN had grown up with the cotton manufacture, of
which in 1815 he had had a quarter of a century's
experience: and as he had been the first spinner of fine
yarn and had made no secret of his processes, he had
always received free admission into other factories. He
travelled much, and in his frequent journeys to and from
London, made use of his opportunities to visit the mills
north and south. He was well aware of the important
consequences likely to result from the vast increase of
machinery.

But the thing which impressed him most deeply, and
which in his eyes was a fatal drawback from the advantages of the manufacturing system, was the condition of
the people employed. He had shown the sincerity and
depth of his convictions, by the efforts he had spontaneously made even in Manchester, to benefit the
factory hands: and at New Lanark, the best of his
energies, and a very large share of his means, had been

for fifteen years, and were still, thrown into his self-imposed task of bettering the state of his subordinates. His heart yearned to extend to the whole kingdom the advantages which his own neighbourhood had experienced.

The sketch which he gives us of the condition of the workpeople generally, may possibly be drawn in lines needlessly dark: but as at any rate it seemed true to him, it fully justified the measures he adopted. He goes so far in his autobiography as to say, that however bad negro slavery was, the white slavery of British factories in 1815 was far worse, " as regards health, food, and clothing." The comparison he makes is between our manufacturing people and the *house* slaves, and not between them and the field slaves. Indeed I think it probable enough that our people were worse off as to physical comforts, than domestic slaves; who as a rule, are well fed, sufficiently clothed, reasonably worked, and treated in a way that does not seem intolerable· to persons reared in slavery. But setting aside this comparison, which tells us little, what was the state of our factory people?

Bad enough I believe. We have seen that at New Lanark, orphan children were made over by parishes in hundreds, to be worked and maintained by an irresponsible manufacturer; who must of necessity have delegated his powers to illiterate subordinates. Children of six years old, condemned to labour ten, twelve, or fourteen hours a day! The mere statement of the fact is enough. We see at once what must follow: sleepiness, weariness, inattention, repeated carelessness, punishment, sulkiness, a degradation of the whole moral being, a perpetual hostility between overlooker and children, followed by frequent and cruel chastisements. We have an account at an earlier period, of the management of a factory where young people were employed. Hutton, the local historian, went to work in a silk-mill at Derby, when he was so short that he was set upon stilts to reach his work: and the treatment he suffered to arouse his flagging attention during the tedious hours, was so unmeasured, that his life was in danger from gangrened wounds inflicted by his master's cane.

A century of suffering had made no improvement. Owen tells us that in his time, children were admitted into some mills even at five years old: that the time of working, winter and summer, was fourteen hours a day; in some mills fifteen; and in a few detestable instances sixteen: besides that in many cases the mills were artificially heated in a way unfavourable to health. Indeed I may repeat what I before quoted: that if New Lanark, under the most benevolent Mr. Dale, was found such a place of torture that the children were ruined in constitution, and were constantly driven to abscond, what must other places have been where a needy and cruel master governed? It is said that there are theorists who deny that even this state of things justified the interference of government: but it would be difficult, I think, to make out what can be the final cause for the existence of men with such narrow minds.

Before England had become a great manufacturing country, it was natural enough that these evils should escape attention. It is painful to apply to such cases the maxim, *de minimis non curat lex;* since this seems equivalent to placing the few poor and unprotected out of the pale of the law's protection. But at any rate, in Owen's time this reason for non-interference had quite ceased. In a previous chapter we have seen what vast dimensions the manufactures had acquired: we have seen that at a meeting of the Archbishop's committee, Owen had been driven into a feeble conjecture, that the mechanical powers of the empire were equal to the labour of five millions of people; and that the result of a careful calculation immediately afterwards, convinced him that this guess reached only one-sixteenth part of the powers employed in the cotton manufacture alone, and only one-fortieth part of the powers employed in all manufactures. This vast extension of the factory system, made it the more imperative on the legislature to carefully protect the people employed.

I have already related that Owen, in 1815, had called a meeting at Glasgow, to petition for the repeal of the cotton duty (a proposition which met with no opposition at the meeting); and also to declare the desirability of obtaining protection for the people employed in textile manufactures. The failure to obtain a seconder on this last topic, was Owen's first taste of what he regarded as the obstinacy of the world. However, he published the address which he had read at the meeting, and distributed it extensively, after his usual fashion, among people of influence. He then went to London to communicate with the Government on both topics. Vansittart (Lord Bexley) promised that the duty of four pence should be reduced to one penny. He stated also that the Government would favourably entertain any bill introduced for the relief of the workpeople, though they would not themselves take charge of such a measure.

Owen felt that a formidable task was now before him; and he knew that he must anticipate a vehement opposition, both from the manufacturing interest in Parliament, and from the manufacturing influence among the electors: but the difficulty only served as a whet to his eagerness. He called on the leading members of both houses, was well received, and had promises of support from men of weight, without distinction of party. Lord Lascelles, M.P. for Yorkshire, a man of great consideration in the Commons, took the matter up so warmly, as to join Owen in calling meetings of Lords and members of Parliament. After it was fully agreed that something should be done, it was needful to consider to whom the bill should be entrusted.

The name of Sir Robert Peel was suggested. He was an extensive manufacturer, a respected member of the Commons, and one who stood well with the Government. But as a manufacturer, would he undertake the task? He had not been consulted, he did not even know what was going on, and his willingness was doubtful. Owen, however, agreed to make the proposal to him: and when he called, explained what was in-

tended, and enumerated the promised supporters, Sir
Robert gave his assent. He attended the next meeting,
and concluded the necessary arrangements for intro-
ducing the bill, in the form Owen proposed.

Owen was of opinion that if Sir Robert Peel had
done his duty, he would have passed his measure
through the Commons in that session, early enough to
have got it adopted by the Lords. He complained that
Sir Robert was too much under the influence of his
brother manufacturers, and that to indulge them he
allowed unnecessary delays. Owen confesses that up
to this time he was quite ignorant of the way in which
public business was conducted; and I regard this as a
sufficient reason for paying little attention to his accu-
sation. It is, no doubt, highly provoking to an enthusiast, to undergo the delays which intervene between
the introduction of a bill and its receiving the royal
ssent: and men like Clarkson may be excused, if they
fret and storm at the long interval which is too often
nterposed between the acknowledgment and the rendering of justice. Yet few politicians of experience
would desiré to reduce or to shorten the stages of legislation; because they would fear the passing by surprise
of many immature measures. In the absence therefore,
of further proof, I acquit Sir Robert Peel of blameable
delay.

On the part of the opposition, there were of course,
the usual ingenuity and fertility in raising objections.
First, there was the argument of the staunch political economists: that Government ought not to inter-

fere with masters in the management of their business. This is now called the free-trade argument: and sorry I am that free-trade, in which I believed long before it became a popular cry, should have so many bastard offspring laid at its door. An attempt was also made, to disprove the injuriousness of the actual practice. People were found with foreheads of brass, to stand up and say that mere infants could without damage, be kept at work fourteen hours a day in heated rooms. Sir Robert consented, probably with wisdom, to have a committee appointed to investigate this statement; and two sessions were consumed in the inquiry.

As the arguments in favour of the proposed bill, rested mainly on the New Lanark experiments, and on Owen as the author of them, it was of vital importance to the opposition, that his alleged success should be disproved, and that his merits should be decried. Two cotton-spinners were sent on a journey of discovery. It was not difficult to find enemies to relate all possible tales of scandal: and application was made to the parish minister of Old Lanark, who was intimately acquainted with every step that had been taken during the sixteen years which had succeeded Mr. Dale's sale of the property; and who doubtless regarded Owen as an heresiarch, worse than Jew, Turk, or schismatic. It is suggested that the moral improvement of New Lanark, was an unpleasing contrast to the stagnant condition of the minister's old burgh. Irregular reform added bitterness to polemical hatred.

Owen professes to know what was the conversation

8—2

which took place between the itinerant scandal hunters
and their reverend friend: and as it seems improbable
that he should have really been acquainted with it, the
statement rather diminishes my confidence in his nar-
ration generally. I must add however, that he professes to draw his information from a member of his
antagonist's committee. The charges made by the
minister are alleged to have been, that Owen had
delivered an address full of treasonable matter against
Church and State: that he gave as much encouragement to dissenting preachers as to the authorized
parish minister, and thus sanctioned the decoying of the
people from the parish church. It is difficult to deny
that an angry priest might make charges so absurd.
But one thing is tolerably certain: that even he would
not dare to mutter a syllable against his enemy's private
character, which was at all times above the breath of
scandal.

Whatever the minister's allegations may have been,
they seemed to the unreasoning anger of the manufacturers, to be of importance enough to serve their purpose. He was carried off hastily to London, and an interview was arranged with Lord Sidmouth. His Lordship listened no doubt, with patience, to the assertions
that Owen was a dangerous man, possessed with infidel
and revolutionary notions, which his high position as a
great manufacturer enabled him to propagate. But
when an attack was made on the address to which
I have alluded, it must have been a satisfaction to his
lordship to be able to say that a copy of it had long

been in his possession, and that there was not a treasonable or seditious word in it. Nothing came of this
attempt at detraction. Owen felt the advantage in
this instance of having made friends of the ministry.

Owen exhibited his usual diligence in promoting the
passing of the act. During two sessions he was present
at every meeting of the Commons' Committee; and he
offered himself as a witness. He was roughly handled
by the manufacturing members, and especially by Sir
George Phillips; who was not contented with the matter
in hand, but questioned him so discursively on general
notions and religious belief, that the whole examination
was afterwards expunged from the minutes on the
motion of Mr. Brougham. Owen's evidence was
favourable to limiting the working of mills to ten hours
a day;* to the shutting out from mills of all children
under twelve years old; to the previous provision of
education, and of special instruction of the girls in
sewing, cooking, and other domestic duties; and to
means for keeping the factories clean and wholesome:
measures which seem even to us somewhat exaggerated, but which must have been monstrous and intolerable in the eyes of men accustomed to licentious freedom in the management of their affairs.

Owen's impatience was, at the end of the second
session, so irritated by the unwearied opposition and by
the concessions made to it, that he yielded his post of
chief promoter, to Mr. Nathaniel Gould of Manchester

---

* In February 1834, Owen asserted that in August 1817 he advertised *eight* hours as a just day's labour.—See *The Crisis*, III. 188, 2.

and Mr. Richard Oastler; the latter of whom at a later
day we all knew as the *king* of the northern operatives.
Perhaps, if there had been any hope of getting a satisfactory measure at last, Owen's perseverance might
have been more sustained. But Sir Robert Peel at an
early period, consented to strike the wool, flax, and silk
manufactures out of the bill; though flax spinning was
said to be a most unwholesome employment.

At last, in 1819, after four sessions' labour, an act
received the royal assent: not such a measure as had
been wished, but yet one of great importance, both for
its own provisions, and for the precedent it gave in
future years. For thirty years after that day there
was a struggle for one improvement after another, until
the passing of the present law; which, as affirmed by
the highest authority,* was destined indubitably to be
the ruin of our factories, but under which they have
flourished more than ever. If Owen had done nothing
more, the originating such measures would have been
an inheritance of fame to hand down to his posterity.

* W. Nassau, Senior.

CHAPTER XIII.

A MAN'S success in life is to a great extent determined
by the fitness of the powers he possesses, for the situation in which he is placed. A punctual, diligent,
tractable clerk in a public office, may perform invalu-
able services: yet give the man a fortune and a seat
in Parliament, and you will find him formal, hesitating,
and as unfit to go alone as a horse who has thrown
his jockey. Porson, notwithstanding his uncultivated
habits, has left a distinguished name; but in any vocation that required decorous regularity, he would have
soon been disgraced and ruined. Owen, as it seems to
me, was singularly fortunate in this respect. I do not
mean to detract from his distinguished merit, when I
say that the circumstances in which he was placed until
middle life, were just adapted to develop the powers he
possessed. His placid disposition showed to advantage
while he was a shopman: his industry and singular

temperance, his thoughtfulness and patience, made him a factory manager above price: the fast growing manufacture of cotton raised him rapidly to the rank of a wealthy master, and thus enabled him to carry into practice the notions early conceived and long cherished. It is true, indeed, that it was to his own qualities he owed his position; and that he had about him a buoyancy of character which would have made it as difficult to keep him down to his original level, as it is to keep a cork under water. But suppose he had been born a Russian serf instead of a Welsh farmer; or that he had been the eldest son of a widow dependent on him for the cultivation of her farm; or that nature had unfitted him by a deficiency of touch, for an appreciation of the finer fabrics. He might still have been a distinguished man, but he would not have been our Robert Owen.

Now I think that this consonancy of abilities with position, existed only during the first half of his life; and that during the second half of it he was placed in circumstances which were altogether unfavourable and disastrous. He was situated like the excellent clerk who proves an insignificant member of Parliament: like Porson in lawn sleeves: like Brinsley Sheridan at the head of an army. It is thus that I account for the singular contrast between the two periods of his life; between Owen young, active, vigorous, and successful, and Owen of mature age, still active, but with obliquity of aim and failure in every attempt. The man was the same, the powers were in their vigour, while the circumstances were adverse. Owen could master difficulties, but he could not make a just use of perfect freedom. Restrained by the necessity of earning an income, and checked by the requirements of his partners, he went straight to a well-defined goal: relieved from what he regarded as hindrances, set at liberty to expatiate as he would over the world, he missed his road, and in search of an ideal good lost himself in devious tracks.

I have mentioned that after two sessions of parliamentary strife about the Factory Bill, Owen had abandoned the charge of it to other hands. But in the meantime he had adopted another hobby, and one that carried him far away from that public approbation which had hitherto waited on his efforts. We have already seen that he had for some time past been dissatisfied with the small progress he had been making; and that he had taken to grumbling at the stupid prejudices of mankind; who, he found, would not listen to the voice of his charming. He told them how most of the ills that afflict humanity might be corrected, and they only shrugged their shoulders: he pointed out the way to restore the golden age, and they turned incredulously away. At the Glasgow meeting, he had found unanimous support to his proposal to benefit the masters, but not even a seconder of his resolutions for the amelioration of the workmen: on the archbishop's committee, he had commanded ready listeners when he had explained to them how war, their great customer, was dead; but when he wanted to introduce them to

the possible triumphs of peace, they declared these
things to be beyond their province, and referred him to
another committee, which, as it proved, refused also to
hear him. Then came the wearing delays of the Factory Bill: the manufacturers' selfish devices (for such
they seemed to Owen); the culpable concessions of
Peel; the reference to an imperturbable committee;
the audacious denial of manifest truth as to the injuries
inflicted; the impudent examination of himself about
matters beside the question; the conspiracy, as it
seemed, of the whole world, to defeat the ends of
justice.

Owen's state of feeling was in singular contrast with
that which he exhibited in his earlier career. When
he first came to New Lanark, bent on putting to the
proof by a grand experiment, the theory which possessed his mind, he was contented to prepare the ground
and wait his opportunity: at present, desiring to act on
an infinitely wider field, he wanted to gather his harvest
at once. His caution and prudence had deserted him;
and I may apply to him what he said of his partner
William Allen, that his head was turned by the attentions he had received from the leading personages of
the world.* His mind was full of the notion that he
was an apostle, if not the prophet, of philanthropy; and
regarding the sacrifice of himself, his fortune, his
reputation, and even his life, as nothing, when compared with the well-being of the race, he was quite
ready to lose everything he had, so that he might

* *Autobiog.* i. 235.

but secure the regeneration of man. In short, Owen was become a fanatic; and he took a step which gratified to a considerable extent his desire for martyrdom.

On the 30th of July, 1817, there appeared in the London papers, a letter of Owen's, dated from 49, Charlotte Street, Portland Place, stating that it was intended shortly to hold a meeting, for the consideration of a plan of relief for the unemployed. The letter was followed by a long document, intended to explain the principles on which the plan was founded. This communication occupies, as reprinted, no less than eighteen octavo pages. It is in the form of a catechism, in which, however, the questions bear a very small proportion to the replies: and it has a long postscript, giving an account of Mrs. Fry's labours in Newgate, and a short sketch of Owen's previous course of life. The particulars of the catechism may be accurately conjectured by any one who has read an Owenite publication. Mrs. Fry's kindly efforts are referred to, as a proof of the truth of Owen's principles.

Ten days later appeared a second letter, fixing the time and place of meeting (the 14th August, at the City of London Tavern); and accompanied by another considerable document, entitled " A sketch of some of the errors and evils arising from the past and present state of society, with an explanation of some of the peculiar advantages to be derived from the arrangement of the unemployed working classes into agricultural and manufacturing villages of unity and mutual co-operation, limited to a population of from 500 to

1,500 persons." The co-operative Owen of our generation begins to appear.

On the 14th of August, 1817, accordingly, the meeting was held. The country had not yet recovered from
the distress which had followed the conclusion of peace:
there were still, destitution and discontent, reduced
profits, falling wages, distress among producers, and
a revolutionary spirit among the people. Any scheme
which gave even a faint promise of relief, was eagerly
listened to; and Owen's promises were of no feeble or
hesitating kind. The meeting was a great success.
The room, in which all large gatherings were then held,
was crowded, the wide stairs were filled, hundreds
outside were unable to gain admittance, and during the
day thousands of persons had to turn back. Owen read
an address in which he explained his plans for the
employment and improvement of the working classes.
He was heard with perfect patience, but subsequently
some confusion was created by the lower radicals who
were present, and to put an end to this uproar an adjournment took place.

Owen was so eagerly bent on publicity, that he
resolved on spending a large sum in purchasing the
assistance of the newspapers. On this occasion he
bought great numbers of the London morning and
evening papers, and distributed them by post with his
own name printed on the corner of the envelope: each
one being franked, as he tells us, by Lord Lascelles,
afterwards Earl of Harewood, " the then most influential member of the House of Commons." Owen sent

no less than thirty thousand of the papers that contained an account of the meeting, the directions having been written previously : and the letter-bags were so loaded with this unusual burden, that the mail coaches were delayed twenty minutes at starting. We cannot wonder that such liberality secured full and favourable newspaper reports of the meeting. Besides this, Owen published and distributed, gratis, forty thousand broadsides. The expense of these doings, at a time when 7d. or 8d. was the price of each journal, would have ruined a man of moderate means; and at the end of two months, after the large sum of 4,000l. had been disbursed, this artificial stimulus was abandoned.

Owen afterwards believed that at this moment he was the most popular man in England : and there can be no doubt that his wealth, and his munificence in using it, added to his earnest convictions, gave him for the time an influence that few popular leaders have enjoyed. He was told that the Government was alarmed. He at once requested an interview with the Earl of Liverpool, and this was granted. It was on this occasion that there occurred the incident to which I have before alluded. Owen, calling by appointment at Lord Liverpool's private house, was at once admitted, and was shown into the apartment of the private secretary, Mr. Peel, afterwards our eminent minister. The secretary arose, and with much deference in his manner, begged his visitor to be seated, while he himself remained standing, and assured him that he should not long be kept waiting. Lord Liver-

pool was soon at liberty, and imitated Mr. Peel in the
humility of his deportment, asking with an appearance
of perfect sincerity what the Government could do.
The notion conveyed, was that place or pension was
to be had for the asking.   Whether Owen misinter-
preted ministerial politeness and policy I will not conjecture: but it is to his credit that the blandishments
stirred up no selfish desires within him; and that his
only request was, that at the adjourned meeting about
to take place, he might be allowed to add the names
of the leading members of the ministry, to the committee of investigation he proposed to nominate. Having
received a favourable reply he departed, leaving Lord
Liverpool, as he thought, much relieved; and he was
ushered out by the formal secretary, with renewed
deference.

The adjourned meeting was fixed for the 21st August,
the original one having been held on the 14th.   Owen
speaks of this second meeting as one "ever to be
remembered in the annals of history;" but it would
be more accurate to say, "ever to be remembered
in the annals of *Owen's* history:" since it was this
meeting which proved to be the wall of separation
that divided his early from his later career; which
neutralized the good opinions he had enjoyed, and cut
him off from the sympathies of the world.   "When
I went to this meeting, I was on the morning of
that day by far the most popular individual in the
civilized world, and possessed the most influence with
a majority of the leading members of the British

Cabinet and Government. I went to the meeting with the determination by one sentence to destroy that popularity," &c. If the ministry had really been startled by the temporary popularity of one who might prove a demagogue, they need only have waited two days to see the gigantic shadow disappear for ever. Owen's popularity was at least as fleeting as it was great.

The meeting was held, and again the large room was so crowded that thousands of persons failed to gain admittance. The reporters were ready to record every word; but they had applied beforehand for copies of the intended address, and Owen had had it carefully transcribed sixteen times, that every editor might be fairly treated. During the interval between the two meetings, Owen had been publicly challenged to declare his views as to religion; and communing with himself what course he should pursue, he resolved to do a deed which should startle the world, and at the same time gratify his new-born desire for martyrdom.

Before this day he had maintained in his publications a moderate tone in speaking of religion. Thus in his second essay he had said, that at New Lanark " it was inculcated that all should attend to the essence of religion, and not act as the world was now taught and trained to do: that is, to overlook the substance and essence of religion, and devote their talents, time, and money, to that which is far worse than its shadow, sectarianism." And again : " To avoid the inconveniences which must ever arise from the introduction

of a particular creed into a school, the children are
taught to read in such books as inculcate those precepts
of the Christian religion, which are common to all
denominations." There was in these sentences a tolerant spirit that many strict persons would regard as
ambiguous, but on which there could scarcely be
founded any charge more serious than that of lati-
tudinarianism. Nor would the ordinary English mind
be much scandalized by an attack upon the sabbata-
rian tendencies of the North. After stating the importance of providing rational and wholesome amusements for the working classes, Owen says that the
Sabbath was originally intended for this purpose; but
that " from the opposite extremes of error, it is frequently made either a day of superstitious gloom and
tyranny over the mind, or of the most destructive
intemperance and licentiousness. The one of these
has been the cause of the other; the latter the natural
and certain consequence of the former."

But at this second meeting Owen adopted a very
different tone. And not contented with quietly drop-
ping a few words, expressing apologetically his real
opinions, he loudly invited the attention of his audience, and resorted to a rhetorical artifice to heighten
the effect of what he said. He had previously determined to " denounce all the religions of the world
as now taught;" and being resolved to enjoy to the
full the greatest cup of martyrdom, he changed his
manner as he came to this part of his address, and
delivered himself of the following rhapsody: " A more

important question has never been put to the sons of
men—who can answer it? Who dares answer it? but
with his life in his hand—a ready and willing victim
to truth, and to the emancipation of the world from
its long bondage of error, crime, and misery? *Behold
that victim! On this day! in this hour! Even now!*
shall those bonds be burst asunder, never more to
reunite while the world lasts! What the consequences
of this daring deed shall be to myself I am as indifferent about, as whether it shall rain or be fair to-
morrow! Whatever may be the consequences, I will
now perform my duty to you and to the world. And
should it be the last act of my life, I shall be well
content, and shall know that I have lived for an
important purpose. Then, my friends, I tell you that
hitherto you have been prevented from knowing what
happiness really is, solely in consequence of the errors
—gross errors —— "

At this moment the speaker paused and assumed
something of the dignity of a prophet. The expectation of the assembly was roused by the previous rant,
and this opportune delay. Owen went on : " —— the
gross errors that have been combined with the fundamental notions of every religion that has hitherto been
taught to men. And in consequence, they have made
man the most inconsistent, and most miserable being
in existence. By the errors of these systems he has
been made a weak, imbecile animal; a furious bigot
and fanatic; or a miserable hypocrite; and should these
qualities be carried, not only into the projected villages,

9

but into *Paradise itself, a paradise would no longer be found!*"

The orator paused again. He thought his martyrdom was at hand. He had nerved himself to die; to be torn to pieces by the hands of an exasperated audience, influenced by these denunciations of their superstition and bigotry. But he found himself as secure as was the destined martyr of old thrown into the lions' den. There was a dead silence: then a few clergymen raised a feeble hiss: but the meeting at large broke out into acclamations of applause. What disappointment to an exalted state of mind! Yet notwithstanding this unexpected first reception, Owen had not the less destroyed his prospects of future usefulness, unless he were prepared, after condemning the old faiths, to produce a new one of his own; and this was the thing the farthest from his thoughts. The manufacturers and the parish ministers were avenged; for henceforth Owen was in the eyes of the public, not indeed a Bayle, a Hume, or a Gibbon, for he wanted their literary and philosophic genius; but a Toland, a Tindal, a Tom Paine, or a Carlile. For the gratification of a mood of his fancy, he had cast prudence to the winds, and was to bear the hatred of mankind as his reward.

Owen, having thus given vent to his fanaticism, and having received immediate applause instead of execration, said to the friends about him: "The victory is gained—truth openly stated is omnipotent." He then went on with his address, which was loudly cheered.

A discussion followed and was prolonged by the opposite side; and, as we are told, the leaders of the political
economists talked against time, hoping that by drawing
out the debate till evening, the workpeople would take
the places of the gentry as they left for their late
dinner. Owen tells us, that well satisfied with his
day's work, he cared little for the fate of his proposal
to appoint a committee of investigation; and that therefore, amidst some confusion, he acquiesced in the asser
tion that he was beaten on a show of hands, although
he felt certain that he really had a majority.   The
meeting had been called for the purpose of explaining
a plan for the relief of the distressed, by means of co-
operative establishments; and the proposed committee
was a means of furthering the design : but villages and
committee were alike abandoned, in the elation that
arose from the consciousness of having dealt a mortal
blow to religion.   *Ecrasez l'infame*, had said Voltaire.

Owen's feat at this meeting, was the most audacious
thing he ever did, and the one which more than any
other, gave a colour to his future career.   One is
curious to know how he afterwards regarded it, when
he found that it brought upon him neglect, hatred, contempt, calumny, and all the ills that follow an excom-
municated man.   I can satisfy that curiosity, if we
may believe his own statement of his feelings.   Writing
in 1851,* he said, that though at the time all had condemned the daring deed, yet he had regarded it and
continued to regard it as the most important act he

* *Journal*, i. 55.

could have performed, and the day of its performance
as the most glorious of his life. Again in 1857,* he
made a similar statement : that the most important day
of his life was that on which bigotry, superstition, and
all false religions, had received their death-blow. On
the other hand, in 1854,† a year lying between the two
I have mentioned, his tone is quite different. He says
that his proceedings for the regeneration of society, had
failed to produce their natural effects, because he had
openly opposed the religions of the world, as containing
too much error, and as being fruitless in practice. But
he adds regretfully, that at that time he was deficient
in the knowledge, which he had since acquired, of the
overwhelming importance of the spiritual condition in
forming the human character. We shall see in a
subsequent chapter, that about the time this was
written, Owen had become a disciple of the American
spiritualists.

Of all Owen's followers, no one has so boldly spoken
out, and no one has so gloried in speaking out, against
the faiths of the world, as George Jacob Holyoake;
and no one therefore, would be more willing to look
favourably at the declaration of August 1817. A man
himself so inimical to Christianity, could not blame
his old friend for having nursed a like enmity : a man
so outspoken himself, could hardly be scared by the
audacity of another. Yet Mr. Holyoake says,‡ that
though the act was a deliberate one, and determined

---

* *Autobiog.* i. 162.   † *New Existence,* i. 15.

‡ *Last Days,* 20.

on two years before, yet no adequate preparation was made for carrying out the work thus begun : and that Owen had followed out the instinct of his conscience without calculation.

For my own part, I think that it was not conscience so much as unreasoning impulse, by which Owen was moved. He had previously been elated by success : then came difficulty and disappointment. In his vexation he resolved, like Lear, that he would do great things; though what they should be he knew not. At last, like a prisoner, driven to revenge himself on his gaoler, by committing self-destruction, he assembled the London world, and publicly put a period to his own political existence. From this day Owen was not a martyr but an outlaw.

CHAPTER XIV.

WE cannot be surprised to find Owen, soon after this
year of the London meetings, away from England and
travelling on the Continent. He had made his native
country an unpleasant abode. All the numerous enemies whom he had provoked during twenty years, by
disturbing their interests or their opinions; the manufacturers who dreaded a servile conspiracy against their
profits; the mere ministers of religion who resented an
encroachment on their province; the conscientious and
pious people, lay or clerical, who saw in the new doctrines the destruction of morality in this world and of
salvation in the next: all these were ready to join in
execrating the infidel-philanthropist, the man who, with
the most benevolent intentions, denied the moral responsibility of his kind. He was denounced at once, and
ridiculed. If he was the prince of cotton-spinners, he
was after all a cotton-spinner; a trader; one who had
fed himself fat on the practices he now pretended to
decry: a moralist among manufacturers, but only a

manufacturer among moralists: an ignoramus who out
of his foolish brain had spun cobwebs a thousand times
more flimsy than his own boasted yarns: a humourist
who thought to impose on the world the maggots of his
splenetic fancy as if they were the creations of genius:
the inventor of a sensuous and gross utopia: not, as he
would fain believe, the restorer of a golden age, but in
truth the creator of an age of brass.

His friends of the best sort lamented his escapade,
as much as his antagonists gloried in it. His opinions
might be pardoned so long as they were kept to himself, and many of them might even be shared. His
denial of moral responsibility, absurd as it seemed to
most of them, and dangerous in its tendency, they were
content to regard as the whim of an untutored mind,
which had been too busily engaged on necessary or
philanthropical tasks, to correct its impressions by the
study of a sound philosophy. But what reasonable
object did he propose to himself by his public declaration against religion? He regarded the creeds of the
world as obstacles to rational progress: did he imagine
that his condemnation of them would effect their overthrow? What would he have said himself of any one
who at Seringapatam, or at Badajos, had rushed un
ordered to the ramparts, and at the risk of his life let
off his musket? Would he have pronounced him a
patriot or a madman? We do not wonder at Brougham's
vernacular address, the day after the meeting: " How
the devil could you say what you did yesterday? If
any of us had said half as much, we should have been

burnt alive: and here are you quietly walking as if
nothing had occurred."

In France, Owen's sentiments, even if they were
known, would be no obstacle to his reception. For a
century past, to the present day, the plainest infidelity
is publicly avowed by eminent men. Emile de Girardin
quite recently, scrupled not to deny in print the existence of a God: "I believe that there is no God, or
what is the same thing, that his existence cannot be
proved." The gross superstitions of the *parti prêtre*,
with the outrageous servility towards Rome of the
ultramontane side, provoke reflecting and self-asserting
men to the adoption of an exaggerated scepticism. It
is natural enough therefore, that at this time Owen
should receive marked attention on the other side the
Channel.

Among the visitors at New Lanark, was the celebrated Professor Pictet of Geneva; and he came, not
merely to satisfy his own curiosity, but also to invite
Owen to Paris and Switzerland; with the assurance of
a cordial reception on the Continent generally. Cuvier,
the great naturalist, was to be shortly in London; and
he, as an intimate friend of Pictet, would go with him
and Owen to Paris. Pictet as companion and interpreter, would make up for Owen's utter ignorance of
French. This was indeed, a flattering offer; and at a
time when for twenty years, travelling into France had
been impossible, had almost as great a promise of
novelty, as a visit to Persia has at present.

Owen accordingly, in company with M. Pictet, tra-

velled to London, where he made arrangements with
his professed disciples for the propagation of the new
views of society.   M. Cuvier arrived;   having been
sent by Charles X. to study the modes of administration
in England, with a view to his taking a part in the
French ministry.   Cuvier was soon satisfied with his
acquirements; and returned to France with his wife
and his step-daughter, in a government frigate, carrying
with him Owen and Pictet.   The same party went on
together to Paris.

Owen now found himself in the Parisian circle most
distinguished for learning and political power: a striking
contrast with that position which, since his voluntary
fall, he was destined to hold in this country.   Before he
had left London, he had received a letter of introduction
to Louis Philippe, Duke of Orleans, from the Duke of
Kent, who had not been driven by popular clamour into
withdrawing his patronage.   The first call Owen made
was to deliver this letter, which found a ready reception.   The future king received Owen with his usual
cordial plainness; and after protestations of attachment
to the Duke of Kent, proceeded to explain confiden-
tially the caution he was obliged to exercise, in order
to disarm the suspicions of his cousin the restored king.
The notorious liberality of Owen's views made any
public attentions to him impossible.   Louis Philippe
appeared to Owen a thoughtful, vigilant person, and
rather timid.

Owen was next introduced by Pictet to the premier:
who gave him a long interview; showed himself ac-

quainted with New Lanark and with the late proceedings in London; expressed himself convinced of the
truth of Owen's declarations, though he regarded them
as premature; and ended with ushering his guests
farther by the length of three rooms than was customary
in ordinary cases. Owen clearly was somebody in the
eyes of French statesmen. Then came Alexander Von
Humboldt, and La Place. The latter, together with
Cuvier, Pictet, and Owen, frequently formed a *parti
carré* for the discussion of social science. These French-
men, says Owen, and especially La Place and Cuvier,
though at the head of their respective sciences, were
remarkable for a simplicity amounting to childishness,
as to human nature and the science of society: and
regarding Owen as an " advanced mind," and as quite
at the head of the science he professed, they sought his
company and eagerly questioned him on his favourite
topics. The pressing invitation he had received, and
the flattering treatment he met with, prove conclusively
that these distinguished men had formed a high estimate
of the English innovator's capacity: and it would be
very agreeable to meet with any record of the impression produced on them by this close intimacy.

After being the lion of Paris for six weeks, Owen,
who had now been joined by his wife's unmarried sisters,
set off with Pictet for Geneva. On his arrival there,
after a delightful journey, he found his "new views"
the regular topic of conversation whenever he was present. He was introduced to Sismondi, and to a daughter
of the celebrated Madame de Staël who had lately died.

He had also the pleasure of seeing his partner, Mr. Walker, who, Quaker as he was by profession, did not allow the extravagance of Owen's opinions to ruin their friendship.

Owen then had the satisfaction of seeing the school carried on by the celebrated Oberlin. He caused this excellent man some perplexity, by assuring him that at New Lanark no punishment was inflicted; and this difficulty was probably not altogether removed by the explanation, that the miracle was performed by winning the affections of the infants before they were three years old. The good father must have been mortified to find another man's success so far greater than his own; but he may probably have found comfort on reflecting, as I should have done under such circumstances, that Owen's testimony to the absence of punishment, would have been more weighty, if he had himself been the teacher of the children, and if therefore, he could have said of his own knowledge, that coercion was dispensed with. Though I have unhesitating reliance on Owen's veracity, I think it far more probable that he was deceived by his subordinates, than that hundreds of children should be kept in order without punishment.

Pestalozzi was next visited: an honest, homely, simple old man: speaking a *patois* which M. Pictet could scarcely understand: and carrying on a school for the poor around him, with arrangements just a little better than those of ordinary persons. But of Fellenberg, a former partner of Pestalozzi, we have a far more flattering picture; and one that would lose nothing in

the vividness of its colouring, from the fact that Owen
made a convert of M. Fellenberg. The one gained a
professed disciple, and the other two pupils in Owen's
sons.

After this visit, Owen set off for Frankfort, in company with his partner Mr. Walker, who had offered
himself as guide and interpreter in the place of M.
Pictet. The Germanic Diet was sitting at Frankfort;
and Owen had introductions to many of the twenty-
two representatives who were there, as well as to other
strangers then expecting the visit of three crowned heads.
Owen was asked by M. Bethman, the great banker, to
a sumptuous banquet given to the members of the
Diet, at which was present M. Gentz the secretary to
the allied Sovereigns. After dinner, M. Gentz and
Owen were purposely engaged in a serious discussion
on the science of society. Among other things, Owen
said, that by means of union, which ought to take the
place of the actual disunion, a provision might easily be
made of ample means of living to every person whatever. "Yes," said M. Gentz, "we know that very
well : but we do not want the mass to become wealthy
and independent of us. How could we govern them if
they were?" If the remark were correctly interpreted,
it was a very foolish one : but I cannot believe that it
expressed the sentiments of M. Gentz's masters, the
allied Sovereigns ; whose paternal administration,
though despotic enough politically, has never shown
itself indifferent to the physical well-being of the subject. Owen however, felt the observation as a heavy

blow to his hopes; because he saw in it a proof of the invincible prejudices and interests opposed to his own views.

Attached to the Russian embassy was Baron de Krudener, the son of Madame de Krudener, whom, as Owen tells us, the Emperor Alexander was accustomed to "consult through spiritual agencies respecting his mundane proceedings." At the time Owen heard this, he must have thought Madame de Krudener about as credible as Moses or St. John; but in after days he became an infatuated believer in the spiritualists of America. Owen was informed by his acquaintance, that Alexander would pay a visit to the Prince of Tour and Taxis at a certain time: and watching his opportunity, he presented himself without introduction to the Emperor, and tendered to him a large packet of memorials: but Alexander, after asking who he was, sharply told him to call on him in the evening. Owen, wounded in his apostolical dignity, failed to keep the appointment, an omission he afterwards regretted.

From Frankfort Owen hastened to Aix-la-Chapelle, to be present at the Congress there. He requested Lord Castlereagh to present two memorials on his part, to the assembled dignitaries: his request was granted: the documents were laid on the table: and a subordinate of Lord Castlereagh afterwards assured the writer of them, that they were regarded as the most important documents presented to the Congress. I fear that the apostle's unsuspicious character was no match for diplomatic smoothness. But I feel bound to add, that years

afterwards, Owen found traces of the impression that
these memorials had made.

Owen now returned to England, to meet with a reception which was the reverse of the flattering one he
had been the subject of abroad.   There he had been
the intimate companion of the most distinguished *savants*
of Paris and Geneva: the trusted of Louis Philippe:
the guest of the Académie : the lion of the *salons :* the
disputant before the members of the Diet: the distinguished author of memorials presented to the greatest
sovereigns.   Here, in spite of his acknowledged services, his model village, his infant school, his interposition in favour of oppressed children, he was the deist or
perhaps atheist: one who had set his hand against every
man's, and whom all would join in execrating. He had
long had the support of the newspapers, glad of the
novelty of his topics, and not untouched by his liberal
purchases: but since that fatal 21st of August, not one
of the editors dared to uphold his cause. He was a
marked and reprobated man.

CHAPTER XV.

The Duke of Kent—1815: Models—Duke presides at Meetings, 1819
—Sends Macnab to New Lanark—Proposes a Visit himself—
Letters: July 18, 1819—Sept. 13, 1819—Oct. 2, 1819—Oct. 8:
the Duchess and Nurse—Oct. 8, 1819—Oct. 31, 1819—The
Duke's Last Efforts—His Convictions and Character—Princess
Olive of Cumberland.

It is a pleasant relief to turn from this record of annoyance and strife, to look for a moment at the disinterested support which was rendered by one of the
highest personages in the realm. The father of her
present Majesty was distinguished among the royal
dukes for his admirable personal qualities ; and the
account which remains of his conduct towards Owen,
exhibits the sincere desire of an upright man to promote what he believed to be the truth, without regard
to party spirit or sectarian prejudice.

As early as 1815, Owen had obtained an opportunity
of submitting the "New Views of Society" to the Duke
of Kent; who was struck with what he heard, and was
induced to study the subject. He occasionally called
upon Owen in London, bringing with him his brother
of Sussex, to whom he was much attached ; and the two
Dukes studied the model of the proposed village, as well
as another model calculated to exhibit to the eye, by

means of cubical blocks, the proportions of the different classes of society. The pin's head at top indicating the royal family, in contrast with the broad and deep base representing the working classes, may have gratified the vanity of the brothers, as much as it alarmed their weakness. Some of the highest nobility from time to time joined in these visits. One day, the Duke of Kent observing one of these glancing from the model to himself, with an ambiguous expression, said boldly that hereafter, no doubt, there would prevail a far greater equality among men than obtained under the present system, but that for himself, he did not shrink from this prospect.

In the year 1819, a committee was formed to promote Owen's plans, and the Duke acted as chairman. Public meetings were also held, and at these again the Duke presided; his exalted position allowing him to disregard public opinion to a degree that might have been dangerous to a man of lower rank. We are told that he was an admirable chairman, firm but impartial, and capable of preserving order among fiery disputants.

The Duke was so much impressed with the importance of the schemes, that he despatched to New Lanark, Dr. Macnab, "his friend and honorary physician," to study the details of the management, and to report upon the practical results. From this gentleman, as well as from General Dessaix who had visited the Clyde, the Duke heard such flattering reports, that his original prepossession was quite confirmed. Macnab had become quite an enthusiast in the cause, and promised to publish the account which afterwards appeared in his name: and both he and the French General expressed themselves delighted with the harmonious working of the complex details, and with the manifest happiness of the people.

The Duke, it may be supposed, had no further hesitation about pushing forward the new schemes. But he said very sensibly, that his opinions would have far more weight with the public, if it were known that he had visited New Lanark and examined every detail himself. He therefore offered to bring the Duchess and her infant (the present Queen) to stay at Braxfield: and he promised that on his return, he would not only continue to preside at meetings, but would also declare his convictions in the House of Lords. Unhappily, his sudden death put an end to this well-concerted scheme of patronage.

I will now quote from thirty letters of the Duke's, some of which are scattered about Owen's various writings.*

"*Kensington Palace, July 18th, 1819.*

"MY DEAR SIR,—For fear of any mistake occurring, and Mr. Rowcroft forgetting to deliver my message to you, I think it best to write a few lines, that you may be apprised of its being out of my power to attend your committee if it should be held on Thursday, as I have been for a long time engaged to attend a meeting at Maidstone at 12 o'clock on that day: but if Wednesday would suit, or Saturday not be deemed too late, I will

---

* For extracts, see *New Existence*, v. app. xii.: and for letters, see *Rational Quarterly*, i. 27, &c.

make a point of attending either or both of those days, if required, from one to three. I am happy to find you have fixed the general meeting for the 26th, on which occasion I shall certainly endeavour to discharge the duties of the chair, to the utmost of my poor abilities ; and to satisfy you and your friends, as well as the public, that I have a most sincere wish that a fair trial should be given to your system, of which I have never hesitated to acknowledge myself an admirer: though I was well aware that to set it agoing, we should have a vast deal of prejudice to combat ; and that in order to make a beginning, many points must necessarily be conceded. Before I conclude, will you permit me to mention that our literary friend—No. 1, Cumberland Street, Cumberland Place, is most desirous to see you at your earliest convenience ; in which request I beg to unite.

"Remaining at all times,
"With friendly regard and sincere esteem,
"My dear sir,
"Yours faithfully,
"EDWARD.

"P.S.—I think it right to mention, that my illustrious friend and relative, Prince Leopold, goes to Scotland next month, and has promised me faithfully to visit the establishment at Lanark. Were it not for my domestic engagements, I should willingly do the same; and I shall envy him his good fortune until I am enabled to accomplish it.

"Since writing the above, I have received your note

of this date, and will not fail to be with you at half-past one on Wednesday."

"*Kensington Palace, September 13th,* 1819.

"My dear Sir,—I received in due course your favour of the 6th, and its enclosures, which I will get Captain Parker to put his name to at the bottom; and will *this day* despatch to our literary friend, who *ought* to be as *grateful* as *I am* for your kind assistance.   Indeed I believe I may safely say *such is the case;* as no one is more heartily engaged in the great cause than is that friend.

" With regard to my own finances, I admit the justice of all you say; and that I am *sincere* in this, I believe my conduct from June 1815, for three successive years, until the day of my marriage—during which time I resigned, out of an income of 24,000*l.*, 17,000*l.* per annum, and lived upon a very reduced establishment upon 7,000*l.*—is *the strongest* proof; nor have I *since that* time, made the *slightest* addition to my *personal* establishment; the only augmentation thereof having arisen from the junction of the Duchess's with *mine;* but certainly *that* has exactly doubled my expenses; and I now candidly state that, after viewing the subject in every possible way, I am satisfied that to continue to live in England, even in the quiet way in which we are going on, *without splendour and without show, nothing short of doubling the seven thousand pounds will do,* REDUCTION BEING IMPOSSIBLE in an establishment like ours, where there is not a single servant idle for a moment from morning to night.

"Exclusive of this, some allowance—say 1,000*l.*—
should be made for the annual expense that must be
incurred for the next five years, while the Duchess
continues Regent of the Principality of Leiningen, and
guardian of her son (a minor)—to enable me to fulfil
the engagement I entered into at the time of my
marriage, that she should not be impeded in fulfilling
her duties conscientiously towards her son, notwithstanding her marriage with me. However, after saying
this, it may be right to add, that were I to confine my
residence to the Continent, I certainly could do with
five thousand pounds a year *less;* and therefore, if my
present exertions to sell Castle Hill for its valuation—
viz. 51,300*l.*—should fail, *I must resort to it.*

"I, however, have very strong reasons to hope that
this point will *yet be effected this season;* and *then* everything else will be smooth.

"Were I *unmarried,* the case would be totally different; and as I have already shown that I *could* make
a sacrifice to a *considerable* extent, I should have no
difficulty in carrying it still further. But having married a princess, who, *when the widow of the comparatively petty Prince of Leiningen,* enjoyed *every comfort
and every indulgence commensurate with her own rank as
Duchess of Saxony,* I never could reconcile it to my
feelings that having become *my wife,* she should be
degraded in the eyes of her own family—*who could not*
be made to view the circumstance as the *English* public
would do—by reducing her below those enjoyments
she has been accustomed to from the period of her

knowing herself. If my services are useful to my country, it surely becomes *those who have the power,* to support me in substantiating those just claims I have for the very extensive losses and privations I have experienced, during the very long period of my professional servitude in the colonies; and if this is not attainable, *it is a clear proof to me that they are not appreciated;* and under that impression, I shall not scruple, in *due* time, to resume my retirement abroad, when the Duchess and myself shall have fulfilled our duties in establishing the *English* birth of my child, and giving it maternal nutriment on the soil of Old England; and which we shall certainly repeat, if Providence destines to give us any further increase of family.

"I have now said enough of *myself,* and shall just add that I received a summons to attend your committee on Thursday afternoon, on my return from Oatlands, which gave me only an hour's notice; and therefore I was unable to comply with it.

"I rejoice to hear that so many persons of respectability are visiting New Lanark this year; to which number I should certainly have added myself, but for my unwillingness to absent myself from the Duchess, and the impossibility of *her* undertaking the journey with me at present. I wish, however, that in addition to Sir William de Crespigny, some other members of the House of Commons, possessing equally philanthropic feelings, but of the *other political* party, might be induced to do the *same;* and this I mention with the view of Parliament taking up the matter seriously next session. At all events, I trust my illustrious relative Prince Leopold, will not fail to fulfil his promise; and in which case I am confident the result cannot fail of being most satisfactory to him.

"Believe me to be at all times, with friendship and esteem,

"My dear sir,

"Yours faithfully,

"EDWARD.

"P.S. I open my letter again, to acknowledge your favour of the 10th instant—this instant received; and to express the satisfaction it affords me to learn that your establishment is at length beginning to become an object of such interest; as I foresee that the most beneficial consequences cannot fail to result from it;—nothing being wanted for the general adoption of the plans, but their being thoroughly understood."

(*Note.*—The numerous italics in these and the following letters, represent the underscoring in the originals.)

The Duke's pecuniary difficulties, his enforced frugality, and above all, his consciousness that his services were not appreciated, account for his dissatisfaction with the existing state of things. A prince with 7,000*l.* a year, while his inferiors by birth are spending twenty times as much around him, suffers some of the worst evils of poverty short of hunger and thirst. Discontent truly, knocks impartially at the cottage door and at the vestibule of royalty.

" Kensington Palace, Oct. 2nd, 1819.

" MY DEAR SIR,—I received yours of the 29th ultimo this morning.

" From a letter I got at the same time from my brother-in-law, I find that he was detained by the troubles at Glasgow, and *by no other* cause from visiting your establishment.

" At the same time, I cannot but admire the justice of your observations upon the subject, and which do equal honour to your head and to your heart.

" As to myself, you know how sincerely I am engaged in the cause; and if any measures are to be taken in Parliament with respect to it, which should render it indispensably necessary that I should be able to vouch for facts, from having had ocular demonstration of them, I shall not hesitate—although we intend wintering in the west, in order that the Duchess may have the benefit of tepid sea bathing, and our infant that of sea air, on the fine coast of Devonshire, during the months of the year that are so odious in London—in posting down to Scotland for the purpose; and if theDuchess's health continues good, and there is no cause to render her travelling imprudent, I have no doubt but she will most readily accompany me.

" In the meanwhile I am delighted to find that you have so many visits from individuals whose suffrages will be of importance; as the more your establishment is seen, the more, I am convinced, it must carry with it the full and entire approval of every benevolent heart.

"With regard to Dr. Macnab, I consider him quite a kindred soul with your own; and am delighted to perceive that you appreciate him, as I thought you would. I long to see him on his return, to hear a full report of his visit to you; as it was entirely undertaken at my suggestion; and from his letters I perceive the result has been to render him quite enthusiastic as to what you have accomplished, and what he foresees *may* be accomplished, if once we can succeed in carrying the public opinion with us.

"Wishing you health, to enable you to continue your zealous exertions for the good of mankind, I beg to subscribe myself,

"With sentiments of friendship and esteem,

"My dear sir,

"Yours faithfully,

"EDWARD."

The following letter will show that the duke and duchess were not above adopting *bourgeois* habits, when right reason dictated that course. Her present Majesty had a mother who was not above the care of her own infant. It would have been a happiness for this country if her example had prevailed with the matrons of the higher classes, so far as to cause the general disuse of wet-nurses; the needless employment of whom robs the mothers of the purest of the intense pleasures of life, and by its fatal effects on the abandoned children, involves the employers in the guilt of infanticide. I know there are mothers who cannot suckle their infants, and unfortunates who having a living to earn, must sell their milk to others.   Such needs may well supply each other: the incapable may innocently employ the necessitous.

"*Kensington Palace, Oct. 8th,* 1819.

"MY DEAR OWEN.—I have this moment received your favour of the 5th.   As yet the duchess has not *commenced weaning her infant;* nor do we expect *at earliest,* to be able to get over that arduous charge until the second week in November; *immediately after which,* her medical attendant thinks it essential that I should take her into Devonshire for the sea air and the benefit of the tepid sea-baths; so that our plan is arranged for going to Sidmouth, should nothing unexpected intervene to prevent it, in about a month from this time. Of course our stay there will depend upon the change agreeing with *her, her daughter,* and *our* little *infant,* who *all* three we hope, will derive the best effects from being near the sea-coast, and having access to the sea-water. Of course therefore, I could not think of attempting the journey to New Lanark, until the period is passed that will allow sufficient time for all the good results we expect from remaining some time by the seaside; but if upon the meeting of Parliament, things take *that* turn which it is to be *hoped* they will do—viz., that your judicious plans to remedy the evil of the want of productive employment, are taken up by the Government or the majority of independent members in such a manner as to ensure them a fair discussion, there will be no difficulty whatsoever,

even if the duchess should be unable to accompany me
on account of the season of the year, for me to run over
by myself, and make myself so far master of the whole
system, as to be able to deliver my sentiments upon it.

" With respect to myself, be assured that I consider
the *trouble* and *fatigue* of the journey as *nothing; nor
would the duchess,* but for the critical moment for her
health, *immediately* after nursing, which requires so
much attention.

"With regard to the *plain* and *simple* accommodation
you will have to offer us, I speak *equally her* feelings
and *my own,* when I say it is *what we should prefer* to
any other, accompanied by the sincerity of that welcome which we know Mrs. Owen and yourself would
give us.

" For *my own* part, I am already *convinced,* that what
I should see on the spot, would amply repay me for any
little trouble and expense which the journey might
occasion me; and the Duchess is as much prepossessed
in favour of .the thing as I am.

" From all I have said, you will therefore infer, that
if the moment shall arrive, between this and the spring,
when, from the certainty of your establishment coming
under the consideration of Parliament, it would become
indispensable for me to inspect it in person, to be able to
take a part in the discussion, I shall not consider the
trouble of undertaking the journey *anything,* but most
cheerfully set out upon it, even if at the time circumstances should not admit of the Duchess's accompanying me; whom I confess, I do not willingly quit *even*

for a day, unless there is an indispensable necessity for it.

"With every sentiment of the most friendly **regard,**

"I remain, ever,

"My dear Owen,

"Yours faithfully,

"EDWARD."

"*Kensington Palace, Oct.* 31*st,* 1819.

"MY DEAR OWEN.—Having been absent for four days, on a visit to the coast of Devonshire, to fix upon a house where we could cheat the early part of the approaching winter, I did not receive till late on Thursday night, your favour of the 19th; since which I have been so overwhelmed with business, as scarcely to have been able to find a moment to devote to you. I will not however, suffer to-morrow's mail to depart without just answering your kind and interesting communication.

"I was delighted to perceive that you had had the visit of General Dessaix, and I look forward *with pleasure* to hear him converse upon your establishment.

"Pray express to Lady Mary Ross, whose brother Lord Robert Fitzgerald is a particular friend of mine, how grateful the Duchess and myself feel for the kind offer of her house in your vicinity, in case we should be enabled to pay you a visit during the period of her absence in South Britain: but as there is an absolute necessity that the Duchess should take the tepid sea-baths in the first instance at Sidmouth, which have been strongly advised by her medical attendant, to strengthen her health after her confinement and nursing, I fear, with every wish on both our parts to do so, we shall not be able to avail ourselves of it, at least for the present year.

" At the same time, I cannot deny that your tempting offer would be a strong inducement to undertake the journey, were we not so circumstanced at present as to preclude almost the possibility of thinking of it. But though this pleasure must be deferred, I by no means think of giving it up. On the contrary, I look forward with pleasure to realizing it at a future day.

" I congratulate you upon having had a visit from some of the particular friends and relatives of that good woman Mrs. Fry; as I am sure they can only have gone to New Lanark with motives of benevolence.

" I think it also extremely fortunate that the celebrated Mr. Ellis of Kent, has determined upon viewing your establishment in person; for it is the opinion of *such* valuable men as *he is*, which, if favourable, must give strength to the cause.

" Lord Torrington who is to accompany him, is certainly a very worthy, well-meaning man; but I am afraid you will not find in him the judgment that you will in his travelling companion. However, it is a satisfaction to find that one nobleman has thought it worth his while to undertake the journey; and I hope his example will be followed by a great many more; being satisfied that nothing can tend so much to establish a conviction of all the good that may result from forming establishments upon your principle, as ocular demonstration. And I say this with the more feeling, being strongly impressed like you, with the belief that the change contemplated for the relief of the suffering poor of the country, must indeed be made more speedily and generally than many seem to anticipate, if the object is to restore the country to a state of order and tranquillity before it is too late. My only fear is that ministers, having chosen to draw the sword, will turn a deaf ear to the representations of those who from motives of benevolence like yourself, and viewing the matter with unbiassed judgment, would adopt measures of a totally different tendency.

"It may be right to apprise you, that I recently received the inclosed papers from Mr. Bourne, who certainly is a most zealous and active member of the committee; but after having so long adjourned our meetings, I should like to have your opinion upon his suggestions, before we act upon them. Pray, therefore, write by return of post; your doing which will, I apprehend, enable me to hear from you on the 9th, or at the latest on the 10th of November, and in the meanwhile,

   " Believe me ever to remain,
    " With the most friendly regard,
     " My dear Owen,
      " Yours faithfully,
       " EDWARD."

Owen, after the last letter which he ever received from his royal correspondent, came to London to see him: and the Duke then reiterated his conviction of the truth of the "New Views;" being confirmed in

his previous opinions, by the favourable report he had
received, both from Dr. Macnab and from General
Dessaix.   He again promised to visit New Lanark,
that he might be able to give his testimony, as one
who knew for himself what he was speaking of.   This
was the last time that Owen ever saw him in the
flesh: though, many years afterwards, the Duke's
spirit was one of those heavenly visitants who condescended to cheer the old age of their friend by mani-
festing themselves to him.   The Duke presided once
more as chairman of the committee, on the first of
December 1819.   His sudden death deprived Owen
of his most powerful supporter; but probably rescued
the Duke himself from the odium which he was incur-
ring, as the zealous advocate of views grossly tainted
with infidelity; and saved him from that contempt
which the unthinking world is apt to bestow on utopian
schemes earnestly pursued.   For my own part, since
I regard Owen's plans at this time as altogether visionary, I cannot imagine that the world lost much in this
respect by the Duke's lamented death: but it is impossible for me to refuse my admiration to one who, brought
up in the corrupting position of son of a king, retained
nevertheless, the vigour of mind required for the earnest
prosecution of schemes which appeared to him to be of
public advantage.

Owen pays a deserved tribute of praise to the Duke's
integrity, firmness, sincerity, and forbearing kindness.
He says that the Duke declared himself to have become
a new man, since his acquaintance with the "New

Views:" a statement which, but for the letters I have quoted, I should have received with caution, inasmuch as a similar statement is made as to the quiet Lord Liverpool and several members of his Cabinet. The letters however, are conclusive as to the Duke's sincerity of conviction. Doubtless he felt invigorated and ennobled by the adoption of a pursuit, calculated as he thought, to relieve his country from many of the evils under which it was labouring.

One more paragraph, and I have done with the royal family. Owen tells us that the Duke of Kent unhesitatingly believed in the soundness of the pretensions of the "Princess Olive of Cumberland," to be regarded as one of the royal family: that he introduced this lady (afterwards Mrs. Serries) as his cousin; and that he showed the deepest interest in her cause and in that of her daughter. Owen, to oblige his royal patron, advanced to Mrs. Serries at different times, sums of money amounting to much more than a thousand pounds, none of which was repaid during his life; the persons appointed to arrange the payment of the Duke's debts not being satisfied with the proof tendered: but quite recently, since Owen's death, the affair having been brought by the executors under the notice of her Majesty, she made no difficulties about legal proofs, but satisfied the claim in a manner the most gracious.

CHAPTER XVI.

Proverb reversed—Peel's Bill, 1819—Owen's Dogmatism—National
Distress—New Lanark not distressed—Why not?—Owen's Reply
—Title of Report — Unbounded Hopes — Fundamental Error—
Machinery in Agriculture—Application to Working Classes—
Owen does not propose to apply—Spade Husbandry—Rashness of
Proposal—Currency—Labour Standard — Details — Report of a
Committee—Favourable Reception—Experiment attempted.

AFTER the unhappy death of the Duke of Kent, Owen
was left without any prominent disciples in England.
But nearer his home he was more fortunate; and in
his case there was a reversal of the proverb which
robs a man of all honour in his own neighbourhood.

In the year 1819 there was great distress in the
country. Owen in his account of it, follows very
complacently in the wake of those who attacked
Mr. Peel with his celebrated Bill of '19, as the cause
of the national calamities. On the greater part of
questions, indeed, even of the highest importance, we
have no choice but to adopt those opinions which are
recommended to us, by the studious application and
sound judgment of persons who have especially investigated them: and in this instance, the first Sir Robert
Peel, by his passionate denunciations of his son's policy,
would have great weight with Owen, whose intimate

acquaintance he had made, by their joint exertions in carrying the factory bill. But in cases where our notions have thus been formed by authority, and not by our own study, we ought to express ourselves about them, not *ex cathedrâ*, not with the excusable dogmatism of a master towards his pupils, but with a modest hesitation. I cannot easily excuse Owen's arrogance, when in speaking of Mr. Peel and the Bullion Committee, he says that " these men knew no more than infants what they were legislating about; and had no knowledge of the amount of most unnecessary misery and severe suffering, which they by their ignorance were about to inflict on millions of their fellow-subjects over the British empire."

The distress, says Owen, was so great, that thousands upon thousands of working people were without work or food; and numbers of active men from twenty to thirty years old, applied at New Lanark for work, and would have taken four or five shillings a week. The absence of any provision in Scotland for the able-bodied who are destitute, must be held accountable for a great aggravation of this evil. The English poor-law, as some tell us, lowers the rate of wages! Why it is the bridge which enables the discharged labourer to pass over that gulf of want and starvation into which, without that friendly aid, he must fall.

The county of Lanark shared in the general depression. Owen's village, on the contrary, went quietly on its way, unconscious of the disturbance in the commercial atmosphere. For Owen had not availed him-

11

self of the stranger workmen's applications, as a means of screwing down his own people, but went on paying at the customary rate. For twenty-five years the scale of wages at New Lanark was unchanged: an example worthy of all admiration, though one which in ordinary cases it is impossible to imitate. Owen practised this munificence not only now, at the head of a professedly philanthropic establishment; but as a younger man, when he advanced 7,000l. to keep the people from want.

In the hope of doing something to mitigate the distress, the county of Lanark held a great meeting; and Owen was present. Persons had noticed the contrast between the county and the manufacturing village. What could be the cause of it? Would Mr. Owen be pleased to enlighten them? The answer might have been a very simple one. New Lanark was under the control of one of the ablest manufacturers of the day; was fed with an abundant capital; was managed on the express condition that all the surplus profit should be applied to the benefit of the workpeople; and therefore, Owen, with his ability, with the capital at his command, and with a vast amount of surplus profits set aside for the improvement, or relief, of the hands, could save his subjects for a year or two from the yawning pit of want. Give to all employers of labourers, Owen's ability, capital and surplus profit, and the distress would never have appeared.

But Owen's notions were of a very different character. He regarded the immunity of New Lanark, not as the issue of accidental circumstances, and of unusual qualities; but as something much higher; as the result of the application of a principle which might be adopted with equal success in the ordinary affairs of life. He eagerly seized the opportunity of explaining this opinion; and must have rejoiced in the field thus opened in the north, just when the death of his royal friend had darkened his prospects in London. He would be glad to give to the county of Lanark the benefit of his thirty years' experience; and to show his neighbours how pauperism might, not merely be mitigated, but once for all extinguished. He thought to himself, that in this public theatre, with the great landowners and nobility among his audience, he would put forth his powers, and with all the skill of a prophet, remove from men's eyes the film which obscured their true interests. He went home and wrote an elaborate report, extending over nearly fifty octavo pages of print: and as he says that this was the first time " he explained the science of constructing a rational system of society," and as he afterwards frequently referred to this report for an elucidation of his views, it is necessary to briefly notice its contents.

The title of the report indicates Owen's notions as to its scope. It is called a " Report to the County of Lanark, of a plan for relieving public distress and removing discontent, by giving permanent productive employment to the poor and working classes; under arrangements which will essentially improve their character and ameliorate their condition, diminish the expenses of production and consumption, and create markets co-extensive with production.   By Robert Owen, May 1, 1820."

After stating that the evil he has to deal with is the want of work and of wages for the labouring classes, Owen goes on to say that without some great measures adopted by the legislature with the support of the country, the existing distress and discontent would become chronic, and the resources of the empire would be gradually dried up. He then advances five maxims, the first of which is, that if manual labour were properly directed, there need be no deterioration of its value for centuries to come: that Great Britain and its dependencies might, under the circumstances, support an incalculable increase of population ; and that so far from fearing a too rapid augmentation, we should be unable sufficiently to stimulate its progress. The gentlemen of Lanark, on hearing this exordium, must have felt only one drawback : the suspicion that promises so flattering could scarcely be trusted.

In the explanation of these five propositions, there peeps out an error, which I imagine to have been at the bottom of all the unsound part of Owen's system. He was himself a manufacturer ; he had floated through life on that wave of prosperity which had arisen from the mechanical inventions of Watt, Hargreaves, and Arkwright ; he had been involved in the turmoil of manufacturing industry ; he had taken an active part in multiplying to the utmost the new mechanical powers applied to production : it was no wonder if the din of machinery and the buzz of the factory, had closed his ears to other sounds: it was in the natural course of events that he should vastly overrate the triumphs, great as they were, of mechanical skill. In the Archbishop's Committee of 1816, he had stated that the increase of mechanical power was one cause of the existing distress: he now said that this increased power, properly directed, was sufficient "to saturate the world with wealth." Now the error I have mentioned, as it appears to me, consists in this: that he fails to distinguish between the different kinds of production: that when he speaks of the mechanical power of Great Britain as producing forty times more than its hand-labour, he omits to remark that this increased productiveness had as yet been limited to manufactures: and that he aggravates this negligence when he says that it has been "introduced more or less into all the departments of productive industry throughout the empire."

If it were true that the labour of a man, assisted by machinery, would produce even twenty times as much, in every department of industry, as it would have produced a century earlier, when machinery was comparatively rare, it would follow that there should be twenty times as many commodities to be consumed. But unfortunately, the whole hypothesis is baseless. In the greatest department of industry, that of agriculture, the amount of new machinery applied is now very small, and in 1820 was still less. We generally say that in England at present, perhaps in Great Britain, but not including Ireland, each man engaged in farming raises food enough for two families besides his own:

which is much the same thing as to say that excluding
those persons who are fed with foreign food, one-third
of our British population is engaged in agriculture.
From Owen's statement, however, it might have been
supposed that one-twentieth, or one-fortieth part of the
population could feed all the rest.

But this error is a most important one in its bearing
on the working classes. The new machinery has been
principally applied to the manufacture of textile fabrics
and of metals. The result has been a great reduction
in the price of calico, silk, linen, iron, hardware, and
such things; while raw produce, and many things easily
formed from it, have not fallen or have even risen. Since
1820, there has been a great, fall in woollen cloth, in
consequence of the introduction of foreign colonial wool.
But what share of a poor man's income is spent on things
that have fallen: what share on things that have not
fallen? The main expense is for food: then there are
shoes, stockings, candles; these have either risen or
have not been materially reduced. He and his wife
get their calico, cotton prints, woollen garments, and
their scanty hardware, for much less money than
formerly. But so small a proportion do these bear to
the whole expenditure, that if they were to be had for
nothing, that would be a trifle by the side of the grand
question of the relation of the rate of wages to the rate
of food. It seems, therefore, that the great mechanical
progress which our age is vastly proud of, has a tendency
indeed, but only a slight tendency, to diminish the expenses of the labourer. If indeed we could apply to

agriculture the same means of increased productiveness that we have applied to manufactures, then the super-abundance of food would justify the opinion of Owen, that our difficulty hereafter would be to get people to multiply fast enough. May Heaven shield us from such a change! as one that would reduce us to the uncultivated condition of a half settled colony, with the illiterate for our masters.

Owen, of course, was not without a dim perception, that agriculture and manufactures followed different laws in their development. Otherwise, he might have suggested the application to farming of the same mechanical appliances which had proved successful in manufactures. It is true, however, that he was no professed admirer of the manufacturing system, and that he even shared the vulgar opinion that labourers and machines were natural enemies; overlooking the fact that though machinery displaces men in the first instance, that effect is only temporary. At any rate, Owen's proposal as to agriculture was far from being the application of threshing machines and steam ploughs.

He was a convert to the supporters of spade husbandry. He had read that delving was more favourable to large crops than ploughing: and in the face of the country gentlemen, who imagined themselves to know something about farming, he laid down the laws of growth and cultivation, without any regard to proverbs about cordwainers and their sandals. A prophet can afford to despise the common sense of mankind. Forty years of active improvement have elapsed since this

report was written; and in that time spade husbandry
has made but little progress: a stronger argument
against it than the one we commonly hear, that to substitute human labour for that of a horse, and the simple
spade for the ingenious plough, is an anachronism and
a rebellion against the law of progress. Spade husbandry, however, had taken up its place in Owen's
mind, and was to be the foundation of his new villages.

When Owen wanted to prove the possibility of improving the condition of a manufacturing population,
his demonstration was short and decisive: "Come and
see New Lanark." People came, saw, and believed.
But when he had to prove the advantages of spade
husbandry, he could merely appeal to the statements of
other people as to the experiments they had made. His
particular authority was Mr. Falla of Gateshead, in
whom he placed implicit faith; with a generous disregard of the statements on the other side, as to the difficulties arising from the slowness of digging in wet
seasons, and from the expensiveness of keeping a man
with a family, to do after all only a portion of the work
of a horse. Owen replied to objectors with the *experimentum crucis*: Mr. Falla had found digging successful.
To this it was rejoined that in another *experimentum
crucis*, digging had been unsuccessful. In short, the
subject of spade husbandry was in an unsettled state;
and to found a new social system upon it argued singular rashness. What should we say of any one who
in 1859, should propose new home colonies, founded on
the alleged discovery by the Rev. Mr. Smith, of the

possibility of cultivating wheat year after year on the same land, by the device of using only alternate strips, assisted by certain complex forkings and hoeings? Such a colonial projector would be reminded of Jethro Tull, who long ago, with wonderful skill and perseverance, forced crop after crop without manure, and as it is alleged, ended with bringing his land into a habit of fertility not a whit better than that of a loose high road. Villages based either on the Lois-Weedon plan, or on that of Jethro Tull, would be nearly as rational as those proposed by Owen on the scheme of spade husbandry.

Another topic on which Owen appears to me to have exhibited blamable rashness, was that of the currency. I have already suggested that the influence of the first Sir Robert Peel was probably that which bent Owen's mind in the particular direction which it took. But he now claimed for himself the authority of a diligent and persevering student: stating that he had deeply studied these subjects, practically and theoretically, for a period of thirty years. When he uses the word studied, he means, I conceive, that he had thought about the subject; and that I fully believe: but study implies an inquiry into other people's thoughts as well as our own, and in this sense I do not conceive that he had studied the currency question. I find in his multifarious writings, singularly feeble traces of study of any kind: and if he had been acquainted with the able treatises written on the gold and paper question, he would not have spoken, as he did, of the suspension of cash payments in '97, as the result of the rapid increase of wealth in this country; leaving out of sight the war and the foreign subsidies. Who that had made himself acquainted with even the elementary writers, could have made such a blunder as this? I do not say this in the character of a partisan of the predominant school: indeed, I do not believe in Colonel Torrens and Lord Overstone: I am convinced by Mr. Tooke's voluminous and very heavy volumes that the ultra bullionists are in the wrong. But I cannot consent to rush with Owen into the extreme of saying that Horner and Peel were as ignorant as infants; nor can I join him in dogmatizing on a topic of remarkable difficulty.

Owen's particular whim was the substitution of labour in the place of gold or silver, as the standard of value: not that this notion was peculiar to him; for other persons in abundance have held that labour, being the first cost of all commodities, forms the natural measure of the worth of things. But to this I object that the hypothesis is untrue: I deny, with an apology to the memory of Adam Smith, that labour is the sole first cost of most commodities. Production can scarcely take place without capital; and capital cannot be accumulated without self-denial: from which it follows that self-denial, as well as labour, is a part of the cost of commodities; and that capital as much as labour ought to have to do with the standard of value. But even if it were true that labour was the first cost of all commodities, the inference drawn is a false one. We do not measure a thing with itself, but with something else. We do not measure apples with apples, but in a quart or a a bushel: we do not weigh sugar with sugar, but by a pound or a hundredweight. So we do not measure labour with labour, or self-denial with self-denial, but we measure them both with gold or silver. The regulation of a money standard, I am aware, is a matter of far greater difficulty than the regulation of a quart or a pound; and if Owen had said, Let us bend our energies to the improvement of our standard, that would have been reasonable. In this matter he was not a reformer, but a wild revolutionist.

I do not propose to state at any length the details of this scheme. Those who think, as I do, that the principles of it are false, will be little desirous of knowing the particular means suggested for carrying it into effect. I will only mention that Owen proposed to cut the world up into villages of 300 to 2,000 souls, with a preference for 800 to 1,200: that every person should have allotted an area of land varying from half an acre to three times that quantity, according as the particular society was more or less agricultural: that the dwellings for the 200 or 300 families should be placed together in the form of a parallelogram, with common kitchens, eating apartments, schools, and places of worship in the centre. I must add, what many will regard not as details, but as the kernel of the whole system, that individualism was to be disallowed in these villages: that each one was to work for the benefit of all; and that as a result, all the members would eat at a table and of viands provided by the community. For myself I regard this communism as one of the subordinate parts of the plan, because, until it is proved that by spade husbandry an increased quantity of commodities can be produced, in proportion to the labour employed, it is quite useless to discuss the best mode of distributing the excess. We must needs kill our bear before we dispose of his skin.

The report, of which I have given this slight sketch, was laid before a committee of gentlemen appointed by the public meeting of the county; and this committee made its report in a cautious and reasonable manner. It could not recommend the adoption of plans, acknowledged to be at variance with the opinions of some of the most enlightened political economists of the age: it had the pleasure of stating that Mr. Owen had consented with his usual liberality to print his report for circulation in te county: it regarded the topic of spade husbandry as being of high importance, and one that would be most satisfactorily investigated by a number of experiments set on foot here and there, on a small scale: it felt bound to speak in terms of the highest praise of New Lanark, of its philanthropic proprietors, of its admirable management, and of the proof it offered of possible amelioration of mechanics, without as it was alleged any pecuniary sacrifice on the part of employers.

Owen's report, though thus shirked by the committee, was favourably received in other quarters. A copy was sent to Paris, and with the four essays, was translated into French and German: and the Académie sent Owen a vote of thanks. At another county meeting it was proposed that a trial of the plan should be made, as a substitute for the erection of a county bridewell. The day of reformatories had not dawned: Owen had not turned his attention especially to the treatment of convicts: the management of a prison establishment was small game for a man, who was bent on parcelling out the world into villages: but had Owen's aims been less ambitious, he might have immortalized himself as a criminal reformer.

Owen always kept the world well informed as to his proceedings; and the circulation of his Lanark report produced a widely spread interest. He was importuned from various quarters to commence an experimental village. He feared that the world was not ripe for it: fifty years of work and success, had perhaps relaxed his vigour: at any rate, he consented unwillingly that a subscription of capital should be opened. He demanded three-quarters of a million to begin with: he lowered his tone to a quarter of a million: under much pressure he consented to make a trial with 50,000*l.* Mr. A. J. Hamilton of Dalzell, who was well acquainted with New Lanark, and who was an ardent disciple of the New Views, offered a favourable site for a village, at Motherwell, a few miles from Owen's residence; and it was agreed that something should be done. The preliminary measures were complex, and required a vast correspondence, so that up to the year 1824 nothing was accomplished.

CHAPTER XVII.

Owen's true Policy—His actual Policy—Inducements to visit Ireland
—Whom Owen visited—Maynooth—The Conference—A May-
nooth Promise—Not of Love—Resolves on Dublin Meetings—
Description of Ireland—A Remedy promised—Meeting on Tues-
day, March 28, 1823—Owen's monotony—Quackishness—Scheme
—Objections—Second and Third Meetings, 12th and 19th April
—An Association formed—Model Illustrations.

I HAVE related how Owen, in the year 1817, laboured
to set against his schemes, all who entertained any
serious thoughts about religion; that is, an overwhelming majority of the middle and upper classes : how, in
company with Professor Pictet, he afterwards travelled
in a sort of triumph through France and Switzerland :
and how, after visiting Frankfort and Aix-la-Chapelle,
and conferring with many of the politicians assembled
at those places, he returned to Britain to receive the
crown of martyrdom, which the London meeting had
obstinately refused to confer on him.　The history
which I have since given, of the years 1819 and 1820,
exhibits Owen as still disappointed of that reward
which his enthusiasm had anticipated.　The newspapers
indeed had ceased to praise him, while the religious
world shuddered at his name: yet there were some
men, from the very highest in rank to the very
lowest, who were his avowed disciples, and who were

bent on carrying his social schemes into practice. If he would now have remained quiet, until by persevering energy he had got one of his model villages into working condition, he might have convinced men of the excellence of his new scheme, just as he had convinced them of the excellence of his New Lanark practices : by saying, Come and see ; here is my village, there are my account books ; judge for yourselves.

But this was not the policy he adopted. Indeed, in the years 1821 and 1822, he seems not to have been much before the world, but to have been busily engaged in the preliminary measures for his Motherwell village. In 1823, however, he again thrust himself conspicuously on public attention ; and again exhibited that extravagant desire for notoriety, which had so seriously damaged his public influence in 1817. In 1823, he made his appearance in Ireland, and acted over again the exciting scenes of the London meetings of 1817. I doubt not that he convinced himself of the propriety of the course he adopted ; nor do I seriously doubt that he deceived himself, and that his passion, not his judgment, was his guide. Just as in 1817, in the midst of the proceedings necessary to secure the Factory Act, he suddenly abandoned his post to others and appeared upon a London platform as the great prophet of irreligion ; so now, in 1823, he left the care of his incipient village and threw obstacles in the way of his friends, by repeating on a Dublin stage the same extravagant part. The love of fame, if it be a weakness, is at least the weakness of a noble mind ; but it

would be difficult to predicate as much good of a love
of notoriety.

Owen tells us that Ireland in 1823, was in a very
pitiable state; a fact we easily receive: and we cannot
wonder that he should desire to see the country for
himself, and judge whether it were possible for his
experience to suggest any mitigations.   He had the
further inducement of receiving many invitations from
leading people in different parts of the country.   He
was fortunate enough also, during the greater part of
the time, to have the company of Captain Macdonald
of the Engineers, with the help of an experienced
agriculturist and a secretary.   One is irresistibly reminded of Arthur Young's tour in Ireland half a
century earlier.   Young, however, did not go as a prophet, nor did he need any agriculturist but himself.   It
would have been natural for Owen, if he had been
acquainted with the notes of that tour, to use them as
the basis of his observations: but he makes no allusion to the work, and he probably was unacquainted
with it.

Owen mentions the names of many of the personages
whom he visited or had communication with in Ireland;
and among them are those of the Marquis Wellesley,
then Lord Lieutenant, the Duke of Leinster, the Marquis of Downshire, the Earls of Carberry, Carrick,
Listowel, and Clare, Lords Cloncurry and Milton, Lady
O'Brien, nearly all the Protestant Bishops, and many of
the Roman Catholic Bishops; and from all these he
received much attention and cordial hospitality.

He penetrated into Maynooth and was well received. He was introduced by the Duke of Leinster, with whom he was staying at Carton, which is near Maynooth; and he accepted an invitation from Dr. Crotty the President, to meet a dozen of the learned Roman Catholic doctors, for a conference on the state of Ireland. A few weeks afterwards, on a second visit to Carton, the conference took place.

A formal introduction was made, and Owen was called on to explain his first principles. He began to do so, and was soon met with objections, by one who seemed the youngest and least experienced of the party. The President saw, as Owen tells us, that the Roman Catholic side was likely to get the worst of it; though what followed seems to me to be susceptible of a different interpretation. At any rate, the President, looking expressively round, suggested the propriety of allowing their guest to give a full and uninterrupted explanation of the principles and practices he recommended. After this, Owen was heard in respectful silence for two hours. At the conclusion of his long harangue, the President said that all the gentlemen were much indebted to their visitor: and (again casting a peculiar glance round the circle) added, that Owen would be secure from any further opposition on the part of the Catholic clergy, at his future meetings. The promise was kept. Was this the language of conviction, of fear, or of contempt?

Owen was afterwards convinced that it was not the language of love. Madame Tussaud was desirous of having his figure to exhibit with those of Napoleon and Thurtell, Washington and Robespierre; and Owen condescended to sit to an artist for the purpose. The figure was moulded, it was dressed in imitation clothes; yet Owen was defrauded of this publication, and the visitors lost the sight of his image. Years afterwards, Owen heard from his tailor, who dressed Madame Tussaud's nonentities, that that lady's Jesuit confessor had put his veto on Owen's appearance.—As many murderers as you please, but not Mr. Owen.—If this hearsay tale be true, the silence of the priests in Ireland was not precisely contemptuous.

After Owen had spent some time in Ireland, and had carefully passed through it from north to south, he determined to communicate to the Dublin people, the results of his labours. Now this is the part of his proceedings which, as I think, his friends have reason to regret.

He commenced with a letter addressed to the " nobility, gentry, clergy, and inhabitants." He opened this, with a description such as many had given before, and many have given since; one which no one disputes the truth of, and which it is impossible to read without horror and shame: a description of a beggarly peasantry without the means of supporting life; of towns crowded with people living in dirt and disease; of merchants and manufacturers losing everything except hope, and that perhaps ill founded; of landowners dreading the swallowing up of rent; of clergy shuddering at the probable extinction of tithe and the consequent starvation of their families; of philanthropic ladies in despair at finding that their labours seemed to create more misery than they relieved; of women clamouring for work at twopence a day; of able-bodied men whining to be employed at eightpence for fourteen hours; of noblemen and gentlemen earnestly desirous of doing their duty, yet forced to barricade their houses as if in an enemy's country. On the other hand, he found a soil fertile beyond description, a fair climate, fine rivers, noble harbours, vast means of production.

Who was to blame? The nobility and gentry? No. The producing classes? None of them, whether capitalist or workman. It was the system, and the system alone, which was wrong. Where then was the remedy? That remained to be told, and he could tell them. Let all parties put aside their differences: let Whig and Tory, Catholic and Protestant, Saxon and Celt, kiss and be friends; and let them all meet him at the Rotunda on Tuesday, the 18th March, and they should hear of something infinitely to their advantage.

The meeting took place accordingly, and was, as might have been expected, crowded. Heavy distress with magnificent promises of relief; an excitable people and a publicist of vast pretensions; a rather idle capital and an orator who promised something new: what more could be desired to attract a throng? Not Irving with the supernatural wonders of an unknown tongue, not Gavazzi with all the enchantments of southern passion, not Kossuth fresh from the struggle for Magyar freedom, was better fitted to arrest the attention of the multitude.

The Lord Mayor took the chair, and Owen proceeded
to *read* a long address, containing his usual notions of
philosophy, and his regular panacea for social evils. I
beg that I may not be understood to complain of this
uniformity of material in Owen's lucubrations. It is the
business of an author to find variety for his readers :
but it is the duty of a reformer to ascertain what is the
truth, and to inculcate his doctrine wherever he goes.
Owen's oft repeated tale, tiresome as it is to the reader
of his works, proves the sincerity of his convictions : for
when a man is sincerely and deeply impressed with any
truth, he must needs bring it forward on every possible
occasion.

Again, I may seem open to censure, for having
assumed a tone of ridicule as to this Dublin meeting,
and for having attributed to Owen something approaching to charlatanism.   But I have done this deliberately,
and I have merely recorded the sentiment excited in
my own mind by reading an account of what took
place.   Not only in the invitation, but at the meeting
itself, there was a something which I can scarcely
forbear to call quackish.   At the end of about ten
minutes' reading, when Owen had alluded to the distress he had observed, and had stated that it was not
the individual but the system which was to blame, he
went on with these words : " I will now disclose to you
a secret, which *till now* has been hidden from mankind." *   A secret forsooth ! and one hidden till now !
Why it is nothing but the proposition which he has

* *New Existence,* iv. App. vi. vii.

been shouting from the housetop, which he has been circulating throughout the world for years, which he has spent a little fortune in publishing. For the alleged secret is nothing more than this maxim: "that the human character is formed, not *by* but *for* the individual."

After adding in his usual trenchant manner, that ignorance of this truth had made all religions a curse * to the world, he propounded his scheme of improvement, which was, of course, his Scotch village, with parallelogram of houses, common table, Spartan education, and abundance of the means of living.

When Owen had finished his address, a Rev. Mr. Dunne rose, and as usually happens in the case of those who are most forward to enlighten the public, exhibited an entire ignorance of facts and unacquaintance with principles. He conceded that Mr. Owen had realized, on a small scale, the plan he proposed: that is to say, he lazily took it for granted, that New Lanark, with its great capitalists and workpeople living on wages, was a communistic village. He dreaded too great an improvement in the means of living on the part of the people: for at the present day, the common artisan must live like a gentleman, and the farmer like a prince. And this was said in the midst of miserable Ireland. Truly, if Owen could have been conceived as arranging a drama for his own benefit, the Rev. Mr. Dunne's speech would have been exactly what he would have placed in the first scene. If people had known the facts of the case, they

* *New Existence*, iv. App. xx.

would have spared themselves all elaborate argumentation, and would have pinned Owen down to one question:
How much money is necessary? He had asked three-
quarters of a million for the construction of one village,
and he had unwillingly consented to begin with 50,000*l*.
But taking this ridiculously reduced estimate, of one-
fifteenth of the original one, what sum would, in the
same proportion, be necessary for all Ireland? If in
Scotland, a village of two thousand people required
50,000*l*. at least, to start with, what would be required
in Ireland for five millions of people? Was Ireland
to remain miserable till a hundred millions sterling
(perhaps a thousand millions) could be found for experiments?

The meeting was ended by the carrying of a motion
of adjournment, without fixing any day for reassembling.
Owen in a second published letter, good-humouredly
approved of this result; but he proposed that a second
discussion should take place on the 12th April. Accordingly, on that day, another meeting was held, but
without the presidency of the Lord Mayor: and a crowd
of ladies and gentlemen were again present. Owen
read another address, which proved so long, that he
proposed an adjournment for a week; and on the
19th he furnished long calculations, the correctness of
which it would have been difficult for any one then to
dispute.

These addresses were not treated by the Irish themselves as the ebullitions of a visionary. It was resolved
by many persons of rank and fortune, that something

should be done; and the result was the establishment of the Hibernian Philanthropic Society. At the first meeting of this society, at Morrisson's Hotel, on the 3rd May, Owen entered the room in company with Lord Cloncurry, the Hon. Mr. Dawson, Sir Frederick Flood, Sir Capel Molyneux, Sir William Brabazon, General Browne, Mr. A. H. Rowan, Dr. Macartney, and others. Loan subscriptions were announced of 1,000l. each by General Browne and Mr. Owen, of 500l. by Lord Cloncurry, of smaller sums by various people; besides a donation of 100l. by Dr. Macartney. Large contributions for the individuals to make, but only a trifling beginning towards the millions or hundreds of millions needed for the village regeneration of Ireland.

Owen, with his unfailing industry, had an address to read, in which among other things he introduced his readers to his favourite cubes, illustrative of the proportions of the different classes of society:* as also to a series of slides arranged as if on a multiplied billiard marker, each slide representing the faculty of a child as it generally is and as it ought to be. The noble lord and the honourable gentlemen must have felt their gravity jeopardized by these devices that savoured of the itinerant lecturer. Owen also promised to visit London, armed with a petition, with a view to endeavour to obtain justice for Ireland, by an entire change of measures on the part of the Government.

* *New Existence*, App. xcvii.

CHAPTER XVIII.

My Authorities—Partners, and Irreligion—W. Allen—Clear Understanding with, in 1815—Allen might have retired—Cordiality in
1818—Interference 1820—Again 1822—Again 1823, 1824. Agreement—Dress of Children—Suspicion of Negligence—Money Matters—Owen's retirement—Bill of '19—Sir Robert Peel's Grief—
Holkham—Offers himself as M.P.—1822 : British and Foreign
Philanthropical Society: the Leaders—Object: Money—Nature of
Communities : Thirty-nine Articles—Another Account—Subscribers.

HITHERTO, the task I have undertaken has not been a
difficult one, because I have had Owen himself for my
guide. When he was a very old man, he published
two volumes of his life : and the first 240 pages of one
of these were properly an autobiography ; the other
volume and a half containing a reprint of the four
essays and other important papers. Even here, some
patience and some method were necessary, to winnow
out the grain from a rather confused mass, and to piece
together disjointed fragments which are presented in
anything but a chronological order. Owen's style of
writing had always been parenthetical and discursive;
and age did not tend to correct these faults. But,
perplexing as the autobiography is, it is better than
nothing: and from this time I am dependent for information on the unconnected and imperfect narratives
which occur here and there in his various publications.

Even my last chapter, on the proceedings in Ireland, was not furnished by the autobiography, which ends with the report to the county of Lanark. But the account of those proceedings was carefully compiled at the time by some unknown friend; and being published by Carrick of Dublin, was afterwards reprinted by Owen in the periodical to which I have given a reference. In order to complete my narrative of the life, which was prolonged a third of a century beyond the point we have reached, I have searched all Owen's publications which I have been able to obtain, and with the help and suggestions of some of his friends, have mastered, I hope, the important facts of his history.

It must have occurred to some readers as a singular phenomenon, that while New Lanark was being conducted by an association of benevolent persons, for philanthropic purposes, one of the number should from time to time make his appearance before the public, and denounce in the loudest and most audacious terms, every religious creed under the sun. Most partners would have felt themselves extremely ill used by this unheard-of proceeding. It could not be said indeed, that it was contrary to the express articles of partnership; because no article would be inserted to restrain a man from doing what no sane man would be supposed capable of meditating: but I do think that Owen, when he induced such men as Allen and his other Quaker friends to join him, did tacitly bind himself not to become a preacher of irreligion; and this under a covenant

stronger than any express stipulation; the covenant I
mean, of an honourable construction of his engagements. The New Lanark partners had, as I conceive,
great reason for complaint.

Owen tells us that some time after he had made his
appearance before the world as the apostle of disbelief,
William Allen began to interfere with his management.
Allen had been travelling on the Continent, had received a good deal of attention, had had some communication with Alexander and other sovereigns, and was
altogether in a rather elated condition of mind, much
resembling, I conceive, that of Owen himself. When
a meeting should ensue, of two bodies both highly
charged, the one with positive and the other with negative theology, what but a thunderstorm could be looked
for? This natural antagonism accounts for the fact,
that Owen always speaks of his partner with less
charity than he exhibits towards others of his opponents. While he acknowledges Allen's sincerity, and
his real desire to do good, he calls him ambitious and
meddling; and implies that he could not rest content
unless the good he proposed, were effected just in his
own way. He says that his mind was hedged round
with Quaker prejudices: that he regarded the Lancasterian system of education as perfect: and that he
thought it gross heterodoxy to attempt to improve it.
The military training in the New Lanark schools was
unscriptural, the music was a profanity, the dancing
was a licentious abomination.

It is mentioned in Allen's Life, that he began to be

uneasy about these matters as early as 1818.* But the truth is that the dissatisfaction commenced almost with the partnership; as we find from a letter† written to him by Owen in 1815, in reply to one from Allen complaining of what was going on. At this time the partners were new to each other, and both of them were in a sober state of mind, free from that exaltation which afterwards made them unsuitable companions. Owen begins with praising the kindness, openness, and sincerity, of the letter he had received; and then expresses his sympathy with his friend's afflictions, which, however, he rejoices to find to be only the measures adopted at New Lanark. I should remark here, that Owen afterwards stated that this praise of his friend's candour was altogether misapplied; inasmuch as at the time when Allen was writing to Owen in the most cordial terms, he was complaining of his "horrible principles" to their common patron Lord Sidmouth. But this came out after Allen's death. In this letter then, Owen goes on to answer the charge that he is an infidel: and he says that this is true, if it constitutes infidelity to believe that men's characters are formed for them and not by themselves. This is clearly an evasion, written for the solace of his friend. He adds another comfort; a good balance-sheet, showing a probable profit for the year of 15,000l.; all to be expended philanthropically of course. When he has administered this agreeable stimulant, he ventures to speak more plainly: and after saying that he will interfere with

* Abridged *Life of Allen*, 160.   † *New Existence*, v. App. i.

no one's religion, he adds that to him, " the mind of every sincere Jew, Christian, Mahomedan, Brahmin, and Pagan, appears to be really insane on the subject of religion ;" and that " it is the evident contradictions which exist in all these systems that compel me, against a strong contrary inclination, to consider them as the effusions of more than infant weakness."

I am not aware whether Allen was acquainted with Owen's notions about religion, before he entered into partnership with him. If he were ignorant of them at that time, it would have been natural enough for him to wish to retire when he made the discovery; and Owen must have had some inkling of such a desire, when he added in this letter: " The profits of this year, to all appearance, will afford some gain above full interest of capital, to open the means by which any who halt between two opinions may *in all probability retire with some gain.*" William Allen did not retire.

Such a thought, however, crossed his mind, either then or somewhat later; for in 1818 we find him* alluding to it, and stating the grounds for not entertaining it:—

" *London, 30th of 3rd Month,* 1818.

" MY DEAR FRIEND,

" How kind and how Christian it is to promise to forgive me my *errors,* upon the good opinion thou art pleased to entertain of my *heart*—this is just as it should be, and a *good Christian* could not have said more. I love *thee* also, for the dispositions of thy heart,

* *New Existence,* App. V. v.

in many respects so congenial with my own feelings; while I deplore that *radical* error which prevents *thee* from deriving the full enjoyment of benevolent exertions, and which, to an extent thou art at present by no means aware of, prevents mankind from benefiting by them. I trust my long silence is not in consequence of diminished affection, or any want of real Christian feeling; and if I may tell thee a secret, it was only this feeling that prevented me from using every means in my power, for extricating myself from the concern at Lanark."

It must be remembered that this letter was written some months after Owen had laboured by his great public meetings in the City of London Tavern to convince the world of his hostility to religion.

Two years later,* in 1820, Allen, on his return from the Continent, in the self-satisfied frame of mind I have already described, took a more forward part; and pressed upon Owen the adoption of a sober and Quaker-like style of education; urging him to abandon the instruction of the children in music, dancing, and military discipline. These remonstrances were disregarded for a time; but as they were strenuously repeated again and again, a disruption of the partnership seemed imminent.

Again in August, 1822,† Allen was at New Lanark, apparently, in company with his partner Foster; and the conviction was now forced on Allen's mind, that he and Owen must part company. Yet he was still so strongly convinced of Owen's rectitude and benevolence,

---

* *Autobiog.* 235, 236.   † *New Existence*, V. v.

and so possessed with a notion of his capacity, that the
horror he felt at his unblushing infidelity was much
diminished: and he. even relished the wild scheme of
a communistic village, and desired that it should be
tried in the neighbourhood of London, " upon Christian
principles." But at this visit, grave discussions had
again arisen about the education; which, it was alleged,
was not conducted according to the articles of partnership: and it was agreed that at the end of the following
month, the present teachers should be dismissed, and
the three partners, Allen, Foster, and Gibbs, should
personally introduce new plans and masters. On reconsidering this arrangement, Owen, after his old fashion,
begged to be allowed to withdraw from the concern:
but the rent was patched up again. At the end of
1823 and the beginning of 1824, there were further
dissensions; and these ended in articles of agreement,
dated the 21st of January, 1824.*

The first clause was to the effect that John Daniel
should be appointed schoolmaster, at a salary of 150*l.*
a year; and that he should be required to teach the
children above six years old, during at least three
hours every day, except Sundays.

2nd. The company no longer to provide a dancing
master.

3rd. No music or singing to be taught, except
psalmody.

4th. Lectures to be delivered to the people, on
chemistry, mechanics, &c.

* *New Existence,* App. V. vii.

5th. Miss Whitwell to cease to be a servant of the company.

Owen had Spartan notions about dress; imagining that our feelings as to decency are conventional and the result of education. Had he condescended to read history, he might have learnt, that the philosophical practices of Lacedemon, are not believed to have resulted in an increase of feminine reserve and chastity. This explains the next clause. " That having considered the dress of the children, we are of opinion that decency requires, that all males as they arrive at the age of six years, should wear trousers or drawers: we agree therefore, that they shall be required to be so clothed."

The next clauses determine that there shall be a reading of scripture, with religious exercises, once a week, for such persons as shall choose to attend; and that a library shall be formed for the use of the work-people.

Then follow agreements to reduce the numbers of visitors, on the ground that they have so much increased as to seriously interfere with the management; to furnish more houses, an ampler supply of water, a washing apparatus, an asylum for the sick and aged, and a savings' bank; and to complete the public kitchen: all these however, subject as to particulars to the approbation of the partners generally. It does not appear which of these improvements were suggested by Owen and which by the other partners. But as Owen had had the management during the ten years which had passed, since the existing partnership was formed, we are left to suspect that he had not been applying himself with the vigour of former years, to rendering his village a model of social excellence. Indeed, how could he unreservedly bend his efforts to the carrying out of new arrangements, at a time when he was attending day by day on a committee of the House of Commons, during two consecutive sessions; or astonishing the world and indulging his own fanaticism, by publicly denouncing religion; or spending months on the Continent in the society of distinguished *savants* and politicians; or elaborating a village scheme for the county of Lanark; or travelling with companion and secretary through Ireland, and holding great meetings in Dublin? These transactions were quite enough to fill his mind during ten years, and to prevent him from working out savings' banks and public kitchens in his village.

The next clause I do not profess to understand. Owen, in money matters, was singularly open-handed, and free from the slightest taint of selfishness: but as I have before remarked, at an early period of his life, he spent 7,000*l.*, most of which was his partners' money, in maintaining the workpeople, after a fashion which nothing but great pecuniary success could have covered. The clause is this:—

" That taking into consideration the case of a partner residing at the seat of business, whose services, in the opinion of the partners, may have been useful, the consideration of the remuneration shall be brought before and determined by the half-yearly general meeting of partners in November in each year; and that no sums of money shall be paid as gratuities to any person em-'ployed in the said co-partnership business without the order of such general meeting."

It must be noticed that it was Owen himself who re-published these articles, thirty years afterwards; a circumstance which acquits him of all consciousness of impropriety as to any of the arrangements to which the clauses refer.

The agreement was signed by five partners, including Owen; though to him it was very distasteful. He regarded the whole proceedings as contrary to the tenor of the original articles, and he was desirous of withdrawing: but at the earnest solicitation of his partners, he consented to suspend his resolution until a Mr. Charles Walker could be made fit to become manager. As Owen was the largest shareholder, it might not have been easy to replace at once, the capital which he would have carried out. He finally retired in 1829;* and he tells us that the first measures adopted by "these religious and intending-to-be-good masters," was an increase in the hours of work and a reduction of wages. As to the first charge I can say nothing: as to the second, I can well understand that it may have been inevitable; since the scale on which Owen worked was formed during the war, when all prices were high, and when provisions and clothing being very dear, a higher rate of wages was necessary than that which would obtain when prices had fallen to a peace-level. I may

* *New Existence*, V. 20.

also mention, that Owen,* writing in 1854, praises the
management of his successor, and says that the village
had not become a mere money-getting place.

Thus ended Owen's connection with New Lanark: a
place which will always be associated with his name;
and one which deserves to be handed down in history,
as the germ of those efforts, that have honourably distinguished the present century, to ameliorate the physical and moral condition of the labouring classes.

A few circumstances which occurred during the
period I am now upon, have been deferred, in order to
prevent confusion. I have already stated Owen's ad-
hesion to the first Sir Robert Peel, in his opposition to
the Currency Bill of '19; and I will now mention a
meeting which was held on this topic. Owen was there,
and gives a short but interesting account. Sir Robert
was deeply impressed with the danger of returning to
specie payments; and he had come to Owen in great
agitation, to ask his co-operation at the public meeting
about to be held. Sir Robert said in his speech, that
the operation of the proposed bill would be, to double
his property, and that of other capitalists; while it would
injure the operative producers and debtors in the same
proportion: that it would double the national debt; or
what is the same thing, would double the amount of
real wealth required to pay the interest. I am not
about to enter on the tedious currency question. I will
content myself with protesting against the gross exag-

----

* *New Existence,* V. 20.

geration, if not the entire falsehood of these statements; made however, in perfect good faith.

I cannot wonder that the first Sir Robert Peel, being possessed with these opinions, should feel deep and sincere grief at seeing this odious measure emanate from a committee of which his son was chairman. That son was the hope of his age: he had persuaded him to enter into public life, at a time when young Peel, fresh from honours at Oxford, had an inclination to a quiet country existence: he had given him *carte blanche* in money matters during his Irish secretaryship: he had watched his progress with the pride of a father. On this day, he told the meeting, with faltering voice and tears in his eyes, that this was the first serious difference which had ever existed between father and son. Owen regarded the stupidity of young Peel as the result of his factitious and servile Oxford education.

Owen mentions, with great satisfaction, a visit which he paid, by invitation, in company with Mr. Rush, the United States' ambassador, to Mr. Coke at Holkham. He praises the manly bearing of his host, who, he says, was a republican in principle, and fond of the company of Americans.   Mr. Coke was a very industrious man, up at five o'clock in the morning, and at work with his steward while his fifty guests were still snoring. According to Owen, he had so improved his estate, as to have raised the rent from 3*s.* an acre, up to 25*s.*, while the farmers had got rich. I should like to know, how much the war prices had to do with this rise; and whether 25*s.* continued to be paid after the peace.

13—2

In the autumn of 1819, Owen had offered himself as a candidate for the representation in Parliament of the Burghs in his neighbourhood. Unfortunately, he was detained in London by public business; and during his absence, four of the old Lanark voters were bribed, by feasting and drinking, to promise the other side: this cost him the election; but he had the gratification of being the popular candidate. Besides his enforced absence in England, a fire which consumed one of the mills at New Lanark, had hindered him by the necessity he felt of finding work for the hands thrown out of employment. He subsequently talked about getting into Parliament, but he never succeeded.

I have already alluded to a scheme that was set on foot, some time after the County of Lanark Report, to carry into effect Owen's projected villages. I presume that this was the same with that started in London in 1822, by " The British and Foreign Philanthropic Society, for the Permanent Relief of the Working Classes." Among the vice-presidents * were Prince Lieven the Russian ambassador; Chateaubriand and Don Luis de Onis, the ambassadors of France and of Spain; the ministers of Prussia, of the United States (Mr. Rush), of Portugal, of Sweden, of Sicily, of Sardinia, and of Baden. Besides these, there were the Earls of Lonsdale and Blessington, the Viscounts Torrington and Exmouth, Lords Archibald Hamilton, and Nugent, Baron de Staël, and Mr. Randolph of

* *Journal,* i. 156. The year 1823 is mentioned here, but at ii. 76, 1822 is substituted.

Virginia.   On the committee were the names of Sir James Graham, of a dozen or two of other baronets, members of parliament, and persons of less distinction.

The object proposed * was " to carry into effect measures for the permanent relief of the labouring classes, by forming *communities* for mutual interest and *co-operation*: in which, by means of education, example, and employment, they will be gradually withdrawn from the evils induced by ignorance, bad habits, poverty, and want of employment." Money was to be lent, and secured on the property of the intended communities; and legal interest to be paid on it.

A community † would, of course, be a voluntary association.   It was to consist at first of not more than five hundred men, women, and children; or something above a hundred families: and it was to be essentially agricultural.   At some future time, the community was to have the management of its own affairs: not however, until it had repaid all the capital advanced to it, nor until education had sufficiently advanced to render the members fit for self-government: in the meantime, the administration was to be confided to a committee of subscribers.   We are furnished with *thirty-nine articles*, regulating all the details of the community: the number thirty-nine being a droll coincidence.

A more simple, and a clearer, account of Owen's own wishes, is to be found in a report made by a Leeds deputation, which visited New Lanark in August 1819. New Lanark was, as we know, a manufacturing establishment; possessing however, 240 acres of land for a

* *Journal,* i. 157.   † Ibid., i. 164.

population of about 2,500 persons. Owen's proposed villages were to be principally agricultural, with 1,000 acres for 1,200 persons, or eight times as much land per head as that actually possessed. Owen would also abolish private earnings, and have all possessions in common. The arrangement of the buildings would of course be different from those at Lanark. The education of the children would not require much change: but the arrangements as to work would be altered: since on the new plan, children at six years old would begin to work an hour a day, in the open air; at seven years old two hours a day; and so on, until by twelve years old they would have arrived at the maximum of seven hours a day: a very different regulation from the existing one at Lanark, by which up to ten years they did not work at all, and then began full hours at once. Though Owen had accomplished great things, he said himself, that he had only reached two points out of twenty that he aimed at.

The necessary money, I have said, was to be advanced, on security of the property of the communities. I annex a list of some of the largest lenders.

Mr. Owen himself . . .	£10,000	Mrs. Rathbone, Liverpool	£1,000
Mr. Hamilton of Dalzell*	5,000	Mr. A. Clapham, Newcastle	1,000
Mr. J. Morrison of Balham Hill	5,000	Mr. George Smith, M.P. .	625
		Mr. J. M. Morgan,† London	500
Mr. H. Jones, Cole House, Devon	5,000	Sir Chas. Grey, Bengal . .	500
Mr. John Smith, M.P. .	1,250	Mr. E. Cowper, London .	500
General Brown	1,250	Mr. W. F. Reynolds . . .	500

* Who offered land also. Mr. Hamilton ended with losing a very large sum by his addiction to communism.

† Mr. John Minter Morgan, author of the *Christian Commonwealth*.

There were many hundreds, fifties, and smaller sums; and the total loans announced amounted to fully 50,000*l*.

Great difficulties were found in carrying out this scheme. There was a prolonged correspondence: and in 1824, when Owen went away on his first voyage to the United States, nothing had been accomplished.

CHAPTER XIX.

BEFORE finally quitting the interesting topic of New
Lanark, I will give a few more particulars of the place,
as it appeared, not to Owen, who looked upon it as a
test of his philosophy, but to the profane world outside,
who insisted on regarding it merely as a manufacturing village admirably administered.   We have several accounts of it, partly republished by Owen himself[*]
so lately as 1854 : the first being that of Dr. Macnab ;
the second that of a Leeds deputation ; the third that of
a Dublin visitor.

Dr. Macnab, it will be remembered, was physician to
the Duke of Kent; and at his patient's request, made a

[*] *New Existence,* V. App. xiv. &c.

journey to New Lanark, to form a judgment of the merits of Owen's plans. He was highly pleased with what he saw; and not contented with giving a favourable report to his royal patron, he published a book, entitled, *The New Views of Mr. Owen of New Lanark, Impartially Considered.* He himself quotes a private account written by *one member* of the Leeds deputation, and I here give part of it.

The deputation, after their arrival at Lanark, went on to Mr. Owen's mansion, which they found situated in a delightful and rural spot; and where they met with Owen in the grounds, with his wife and children and Sir W. C. de Crespigny, M.P. In going from the old town and back again, they questioned their two guides, and found their answers corroborative of the alleged well-being of the people. One of them had a wife and eleven children; five employed at the works, together earning 36s. a week, and the remainder under ten years of age. The man had no fear of Malthus before his eyes; and if he had had a family of twenty, would not have been alarmed: he found his children well-taught, religiously disposed, and properly behaved: the education of the whole cost him threepence a month, including books and stationery: during a four months' illness of one of them, excellent medical attendance and drugs were supplied gratis: his house and furniture were excellent.

Another of the deputation set off on a voyage of discovery on his own private account, and was convinced that Mr. Owen was regarded in Old Lanark, as the

" landmark " of beneficence and goodness. Mr. Dale, he heard, was an eminently good man, and Mr. Owen was just as good. In a Methodist chapel, he found two men from New Lanark, conducting public worship.

The writer does not seem to have seized on the striking features of infant education. He only states in general terms, that he and his friends were particularly gratified with the sight of the children from two to four years old; and that nowhere could be seen a more pleasing sight, than the " glow of health, the innocent pleasure, and the unabashed childish freedom " of their appearance; a scene so charming as to be of itself enough to repay the toil of the journey.

The elder school was remarkable for its neatness and cleanliness. At the time of the visit, a psalm was being sung; after which there was a prayer. Then followed the reading of a chapter in the New Testament: the boys and girls standing on opposite sides of the room; and portions of three verses being read alternately by a boy and a girl. A catechiser in another part of the room, was hearing the Assembly's catechism. This visit seems to have been made on a Sunday.

Afterwards, the deputation, with other visitors, as well as Owen and part of his family, attended worship in one of the chapels; where the people seemed devout, and the service was decorously and rationally conducted. Then came lunch at Braxfield; a long discussion (how tiresome to Owen if he had not been an enthusiast!) on the effects which would follow from the universal adoption of the system. After that, the party

turned out to see the people returning from Old Lanark,
whither a large part of the population repaired on a
Sunday morning, to attend two services. The writer's
mind was much excited by seeing a thousand persons
out of so small a place, returning from this errand of
religion, with smiling faces and decent apparel: re-
butting the charge ignorantly made against New
Lanark, of irreligion or profanity.

An example is given of an old Highlander, who had
been at the place ever since, twenty-five years earlier,
he had come with sixpence in his pocket. He held the
undignified office of general scavenger: but he had
made so good a living, as to be able to educate a son for
the ministry; and to have his daughter, who kept his
house, taught mantua-making: besides having a reserve
in a savings' bank. He and his fellows, regarded Owen
as their friend, and were not required to exhibit any
servile homage towards him.

The deputation, the following morning (as I suppose),
walked with Owen to the play-ground, where there was
all the happiness of well-trained children. Here did
Owen appear especially in his element, as if in that improved state of society on which his imagination was
always running, and in the possibility of which he without hesitation believed. Here he loved to preach his
sermon :—Give me a colony of infants; I will suppress
all erroneous reasoning and all false conclusions; nothing
shall be believed but what is thoroughly understood; I
will then so educate my children that they shall grow
up to despise those things which now they most value,

and unite in a community of interest which will end in universal brotherly love and unity.

After this, the deputation visited the playroom for bad weather, generally appropriated to children from two to six years old, though some of the forwardest pupils were drafted off into the higher schools, at four years old. In another large room, six boys entered in Highland costume, playing a quick march on the fife, with all the boys and all the girls following in order, the rear being closed with other six boy-fifers. The whole body, on entering, formed a square: then, after practising *right face* and *left face*, they marched round the room in slow and in quick time. At the word of command, fifty boys and girls, by means of a sort of dancing run, met in two lines in the centre of the square; and sang, with the accompaniment of a clarionet, *When first this humble roof I knew*, *The Birks of Aberfeldy*, *Ye Banks and Braes of Bonny Doon*, and *Auld Lang Syne*. The square having been re-formed at the word of command, other children came to the centre, and went through several dances in an elegant style. In England there would be great awkwardness in such a case, from the clumsy, or ragged, shoes; but these youngsters went barefoot. The narrator describes the whole scene as most exhilarating, and as bringing tears to his eyes.

The next visit was to the large schoolroom, which could seat four hundred children to practise writing and arithmetic. It had a pulpit at one end, and with the help of some neat galleries, would hold twelve hundred people. The children's acquirements seemed highly respectable. In another place, a dancing-master from Edinburgh was training four boys and four girls to bow, curtsey, and perform steps. There were also two paid violin players.

A woman who was casually met, carrying a piece of beef, stated that in Glasgow market it would have cost her 10*d.* a pound; but that she had only paid 7*d.* a pound for it. Mr. Owen's attention had been directed to the management of idiots; and he had succeeded in so far improving the only two under his care, as to fit them for earning a subsistence in the works. He had also received from a neighbouring magistrate five criminals to experiment upon: two had absconded very soon; the other three had become decent, industrious persons.

A short account is given of the public kitchen mentioned in the articles of agreement of 1824, as detailed in my last chapter. The building was 150 feet by 40 feet, and was finished but not fitted up; having kitchens and store-rooms on the lower story, and an upper story consisting of a large elegant eating-room, with a gallery for an orchestra at the end, and a library, with lobbies in the centre; and of a room, of equal size, at the other end, constructed for a lecture and concert room. The intention was to furnish a dinner at a fixed price, to all who chose to come.

The manufacturing department does not seem to have been anything very striking. There were ordinary cotton mills, spinning annually a million and a

half pounds of cotton: a foundry of iron and brass,
judiciously constructed, with an elegant cupola, and,
aided by good sand, turning out excellent castings: a
smith's shop, 140 feet by 30, containing many excellent
lathes and several hearths: and over this, an engineers'
shop, employing about thirty people.

The narrative I have given above is an abridge-
ment of one supplied to Dr. Macnab by a Leeds gentleman, who was acquainted with manufacturing processes and arrangements. The impressions made on
the mind of the doctor himself were, of course, very
different, though they were equally agreeable.

In conducting this large establishment, Owen was
obliged to trust very much to the services of agents.
Of these there were six principal ones, all of whom
had been regularly trained for the performance of their
duties, and who were required to go beyond the formal
execution of a bare routine, and to carry out the benevolent and orderly intentions of their principal. Their
salaries were raised gradually, until at last they reached
a very liberal standard: as, for example, a Highland
boy who began with a few shillings a week, was at
last allowed 350*l.* a-year, as director of the mills. In
conversing with these men, and observing the spirit
infused into them, Macnab felt the truth of some remarks made by Major Torrens: that Mr. Owen was a
surprising man, persevering in his exertions, and when
opposed, only exhibiting fresh ardour: that whether he
was right or wrong, *there was a moral grandeur in his
character:* that reflecting on the philanthropy of his

motives, we might excuse his virtuous enthusiasm, without conceding his extravagant claim to be regarded as the high-priest of reason.

The arrangements of New Lanark seemed to Macnab as precise as those of an army.   But with this difference : that soldiers are ruled by fear of punishment ; Owen's soldiers of industry by appeals to the social affections.   (I repeat here that if punishments were rare, they were by no means disused.)   The agents were required to conduct their own departments, without any appeal to Owen, except on extraordinary occasions : and from this arrangement it followed that when he was absent, in London or in Paris, the business went on with its usual regularity.   Macnab, until this visit, had been a sceptic as to the possibility of such moral machinery, but he was now convinced of his error.   For my own part, I readily believe that a man of administrative ability, who had himself formerly managed each department of his business, and who knew every machine in his mills and every corner of his village, might, without any surprising effort, control successfully, and carry on profitably, the large concern of New Lanark, even though he was absent a large part of his time, and during the rest of his time had his attention principally directed to other pursuits.   The manufacture was not one that required a constant variety of patterns : nor was it in any degree dependent upon the whims of fashion : it had an abundant capital and an established reputation.   With Owen's mature judgment and practised shrewdness at the helm, such a vessel would run for twenty or thirty years by the mere force of its previous impetus.

Dr. Macnab mentions a practice, which persons better acquainted with business, would have highly approved, but would not have thought worth recording. When orders for yarns were received at New Lanark at a time when a fall of prices was imminent, the company, instead of grasping the opportunity of protecting themselves from loss, always wrote to the buyer to state that by waiting he might probably buy better: as on the contrary, when a rise of prices was expected, the principal customers were informed of the fact, and recommended to buy in anticipation.

Macnab calls these proceedings, honesty: I call them by a different name, liberality. If they were mere honesty, every manufacturer is bound to do the same: if they were properly liberality, the cogency of the practice will vary according to circumstances. A holder of any commodity, who allows an ignorant buyer to take it in the face of an approaching fall, can hardly be pronounced honest: but as a rule, the buyer is just as able to judge of the future as the seller is. And the second part of the practice is in many cases quite inapplicable. An iron-master who has been working for years at unremunerative prices, and who sees a better time coming, will certainly not feel himself bound to invite his customers to load his books with orders in anticipation. On the contrary, if he have capital at command, he will contract his sales, and pile up his iron towards the clouds, in the hope of making up by an advanced price on his stock, for the losses of former years. The New Lanark practice was, I doubt not, a prudent one: but it should be called a wise liberality, and not mere honesty.

Dr. Macnab notices the measures adopted to discourage excessive drinking. He praises Owen's wisdom in not attempting any direct interference with his people's habits; and states that in the storehouse opened by the company for the sale of useful commodities, liquor was sold at prices twenty per cent. lower than those charged in the pothouses. The immediate tendency would certainly be to increase the quantity of spirits bought; just as happens in Norway and Russia, where the cheapness of potato spirit is accompanied by a vast consumption. On the other hand, the temptations of credit and of jovial company, were taken away; and a check was introduced by the usual presence at the storehouse, when open, of one of the chief managers of the works. As a result, it appears that the pothouses were gradually closed, and that drunkenness was much diminished. It is stated indeed, in the *Life of Allen** that he learned from two ministers of religion, that during more than a year, even a single case of drunkenness was unknown at New Lanark: strong evidence coming from a hostile quarter.

Dr. Macnab's writing generally, is too declamatory to be very instructive. He appears to have been quite possessed by the genius of the place; and to have surrendered his mind to the fascination which the sin-

* *Sherman*, 161.

cere and placid enthusiasm of Owen commonly exerted over those around him. Macnab during the first two days of his visit, was so full of pure enjoyment, that he felt himself quite unfit for cool and deliberate observation; and prolonged his stay to allow this access of moral fever to pass away. Many persons may think that this was the highest compliment Owen could have received. When a physician, commonly in attendance on a royal personage, makes a visit to a manufacturing village, and instead of dirt, drunkenness, squalor, and stunted children, finds comfort, plenty, ruddy cheeks, moral conduct, and happy faces; an Arcadia in place of a Pandemonium: he may be excused a little wildness of delight and looseness of rhetoric.

I have already quoted part of an account given by a gentleman from Leeds.* He was one of a deputation sent by the Leeds guardians of the poor, to see if there was at New Lanark, anything worthy of their adoption. The deputation consisted of strangers to Owen: " Mr. Edward Baines of the *Leeds Mercury,* a Dissenter; Mr. Robert Oastler, a Wesleyan; and Mr. John Carwood, a Churchman." The report handed in by these gentlemen, is of necessity, a formal document and therefore uninteresting: but it confirms the accuracy of the individual narrations. It states generally, that " Mr. Owen's establishment at Lanark, is essentially a manufacturing establishment, conducted in a manner superior to any other the deputation ever witnessed; and dis-

* *Autobiog.* 1 a. 253; and *New Existence* V. App. xxiv.

pensing more happiness than perhaps any other institution in the kingdom, where so many poor persons are employed: and is founded on an admirable system of moral regulation."

The whole of the population of the village was in connection with the works, and consisted of 2,293 persons; besides 188 Old Lanark persons who came over for daily employment: making up Owen's subjects to about 2,500. Of these, there were 103 under two years old, and 380 between two and ten: and as no one under ten was allowed to work, the number employed was about 2,000.

The deputation was highly satisfied with the education imparted: with the spirit of kindness exhibited by the teachers; with the amiability towards each other of the children; with the careful banishment of everything morally hurtful; and with the quality of the instruction given: and it seemed certain that if the orphans and pauper children of a town, could be brought up under the same favourable circumstances, employers would seek for their services instead of shunning them as they have done.

The young people from ten to seventeen, were employed all day; and in the evenings, from 7 to 8.30, had lessons in continuation of what they had been taught as children. These youths were steady and industrious in their conduct, and singularly pleasing in their manners. As the population of the place had increased beyond the demand for labourers at the works, many of the boys had been apprenticed elsewhere by

14—2

their parents ; but there was no record of their conduct in their new homes.

The adults appeared clean, healthy, and sober ; and as might be expected in the absence of drunkenness, well fed, warmly clothed, and excellently housed. Making all allowance for the disposition of the Scotch to a strict observance of Sunday, it would still seem that the tendency of the New Lanark practices was to foster a religious character ; so that Mr. Owen might be believed without hesitation, when he asserted, that he presided over the most religious manufacturing community in the United Kingdom. The people did not spend their evenings in taverns : there was in public no cursing or swearing, nor any brawling women. A sick-fund and a savings'-bank, had been successfully established. One or two other points I will mention afterwards : and some remarks on Owen's future aims, I have already abridged in my last chapter.

I give some portion of another narrative, of a visit made rather later : in 1822 : and I do this, not from a wish to heap up authorities, but because different observers, standing in the same place, do not see the same things. This account was published in the *Dublin Report* : and judging by the learning it displays, in justifying the absence of shoes and stockings, by the injurious influence those articles exert on the *extensor pollicis*, I should pronounce the writer to be a medical man. He noticed that in the large room where the children assembled, there was a belt several feet deep, half way up the walls, painted by a lady of great artistic power, with figures of quadrupeds and birds as large as life, and in their natural colours: the room altogether being singularly elegant. The boys all wore the kilt, or rather a shirt and plaid jacket reaching almost to the knees: the notion being a very just one, that this dress was favourable to activity and hardihood. The children were wonderfully handsome; and all of them had straight, well-formed limbs. The little ones, as young as four years old, showed great prowess in climbing the smooth iron pillars. All seemed unhappy if they failed to attract the notice of Mr. Owen. The writer, while he admired the dancing and singing, feared that in practice, judging by experience, these accomplishments would be found detrimental in after-life. On paying a second visit, he was again struck with the affection displayed by the children towards Mr. Owen; even some little ones who were too young to walk alone, being eager to get within his reach. He was also confirmed in his estimate of the unusually handsome and athletic appearance of those who were natives of the place; and he observed a striking contrast in the case of a few whose parents had lately come to the village: these late comers looking pale and unhealthy by the side of the others. The young women also, he pronounced to be the handsomest he had seen during an extensive tour through Scotland.

Any one who desires still further authority for believing in the excellence of New Lanark, may find it in an account of a visit paid by Mr. James Smith, which was lithographed in Liverpool in 1824, and

reprinted by Owen in 1852.* The only observation
which I think worthy of quotation is this : that Owen
was an enemy to the use, in education, of individual
rewards and of the incitements of emulation.   In this,
as in most of his notions, he set at defiance the opinions
of the most experienced men.   For my own part, after
many years' observation of the working of schools, and
after anxious inquiry into the means of restraint and
of stimulus, I arrive at the conclusion that if masters
are on the one hand to be debarred from the occasional
infliction of punishment, and are on the other hand to
be forbidden the use of inducements to individual
exertion, they are the most unhappy of men ; and must
resign themselves to the mere dull performance of their
duty, without any hope of seeing their pupils acquire
even the rudiments of any difficult branch of learning.
Take away from grown men the passions of hope and
fear, and you reduce them to a mere epicurean existence, and drive them to seek excitement in sensual
pleasures or in gambling : take away from boys the
stimulants of rewards and punishments, and the play-
ground, or forbidden delights, become the only objects
of their thoughts.   Why would Owen be wiser than
nature, and aim at perfection by emasculation ?

> On life's vast ocean diversely we sail,
> Reason the card, but *passion* is the gale.

True education should aim, not at extirpating, but at
regulating, the affections.   I may add that I have seen
an attempt made to adopt Owen's notion of educating

* *Owen's Journal*, iv. 191.

without the use of emulation, of rewards, or of punishments: and with this result; that the boys were amiable and good enough, but very deficient in knowledge, and wanting in the power of close and continued application to dry and distasteful topics: a power which is the great characteristic of a highly-trained mind.

I mentioned in my last chapter, that Owen postponed his retirement, until Mr. Walker could be fitted to take his place.   I have met with a short account of the state of New Lanark under that gentleman's management in 1833.   It appeared originally* in the *Glasgow Free Press*.   At this time there was still a constant stream of visitors to see the celebrated village.   The writer says, that though there had been a diminution of what may be called the ornamental parts of education, as compared with the time when Owen was paramount, yet singing, and even dancing, were still regularly taught; and that the girls enjoyed that pre-eminence of bloom and beauty which my Irish authority assigned to them, eleven years earlier.   The mill which was burnt in 1819 was at length about to be set to work again: and the business was highly prosperous.   " The population, if not entirely happy, were apparently contented."

On the whole; that man must be obstinately sceptical, who entertains any doubt of Owen's success, in making his people happy and good.   It is certain that drunkenness was very unusual at New Lanark; and this alone may be taken as a satisfactory proof of a high condition.   Drunkenness is truly said to be the cause

* See *The Crisis*, iii. 29.

of a large portion of the offences committed. Men who would not rob to satisfy their hunger, will do worse than that when maddened by drink, and unable to gratify without crime, the passions which their excess has awakened. But drunkenness is also a proof of a generally bad state of manners in the place where it prevails: it is the amusement of a coarse people: it is the solace of the discontented. Owen had got rid of the vice by undermining it, and not by a direct assault: he had not employed fines and punishments; but had provided other recreations, had discouraged the vicious habit by precept and by example; and, above all, had rendered his people happier and more refined, and had forborne to overtask their powers of labour. Nor had he had recourse to a Maine law; which restrains the poor who must buy by retail, and spares the rich who can supply themselves in large quantities: which may reduce the present amount of drinking, but which creates a risk of a frightful reaction. Nor did he resort to a pledge of total abstinence: to an oath too weak to master the passions of ordinary men, but strong enough to be a snare to a scrupulous conscience. These were devices of a later day, and of men less wise in this respect than Owen.

The morals of the young women were also highly satisfactory, when compared with those in other places. The number of females employed was latterly about 1,380.* The illegitimate children were as follow: 1810, 1; 1811, 3; 1813, 2; 1814, 5; 1815, 6; 1816, 5;

* *New Existence*, V. App. xxvi.

1817, 3; 1818, 2; or an average of three a year; a number far below the average of Great Britain. It is stated that the putative fathers were not generally men belonging to the village, but strangers: two of the number in 1815 having been French officers.

It cannot have been forgotten, that the principle on which the last partnership was framed, was the applying to the benefit of the workpeople all profits beyond five per cent. on the capital. This exempted Owen from the necessity of squeezing the greatest possible quantity of work out of his mills: and it enabled him to reduce the working hours of his people to ten hours and a half per diem, at a time when other mills were running their thirteen or fourteen hours.* The profits however, seem to have continued large. In the first thirty years of this century, the clear profits, after paying the 7,000*l.* of gratuities in 1806, and the expenses of benevolence, amounted to 10,000*l.* a year: but we are not told how much of this accrued before, and how much after 1814.

The fact that these large gains were made, is a proof that the happiness of the people was not merely the result of an unreasonably high scale of wages, taking the average of the thirty years. Dr. Macnab† states that less wages were paid at New Lanark than elsewhere: and the Leeds deputation,‡ a safer authority, says that in Yorkshire the earnings would be thought

* *New Existence*, V. 55.   † Ibid. V. App. xxi.
          ‡ Ibid. V. xxvi.

low. Particulars are given thus : under eighteen years of age, youths working by time 4s. 3d. a week ; working by the piece 5s. 4d. a week : females 3s. 5d. and 4s. 7d. respectively. Above eighteen, men 9s. 11d. and 14s. 10d.: women 6s. and 8s.: by time or piece respectively. To an Englishman, the men's wages at 10s. for a week's work, seem even scandalously low : but labourers are far worse paid north of the Tweed than they are among ourselves : a fact worth the careful attention of those who regard our poor law, with its accompanying law of settlement, as a cause of improvidence and destitution.

We have now done with New Lanark : a place associated for ever with the name of Owen. We of this generation, have reason to be deeply grateful to the man, who growing up with the vast modern manufacturing world, had the sagacity to see, the disinterestedness to denounce, and the courage to grapple with, the social evils that accompany it. It may be that we have not done nearly what we ought ; but without Owen we should have done still less. As it is, the most crying evils of our worst populations, are not to be found in our great English manufacturing towns, so much as in London, in Liverpool, and some of the agricultural districts. But when Owen began his career, the condition of some factories at any rate, was a disgrace to a civilized country. He had great reason to be proud of his achievements as a social reformer: and I do not wonder that, in after life, when his other schemes of philanthropy had melted away, one after another ; when the

United States, and Mexico, and Ireland, and Scotland, and London, bore witness to his failures; it was his consolation and delight to fight over again the victorious battles of his youth, and to say with just exultation, that New Lanark and its glories were his own.

CHAPTER XX.

IN my seventeenth chapter, I have recorded that Owen,
in the year 1824, took a voyage to the United States.
During the two years preceding this, there had been a
long correspondence about the details of a community
which was to be established in Scotland; and it will
appear in a future chapter, that the communistic society
which was commenced immediately afterwards at Orbiston, near Glasgow, was subjected to certain regulations of which Owen highly disapproved: a fact which
may account for his disappearance from Great Britain
at this juncture.   Amiable as he was, and of a temper
the reverse of overbearing, he had yet an invincible
dislike to being interfered with in carrying out his
schemes; and we have seen in his surrender of Mr.
Drinkwater's partnership, and in his subsequent changes,

how decidedly he indulged his antipathy to the intermeddling of other people.

He determined therefore, to make a trial of his plans
in another hemisphere, where he could buy an expanse
of country, at so small a cost as to be within his own
means; a circumstance which would free him from
all claims on the part of others to dictate laws for his
guidance.   He accordingly entered into a treaty for a
large tract of land, partly cleared; and by April,* 1825,
the bargain was completed.

This estate consisted of thirty thousand acres of fertile land, in Indiana and Illinois;† and was situated on
the river Wabash, about thirty miles from its mouth.
It was stated that it was a very healthy spot: for that
though when it was first settled on, the deaths were
rather numerous, yet afterwards, when a larger portion
was cleared, there occurred fewer deaths than happen
in other parts of the world.   This statement, however,
was made in ignorance of the laws of mortality since
discovered; and therefore, without making allowance
for the fact that the people in question had scarcely any
young children among them, and probably, as recent
settlers, very few old persons.   Thus, the fewness of the
deaths fails to prove that the site was healthy.

The purchase was made from a community of 700
Germans, who called the place Harmony, and themselves Harmonians.   They had lived here eight or nine
years, and had had great success in providing them-

* *Co-operative Magazine,* i. 12.
† *Owen's Second Discourse at Washington,* p. 24.   London, 1825.

selves with the means of living, which they consumed in common. Owen describes the town as consisting " of log, weather-boarded, and brick dwelling-houses; of infant manufactures of wool, cotton, leather, hats, pottery, bricks, machinery, grain distilleries, breweries, &c. : with granaries, and two large churches and other public buildings, laid out in regular squares like all the modern American towns." The country is described*
as thickly wooded, generally flat for about a mile and a half from the river, after which the surface is hilly and pleasantly undulating. The neighbouring hills were covered with vineyards and orchards: and the town seen from these heights, had an inviting appearance; with the ample stream of the Wabash winding in its front, and the luxuriant and lofty woods seen on the opposite banks of the Illinois. One observer admired the brightness of look given by the red bricks of the houses; a peculiarity which few Englishmen will envy: though they will sympathize with the approval bestowed on the practice of planting trees along the streets; Lombardy poplars originally, but these failing, then mulberry trees. The land was well adapted for irrigation, and there was abundance of water-power.† This town, with thirty thousand acres of fertile land, was bought by Owen at his own expense; and from its facilities for both agriculture and manufactures, it seemed as if made expressly for his purpose.

The previous occupants were leaving their delightful site, not from any disappointment as to its capabilities,

* *Co-operative Mag.*, i. 13.   † Ibid. ii. 415.

but because they found the outer world of men, pressing too closely upon them, and urging them to flee still
farther into the depths of the wilderness.   Indeed, their
singular success in providing themselves with abundance of means of living, was laid hold of by Owen's
followers, as a striking illustration of the advantages of
a life in common.   How far any inference could justly
be drawn from this case, it is not difficult to judge,
when the peculiar circumstances are known.

The Harmonians were a European colony, chiefly
from Wirtemberg and its neighbourhood, and went out
under the direction of a Mr. Rapp, a pastor or prophet.
They originally settled in Pennsylvania, near Pittsburg,
and at starting were nearly annihilated by starvation,
and would have been altogether destroyed, but for an
interposition, which they doubtless regarded as mira-
culous.   They had applied to a neighbouring merchant
to assist them with food while their first crops were
ripening; and he had consented: they went to him
again; he refused: they resigned themselves to die;
it was the will of God: but the merchant had a
vision; these poor people appeared to him in the
pallor and emaciation of want; he put aside his fears
of loss, and hastened to their aid.   In after-days,
the society flourished and the merchant fell into
destitution: he was always a welcome guest among
the Harmonians.

After a very few years,* they left Pennsylvania,
being elbowed by an increasing population around

* *Visit by W. Hebert in* 1822. London, 1825.

them; and having sold their clearing and plant, for a considerable sum of money, removed to the Wabash and Illinois. Here they fully carried out their communistic principles. They laboured from sunrise to sunset, with great industry, though without that excessive application which often ruins the health of ordinary men: and they did not grudge the nightwork necessary for their brewery and distillery. If any one, secure of a maintenance, became apathetic and remiss, he was not punished, but was "sent to Coventry" or reprimanded. Every one was entitled to his share of the produce of the community, though some sort of accountability was kept up.

They were a grave and even saturnine people, who seldom smiled, and among whom laughter was an offence: and the sounds of mirth and conviviality, if heard at all among them, proceeded from their profane neighbours, on a visit for purposes of trade. Literature too, was an abomination: what had Christian people, mere sojourners in this valley of weeping, heirs of an immortality of happiness, to do with the literature of a heathen antiquity, or with the frivolities of the modern profane? So little did they care for books, or for information of any kind, that among the mechanics of various kinds among them, not one printer was to be found.

They appear to have been completely governed by Mr. Rapp; who did not confine himself to spiritual ministrations, but superintended their work in field or factory, and himself diligently explored their woods for any tree they might want. He had adopted a son, who was called Frederick Rapp, who was now about forty years of age and unmarried, and in whose name all the money concerns were carried on. Some power was in the hands of the superintendent of the general store, of the doctor, of the saddler, of the smith, and of the keeper of the house of " private entertainment," which the unenlightened call a tavern. Very little was known about the internal arrangements, as the policy of the managers was silence, and therefore free discussion was as rare as were newspapers.

The Rappites were professedly Lutherans, but very unlike the hearty, jolly Norwegians, or Prussians; who think it no shame to sit down to dominoes or cards on Sunday evening, after the sacred twenty-four hours have expired, or perhaps a little earlier. It has been said that the Rappites accepted from their pastor a positive prohibition of marriage, but this is not true. Marriage was only discountenanced; but the discouragements to it were so severe that they produced nearly the effect of forbidding it. During three years there was but one wedding; and this while there were probably young persons enough to furnish fifty weddings, and without the ordinary restraint of want of the means of living.

An extensive commerce was carried on by the Harmonites. They could boast indeed, that they produced within their settlement everything they wanted except groceries, and these they bought in exchange for their surplus commodities. They also sent out quantities of

15

grain, beef, pork, whisky, beer, wine, and manufactures, to New Orleans and elsewhere; besides selling
by retail at their general store. They had agents even
in various cities, who sent them goods for re-sale in
the neighbouring country. When a man, instead of
having to maintain four or five persons, had no one
but himself to feed and clothe, and yet laboured as
hard and as steadily as other men, he would, of course,
produce a great excess of commodities. What became
of the money for which all these merchantable articles
were sold, the profane world did not know; but the
members seemed generally quite contented. If any
one of them had turned litigious, and had brought the
affairs of the community before a law-court, as recently
happened to the ancient Jaults in France, strange revelations might have been expected. It is alleged that
the same fault prevailed at Harmony, which John
Wesley complained of in his followers, when he said,
that having cured them of the love of gaieties and
sensualities, he found that they addicted themselves to
the love of money and the desire of worldly success.
Avarice took the place of levity. This money-getting
spirit of the Rappites has been unfavourably contrasted
with the more moderate tone of the Shakers, about
a hundred miles more north; who decline commercial
dealings with the world outside them, and are contented with the plenty which industry and forbearance
from marriage secure to them.

In one respect, these people showed themselves superior to the ordinary coarse-grained backwoodsman:

they reared a noble building for public worship. The form of this church was that of an equal-limbed cross: the roof was supported by a number of stately columns, turned out of black walnut, cherry, and sassafras trees: the masonry and woodwork were fine: and entering at either of the four doors, placed one at the end of each limb, the effect produced on you was striking and grand. Some personal sacrifice was made for the erection of this edifice; for while it was going on, it was necessary to defer the building of the private houses. It is probable that this noble work was much promoted by the priestly influence of the predominant pastor; and it is remarkable that the love of utility showed itself, in converting the vaults of the church into storehouses.

Whilst Owen was settling his purchase of this large property, he had an opportunity of publicly explaining his views and projects. We have seen that it was always his policy to make friends of leading and influential people, under the notion that it was to them, and to governments led by them, that he must look for such an alteration of circumstances, as would bring about the moral revolution after which he panted: whereas, to expect such an alteration from the people themselves, was to sit stupidly down and await the voluntary cessation of a river. Certainly there was much to be said in favour of this policy; which is in fact, nothing more than that of most educationists of the present day; who loudly declare that, in one way or other, instruction should be brought to every one's door, and pressed on every one's acceptance, as being a thing far out of the sphere of the common law of demand and supply. Owen, as we have seen, was eminently successful in carrying out this policy. While the middle classes of society were learning to hate him as a great heresiarch, or something worse, men of noble, and princely, or even royal blood, freely used their influence in his favour. The United States contained no men who came under this description: but they had presidents and vice-presidents, and ex-presidents and men honourable by virtue of office: and these men listened freely to the English innovator.

Owen then, being at Washington, early in 1825, obtained the use of the "Hall of Representatives," in which to deliver a discourse. A slight misrepresentation of this event has been unconsciously made by some of his followers, as though the Congress itself, or at any rate the Lower House of Congress, had formally assembled to listen to a lecture. The title prefixed to the printed discourse disproves this assertion: for it states that the discourse was delivered " in the presence of the President of the United States, the President elect, the heads of departments, members of Congress, &c." The truth is simply, that Owen applied for the use of the hall, which was granted; and that the leading people who were at Washington, with many of whom Owen had an acquaintance, paid him the compliment of going to hear him.

Owen on this occasion exhibited his usual brave candour. He told the Americans, that they laid claim to the possession of more privileges than any other nation; and that this claim was in many respects well founded: but that even among them, where the laws were unusually mild and less than commonly irrational, such absurd notions prevailed, as led to the infliction of death upon persons for acting as they were compelled to act, and as led to the rewarding of other persons for actions without a particle of merit. He explained afterwards * what he meant: that the practice of rewards and punishments under any circumstances whatever was " a grievous error of a past wretched system."

This might pass for the whim of an eccentric philosophy. But many of the hearers, testy men, jealous of any censure from an Englishman, must have thought of pistol and bowie-knife, when he told them that they did not possess real liberty. Political liberty no doubt they had by a hard struggle attained; but real liberty, the liberty of the mind, was still to seek. Which of them dared to speak his real sentiments, freely and openly, on subjects of vital interest to man? How many of them had so cast off the old mental bondage, as to be able without a thought of inconvenience, to convey to others without concealment the genuine, incorrupt sentiments of their own minds? Not one of them: there was no such man: all, all were mere slaves to the opinions of their fellows: hampered, tongue-tied, veritable cowards, when truth was to be told. And did they call this liberty or mental servitude? But he would make them acquainted with a

* *First Discourse.* London, 1825. Page 13.

new system, under which they should be really free:
he would tell them of social arrangements under which
there should be no privileged [thoughts or belief, but
every one should be free as air to tell the world the
undisguised impressions and reflections of his mind.

Another part of the discourse, which must have surprised the hearers, was a denunciation of commerce.
He said that the practices to which we are trained, of
buying cheap and selling dear, were degrading and pernicious: that the whole trading system was one of deception, in which every person makes it his business to
take advantage of his neighbour: and that the inevitable
result was, to give excessive wealth and power to a few,
leaving the many in poverty and subjection. Now if
there be a country in which trade and traders are held
in honour, it is the United States. In reading the best
periodicals of that country, nothing has struck me more
than the tone adopted as to mercantile life, when compared with the tone of the corresponding publications
here. Among us, a man is not ashamed of being a
merchant or a leading manufacturer: to be a first-rate
man of business is, among the Americans, a matter of
congratulation and boasting. Their lower classes govern,
and their traders are their aristocracy: our middle
classes predominate, and our landowners give the tone
to society and to literature. It must have been therefore, with great surprise, that the industrious community heard trade and commerce condemned as iniquitous.
But I do not imagine that these sweeping invectives
against commerce tended to arouse any evil passions.

If they had been directed against the excesses of the Americans, against their worship of the silver dollar, against their perpetual talk of adventures and gains, against their boasted smartness in driving a bargain, against their reckless trading, which substitutes gambling for industry, their withers would have been wrung, and they would have winced under the infliction. But they could listen patiently to a general condemnation of the system, just as we drowsily receive from a preacher the perpetual assertions of the wickedness of humanity. We are all willing to confess that we are miserable sinners: but woe to him who points out a specific sin!

Having thus condemned society as it is, Owen went on to exhibit his specific remedy; and he assured his hearers that so wonderful were its effects on the body politic, that it would correct all the crying evils he had pointed out, would cure the avarice and remove the anxieties of capitalists, while it rendered improvidence and destitution impossible among the labouring people. So strongly was he impressed with the advantages to be obtained, that his only wish was, to communicate them in the shortest time to the greatest number of persons, though with the least possible injury to those who benefited by the actual system. This last consideration gave him some anxiety: for he was convinced that as soon as his principles and practices were fully understood, they would be adopted with great rapidity: and therefore he was glad of this opportunity of publicly announcing what was about to happen, that no one might complain hereafter of having entered on new speculations in the very face of this approaching revolution.   No interpreter of prophecy, no seer of the millennium, was ever more confident, or more egregiously mistaken, than was Owen.   He had no hesitation in saying " from that chair, from which they had been accustomed to hear so many important truths," that his system was competent to turn their States into countries of palaces, gardens, and pleasure-grounds; and in one generation to make the inhabitants a race of very superior beings.   Poor America!   Its fields are not yet covered with palaces and pleasure-grounds : nor will its most ardent admirers assert, that comparing its inhabitants with those of other countries, they can be called a superior race.   The dollar in the north, and slavery in the south, are still the idols which men worship. Owen's principles and practices were well known, yet they did not prevail.

After delivering this discourse, Owen had intended to leave Washington, on a visit to Mr. Jefferson and Mr. Madison : but many of his hearers were so well pleased, and so desirous of having more particulars explained to them, that they begged for a second lecture, and this was granted.   Much that was then delivered may have been new to those who heard it, but it would be tiresome to those who having followed Owen thus far, know pretty exactly what he would say to an admiring audience.

CHAPTER XXI.

New Harmony: object proposed—Means—Persons: Work: Means
of Living—Disposal of Assumed Surplus—Discontent or Misconduct—Future Proceedings: Anticipations—Rules of the Advanced Society—Actual Beginning—Morris Birkbeck—Owen
crosses to England and back again—Resolves on real Community
—A Convention for a Constitution—Principles agreed on—Practical Illustration—Owen's View of it—Conclusion.

In the second discourse at Washington, which I mentioned at the conclusion of my last chapter, Owen, after
explaining his principles, proceeded to give many particulars of what he proposed to do to carry them out.
He stated that he was about to commence a new society
at Harmony: that the aim of the association was, to give
and secure happiness to all its members :—

> " O *happiness !* our being's end and aim,
>   Good, pleasure, ease, content—whate'er thy name,
>   That something still which prompts the eternal sigh,
>   Which bids us bear to live, or dare to die."

(Owen was not addicted to quotation: and his memory
must be exonerated from the imputation of an undue
familiarity with Alexander Pope.)

This object was to be secured by " the adoption of a
system of union and co-operation, founded in a spirit of
universal charity, derived from a correct knowledge of
the constitution of human nature." This knowledge

would be found perfectly efficacious in preventing mis-understanding, whether from religion or from other causes. But it was thought safer to organize at first a preliminary society, to be conducted by persons of experience.

Into this preliminary society, would be admitted two classes of persons: those with capital, and those without it. Capitalists indisposed to labour, might be maintained on payment of a fixed annuity. Persons without capital would be employed in farming, manufactures, building, gardening, or giving instruction; and would receive in return, the best food, clothing, and lodging, the association could afford: besides having a provision in sickness and old age. All the children would be brought up together, and would receive a superior education.

At the end of every year, an account would be taken of the services rendered by each family, and of its expenditure; and in proportion to these, a certain sum would be placed to its credit: it being assumed that the gains of the whole body would far exceed its outgoings.

Any person might quit the association at pleasure, taking away in productions as much as was placed to his credit at the previous balance-day. And any incorrigible offender against the laws or happiness of his fellows, would be dismissed: but it was anticipated that in a short time, such a spirit of justice, charity, forbearance, and kindness, would be found to prevail, as to render this apparent harshness unnecessary.

The above arrangements were purely provisional. It was proposed shortly to organize a society of a higher grade, " consistent in all respects with the constitution of human nature;" in which there would be a perfect equality of rights and of property; the only distinctions being those of age and experience. Members of the preliminary association would be invited to join the more advanced body: and they would not hesitate to do so when they were assured on the authority of thirty-five years' experience, that the proposed arrangements would be found valid enough to *banish* from among men, almost all, *if not absolutely all*, the evils which had hitherto afflicted them.

When this perfect community should be established, it should be governed by the thirty-nine articles which I have mentioned at the close of Chapter XVIII.; of which I will recapitulate a very few. The number of persons should not much exceed five hundred, including women and children. · The establishment was to be managed by a committee of all persons of a certain age; but this arrangement was not to take effect, until some indefinitely distant period, when the capital advanced to the community was repaid, *and* the general education was *sufficiently* advanced; and until that far-off era, the government was to be in a committee of twelve, of whom eight should be persons who had advanced 100*l.* or upwards. The committee howsoever constituted, was to determine the employment of every person, with a due regard however, to his wishes; and giving to every one the option of spending part of each day in agriculture. The members generally would have a common table; but any sick, or fastidious, person might eat alone.

These were the regulations framed by Owen for his colony. Almost immediately after delivering his addresses at Washington, he proceeded to Harmony, took possession of his estate, and received his members. Of these there was no lack, and his little town was soon full to overflowing; 900 persons having come to it, and more desiring to do so. In the first instance, as sole proprietor of the place, he took upon himself to nominate the committee of management.* Then, having seen his people fairly at work, carrying on the operations which the Germans had begun, he went to other parts of the States: and returning in about a month, he was so well satisfied with the progress made and the excellent spirit manifested, that he dissolved his committee, and called upon the members to elect one for themselves: and they at once re-elected most of his nominees, including his son William.

A proof of the success of the incipient community was given by Mr. Morris Birkbeck, who was settled near Harmony. He had not been a disciple of Owen; but coming across to visit him, and being induced to remain several days, he was greatly struck with what he saw; and when he left, declared his intention of winding up his affairs and migrating to New Harmony. Unfortunately, returning home in haste after his prolonged absence, he attempted to cross the river while

* *Co-operative Magazine,* i. 16.

the tide was running strongly; and as he was turning to the assistance of his son, who like himself was on horseback, he was carried away and never seen again.

Owen at this time was not free from his engagements at New Lanark; and he was soon obliged to return to Scotland. No doubt he crossed the Atlantic, congratulating himself on the success of his first step towards a real community; and was convinced that the society he had left, though it was only a half-way house to the ultimate object of his efforts, would enable him hereafter to complete the rest of his progress towards thorough co-operation and equality of rights. After he had remained a few months in Great Britain, he again, in the winter of 1825-26, sailed for America, and reappeared in Indiana. He had the high gratification of finding New Harmony in a condition worthy of its name. In the first three or four months from its establishment indeed, about a dozen persons had left: rovers no doubt, always looking out for novelty and unwilling to labour: and three had been dismissed; one for turbulence, one for misconduct, and the third for idleness. Some slight disagreements had occurred, and there had circulated reports unfavourable to the commercial soundness of the establishment.

By the time of Owen's arrival, however, about three-quarters of a year after the first start, these little asperities had been smoothed down, and everything was going on prosperously. He had originally resolved that the probationary condition of the colony should

continue at least two years, to give time for the people
to become acquainted with each other, for testing the
steadiness of the members, and above all, for instructing and training every one in the knowledge and practice of the true principles of society. But when he
witnessed the excellent state of his people, he was
moved by an emotion of generosity, by the impatience
of a projector, perhaps by an honest emulation with
the conductors of a similar experiment in Scotland, to
shorten the noviciate, and at once to try the grand experiment. How would it succeed?

On the 25th of January 1826, about nine months
after the commencement of the colony, a convention
was held* for the "formation of a constitution of a
government for the New Harmony community of
equality." Hard-handed men, fit for a struggle with
the wilderness, may be pardoned if they fail to write
silken English. Dr. Philip M. Price was elected president, and Thomas Pears secretary: by means of the
ballot, seven persons, including W. Owen, were chosen
as a committee to form a constitution: the plan was
drawn and presented; the convention discussed it at
several sittings, and sent it back again to the committee: that body again reported: and the convention
at its seventh sitting finally adopted a constitution.

Persons sitting down anywhere between the Atlantic
and the Pacific to frame a constitution, would do well to
remember the ill fortune of the grand words about the
equality of men, which form the basis of the government

* *Co-op. Mag.* i. 301.

of the United States: for the sentiment, true and important as it is, is a perpetual blister to those who, in its despite, declare the fitness and righteousness of holding blacks in the subordinate condition of slavery. Men who aim at the practical should leave maxims and wise saws to philosophers and poets; but where Owen was the presiding genius, this was not to be expected. The "constitution" begins with a declaration that the object proposed is happiness: that the principles are, equality of rights among adult men and women; co-operative union in business and amusement; community of property; kindness in action, courtesy in intercourse, &c. &c. Then follows a statement of belief in Owen's pet dogmas, with just that variation of language which marks the *location* of the writers. Community of property is adopted, in order to get quit of " competition and opposition, jealousy and dissension, extravagance and poverty, tyranny and slavery."

I need scarcely repeat that one of Owen's fundamental conceptions, was the irresponsibility of man. People are what they are made to be: cannibals in New Zealand, thieves in St. Giles's, pedants at Oxford, money-grubbers in the City. Will you reward or punish them for the inevitable result of circumstances? Or, as the backwoodsmen expressed the opinion: Man's character is the result of his formation, his location, and the circumstances within which he exists: his character is not of his own formation: therefore, artificial rewards and punishments are inapplicable to him: kindness is the only consistent mode of treatment, and courtesy the only rational species of deportment. An amusing illustration of the doctrine is furnished by the *Co-operative Magazine* itself, the chosen organ of communism. An English member of the society at New Harmony was descanting with energy on this favourite topic: but in the very whirlwind and tempest of his denunciations of the world outside, turning his head, he saw a young pickle eating the plums in the orator's little garden; and forgetting at once philosophy, kindness, and courtesy, he rewarded the boy's faith in his forbearance by a hearty flogging. Truly, the figments of Owen's brain were all too weak to bind the passions of men.

But in Owen's eyes, this was only an accidental departure from the rule of right, resulting inevitably from the nature and circumstances of which the inconsistent member was the victim. If the man in his fury had killed the boy, the homicide ought not to be punished; since not he, but destiny was to blame. The offender was to be pitied, just as he would be if he had chopped off his foot, or succumbed to the yellow fever.

At length then, a community, a society of equal right and equal property, was established. Away competitions, rivalries, and emulations! Avaunt improvidence and avarice, luxury and destitution! Your reign is at an end: your sand has run out: you must give place to peace and kindness, health and cheerfulness, wholesome labour and abundant living. The new era of the world has begun, and no obstacles can impede the steady march of Owen and communism.

CHAPTER XXII.

Split about Religion—Unfavourable Reports—Correction of a former Statement—Another Version—Conduct as to Religious Teaching —Imitation Communities—Another, July 1827—Maclure—Independence and Munificence—Maclure's own Account—Separation of New Harmony—Two Societies dissolved—Another Attempt fails—Remedy: New Distribution—Comments on the Changes: Owen resigned—Causes of Failure—Alleged Causes—Owen's Account: not dispirited—Caution necessary—In London—Owen's Munificence—Progress during another Half Year—Terms granted by Owen—Owen's Inference: not Angry—Communism abandoned—Conclusion.

I CLOSED my last chapter with a song of triumph: at present I have to assume a less agreeable tone. The communistic system was agreed upon early in 1826; and it might have been hoped that the zeal of a new society would have carried it on a few years, without any serious difficulties. This was far from being the case. So soon as June 1826, it was known in England* that the course of the colony had not been a smooth one; and taking into account the slowness of mails thirty years ago, we must conclude that Owen and his friends had hardly enjoyed many weeks of peace and concord. It was stated that religion was the cause of dissension; and that some persons whose opinions on that topic were those of the world generally, had split

* _Co-operative Mag._ i. 193.

16

off and formed a new community of their own. The old and the new bodies, however, were represented to be on the most friendly terms. As Owen's anti-religious notions seemed to every one but himself, independent of his new views about the constitution of society, the loss caused by this schism, would fall on New Harmony rather than on the cause of communism. This dissension however, besides a multiplicity of details to be attended to, were sufficient to detain Owen in Indiana.

We cannot wonder that there arose reports unfavourable to the new settlement. About the time I have mentioned, Owen's enemies here were gratified, by a paragraph copied into the London papers from a Philadelphia letter, to the effect that the condition of New Harmony was so unsatisfactory, that the experiment would probably have to be abandoned, with an entire loss of the money laid out. To this it was replied* that the account was part fabrication, part exaggeration: and it was alleged in proof, that a gentleman of some property who had gone out with Owen, had now sent to his wife in London to join him at New Harmony.

Out of this discussion however, there emerged a fact, which much reduces the satisfaction of the last chapter. I there allowed myself to believe the statement, that Owen's premature adoption of a real communism, in place of his intended two years' probation of his people, arose out of his approval of the conduct and tempers of the New Harmonites. But we are now told that Owen on his return from England in the winter of

* _Co-operative Mag._ i. 227.

1825-26, had found matters to have been conducted not so skilfully as they ought; though the deviation was soon corrected by his presence. But since he was dissatisfied, why did he shorten the noviciate? I assent to the statement of the unreasonableness of looking in a new colony for the comforts of an established society, and of anticipating regular and systematic industry from an heterogeneous collection of people greedy of novelty: but I cannot see in these circumstances any justification of the premature adoption of a system, requiring at any rate much self-denial, mutual forbearance, and public spirit.

Early in 1827,* we meet with a still more candid account. From this it appears, that when the Rappites quitted their settlement in April 1826, a crowd of people rushed in from all sides, on the faith of the general invitation which Owen had issued in his public addresses. Strangely enough, such an event had not been anticipated: no arrangement had been made to inquire into the character and history of the self-proposed members; none to prevent the intrusion of persons however unfit or disreputable: and as an inevitable result, New Harmony was filled with a mixed crowd of good and bad, rough and gentle, thrown together to jostle each other as they pleased. To make the matter more hopeless, Owen, soon afterwards, set off for Great Britain, leaving only his son William, a young man, as the depository of his secret intentions; without any arrangements concerted for winnowing out the desirable

* *Co-operative Mag.* ii. 48.

16—2

from the obnoxious members. We have already seen that in a very short time, there broke out religious dissensions, which led to the shelling off of part of the members to form a new community.

On Owen's return from Great Britain in the winter of 1825-6, the condition of his settlement, far from being the agreeable one which it was at the time represented to be, was actually distressing. "The ignorance and bad passions which existed,* were most annoying, and required all the forbearance which the new system inculcates, in its highest perfection." Owen's placid temper and predominant influence did wonders to still a tempest, which, it is said, any one else would have run away from in a month. The strength of the expression indicates the virulence of the disorder. Religion seems to have been the earliest topic of disagreement, and the evil seems to have been aggravated by visits from itinerant preachers, whose interference, however, was checked in a characteristic manner. It was professed that free discussion on religion and every kind of teaching, was tolerated and even sought; and therefore, all ministers who came for the avowed purpose of preaching publicly, were entertained at the tavern free of expense: but with this unusual condition; that at the conclusion of a sermon, any one of the congregation might ask whatever questions he pleased. This catechizing was so little liked by the subjects of it, that during many months no preacher visited New Harmony. The absence seems to have been a great relief to the settlement; for it is alleged* that illiterate and bigoted men came, and made violent attacks on everything they found established; and with such success as to alarm many timid members, and make them fear themselves on the high road to perdition. It is added, that some of these reverend persons spread scandalous and untrue reports about the moral condition of New Harmony: asserting that there were enacted scenes of insubordination, confusion, and debauchery; that wives were unfaithful, children disobedient, daughters unchaste, and sons dissolute. Thousands of persons conceived unjust prejudices, in consequence, and turned away from New Harmony in disgust. The charges no doubt, were utterly unfounded, and were the inventions, or gross exaggerations, of men who in their ignorance, could not even conceive that followers of Owen were industrious, moral, and amiable. Theological hatred is no new disease.

There seems to have been some difference of opinion as to the wisdom of Owen's measures. But the friends of co-operation were much encouraged by hearing of many other settlements in America, besides the one that bought out the Rappites. So soon as October 1826, we find mention made† in an American paper, of several communities established on Owen's principles, though with some modifications: the names mentioned are the Yellow Spring in Ohio; the Alleghany Association at Pittsburgh; one at the Blue Spring, near Bloomington, Indiana; and the Philadelphia Association.

---

* *Co-operative Mag.* ii. 217.   † Ibid. i. 329.

Another paper speaks of a community, beginning from families of Wilmington and Philadelphia, and intended to be "located" in the Great Valley, twenty miles from Lancaster and forty from Philadelphia. A little later,* we hear of two communities in the immediate neighbourhood of New Harmony: of which the one was named Macluria, as a compliment to an able coadjutor of Owen; the other *Feiba Peven*, a name intended to express by a pedantic *memoria technica*, the latitude and longitude of the place. Macluria was settled by backwoodsmen, men with large families, much addicted to camp meetings and revivals, and strongly prejudiced against new-fangled methods of cultivation. These people were about 150 in number, with 1,200 acres of land; and with the help of some capital lent to them by Owen at 4 per cent., they built a few cabins arranged in something like a parallelogram, and laboured hard at their land in the slovenly fashion of their country. The community of Feiba consisted of a few Englishmen from the neighbourhood of Messrs. Birkbeck and Flower, with few children, and, like the Maclurians, with 1,200 acres of land, situated between New Harmony and Macluria. They were skilful and neat farmers, but, as was said, a little too much addicted to whisky.

Six months later,† another community makes its appearance; that of Kendal in Ohio: a flourishing concern, with more and more dwellings rising up, though still insufficient to house the families which are pouring in;

* *Co-operative Mag.* ii. 46.　　　† Ibid. 325.

and with a great building in course of erection, 170 feet
by 33, intended for workshops, but to be used first for
houses; a pleasant and healthy place, without any one
on the sick list: with mechanics flocking in, and prose-
cuting the trades they knew, including that of working
wool: with schools at first on the old plans, but shortly
to be arranged *à l'Owen*, under a competent principal
educated at the Canton Academy: with a spirit of concord and bustling emulation: with a habit of industry:
and if not without anxieties, yet in the enjoyment of
health, peace, and competence. Truly, the pre-eminence of New Harmony was in danger.

Of the members of New Harmony, the most remarkable, next to Owen, seems to have been Mr. Maclure,
after whom one of the communities mentioned above,
was named. Maclure was at this time about sixty, the
possessor of a large fortune, a bachelor, and very open-
handed. He was a man of scientific pursuits, had been
President of the Philadelphia Academy of Natural
Science, and had travelled much. He had become a
convert to Pestalozzi's educational system; and had
devoted much time and money to the introduction of it
into the United States. He had subsequently been
struck with the notions of Owen; and was so far in
accordance with him, as to migrate to New Harmony,
bringing his extensive library, his important museum of
mineralogy, and his valuable scientific apparatus; besides inducing some friends to accompany him. He had
associated these with himself in the education society,
which was one of the three communities that had

branched off from the parent trunk of New Harmony: and especially he had for a coadjutor, one
Peter Naaf, who, as it was alleged, was the real author
of the system which went under the name of Pestalozzi; that excellent man being merely an intelligent
patron.

Maclure was a man of independent thought, and was
no unreasoning disciple. He was convinced of the
truth of Owen's assertions, as to the possibility of training the young to almost any mode of thought or excellence of conduct: and he exhibited the sincerity and
depth of his convictions, by this migration to a settlement of rude and ignorant people, far from the society
of men of cultivation and science; as well as by taking
the education community under his direct patronage,
and by advancing to it a large sum of money to buy
land and buildings from Owen. At the same time he
made no secret of his dissent from Owen in one fundamental particular. By all means, said he, educate the
young, and train them for your purposes, while they are
unformed and docile:

> " 'Tis education forms the common mind :
>   Just as the twig is bent, the tree's inclined."

But the case of adults is quite different. You cannot
bend to your will the mature poplar or ash, and still
less the gnarled oak. The communists gladly accepted
their patron's assistance, and could not quarrel with
opinions munificently backed.

In July 1826, when Maclure had been at New Harmony nearly half a year, he addressed a letter to the

Revue Encyclopédique.[*] It appears from this letter, that he regarded his proceedings at New Harmony, as part of a philosophical experiment; for he spoke of having, during the twelve months, made considerable advances in his "researches on education." He mentions two foreigners, a lady and a gentleman, who had been highly successful in teaching on Pestalozzi's plans; but who had made the great sacrifice of migrating to New Harmony, on condition of receiving as remuneration, their maintenance and nothing beyond. Maclure, with his friends, had established a school; and had purchased from Owen for that purpose, seven large brick houses, each sixty feet by forty, as storehouses for the children's provisions; eight or ten smaller brick houses for the married teachers and others; ten or twelve wooden houses for workmen; two large granaries and stables for an experimental farming school; a large public building, converted into a workshop for the instruction of boys in useful arts; and a hall to be used for a museum, as well as for lectures, meetings, concerts and recreations generally. There was room enough for 800 or 1,000 children; though there were at present only 300 to 400, and these were classed as follows : 100 from two to five years old, under Madame Frétageot; 180 to 200 from five to twelve, under M. Naaf assisted by his four daughters and his son, all five pupils of Pestalozzi; and 80 in the church instructed by M. Phiquepal, in mathematics and the useful arts. It was thought that the schools would soon be full, both because the charge

[*] *Co-operative Mag.* i. 373.

of one hundred dollars a year for maintenance, clothes, and instruction, was very moderate, and because the knowledge imparted was of a solid kind. Chemistry, drawing, and natural history, were lectured on by MM. Troost, Lemur, and Thomas Say, respectively: and the last of these, having resolved to publish his superb work on entomology, with coloured plates, had sent to London and Paris for the necessary materials. Mr. Owen's two sons, with Mr. Applegarth, were at the schools; and men of high ability were expected from England. For the schools in experimental farming, 900 acres of land had been bought from Owen; and judging from an experiment made by M. Phiquepal, it was anticipated that the children in this particular department would maintain themselves by working a few hours a day. The purchases from Owen might be worth 6,000*l.* to 8,000*l.*; and Maclure had enabled his society to pay ready money. He had eagerly availed himself of the opportunity to promote during his lifetime, a system which he had always regarded as the greatest boon men could obtain. The scheme of communism was fast extending: the notion of perfect equality, and the simple thought of labouring for a maintenance, possessing a charm which was wanting to the thirst for precarious gains.

We have seen that originally, New Harmony was not constituted on communistic principles; but that in less than a year the change was made of converting it into a society with equal rights and community of property. Soon afterwards when difficulties arose, it was again restored to its original condition, and the inhabitants were allowed to possess private property.*   But three other establishments on really communistic principles, were formed in connection with the town: the largest of the three being that for manufactures; the next that for education (under Maclure); and the smallest that for agriculture.   These three, together with the two neighbouring communities of Macluria and Feiba Peven, all bound themselves to carry out the same general principles, though each had its own mode of government.   New Harmony therefore, was no longer a community,† but a central village; " out of, and around which, communities have formed, and may continue to form themselves; and with the inhabitants of which these communities may exchange their products; thus obtaining those manufactured articles, which the limited operations incidental to an incipient colony do not enable them to produce themselves."

Soon a further change took place.   Of the three communistic societies revolving like satellites round New Harmony, two found themselves in trouble; caused, it is said, partly by the admission of unsuitable members, and partly by the excessive numbers.   These two abandoned their independence, and put themselves into the hands of Owen, with four trustees: leaving only Maclure's education society standing.

Under the management of Owen and the trustees, another‡ attempt was made to unite these people in communistic bands; but unfortunately, it soon became

* *Co-operative Mag.* ii. 46.   † Ibid. 322.   ‡ Ibid.

clear that this new establishment did not pay its expenses. Various causes were assigned for the deficiency: carelessness on the part of many members, as to the common property: absence of interest in the experiment: mutual distrust, generated by inequality of industry and discordancy of habits: an incapacity among ignorant people to look beyond what they saw, and to understand the whole social machinery: and fears arising from previous failures.

It was now proposed to get rid of some of the obstacles to success, by forming a new communistic society; to consist only of such persons as from previous friendship, would feel mutual confidence and attachment. A number of volunteers appeared, and with the help of land and of maintenance for the first year, formed an association, and settled in the neighbourhood of New Harmony. Within the town itself, communism had been abandoned. The inhabitants were divided into trades or occupations; each of which formed an independent body, framing its own internal regulations, administering its own affairs, and paying only a small weekly sum towards a general fund for the town expenses. It had been found that the present inhabitants, trained from childhood to think of little but the pecuniary interests of themselves and their families, were unable to devote themselves heartily to the general welfare of five hundred or a thousand persons: and it was thought that by circumscribing the body to which each person belonged, that indifference would be diminished; and the more, as it was left to each trade to allow as much or as little individualism as it pleased. The town was now an aggregation of self-governed guilds : the communism was banished to the country.

Those who wish to read accounts of still further changes, may consult the *Co-operative Magazine.** To record them here, would be perplexing and disgustful. I have given so many, only because I know no other way of conveying a correct notion of the confusion that really prevailed : of the constant hopes entertained ; of the difficulties, mere trifles at first, that intervened ; of the fears, growing gradually into certainties, as to the failure of each experiment ; of the undying labour, accompanied with sighs and groans, of heaving up hill a " huge round stone," only to see it " result with a bound," and " thunder impetuous down " again. If Owen ever indulged in poetry, he must have compared himself with Sisyphus. The philosopher Maclure had uttered many unfavourable prognostications. When he saw one adventure after another fail hopelessly, he must have been confirmed in his conviction, that to change essentially the character of adult men and women, was almost impossible: if he were a good-natured man he must have looked grave ; if he were a sympathetic man he must have pitied his Sisyphean friend; if he were a cynic he must have grinned sarcastically. To myself, Owen's troubles seem much like those of a patentee of a mechanical invention. Here and there no doubt, a new process amply repays the expense of carrying it out and of protecting it by royal letters ; but

* ii. 223.

in most cases there are alternate expectations of fortune and anticipations of loss; sleepless nights, and days of anxiety; public acclamations it may be, followed by private lamentation; disappointment rendered more bitter by the long-continued hopes of success. Such was the course of New Harmony. We cannot wonder that Owen in despair, resigned the management: * and I am only surprised that he and his two sons remained on the scene of their troubles some time longer.

What were the causes of these various failures? People will give different answers, according to the general sentiments they entertain. For myself I should say with Maclure, that such experiments must fail, because it is impossible to mould to communism the characters of men and women, formed by the present doctrines and practices of the world to intense individualism. I should indeed go further than Maclure, by stating my conviction, that even with persons brought up from childhood to act in common and live in common, it would be impossible to carry out a communistic system, unless in a place utterly removed from contact with the world, or with the help of some powerful religious conviction. Mere benevolence, mere sentiments of universal philanthropy, are far too weak to bind the self-seeking affections of men. In the middle ages, when governments were feeble, men combined together for mutual protection; and in some cases, though principally those of near kindred, they established small societies with community of property:

* *Co-operative Mag.* ii. 243.

but now that governments are able to shelter their subjects from wrong, each individual walks alone, and grudges the surrender of liberty to work and live as he pleases, uncontrolled by his friends and neighbours. People generally would regard communism as a voluntary slavery. Thus, as I believe, Owen's attempts must have broken down, because his principles were entirely opposed to the spirit of his age.

But professed co-operators refused to see the affair in this light. They retained their conviction that Owen's principles were true; and casting about to find the causes of the collapse of New Harmony, they laid the disasters to the door of Owen's injudicious conduct.* He ought, said they, to have set to work as if he had been raising a regiment; by selecting a staff, by appointing officers, by nominating managers, by joining with himself such numbers of persons skilled in his system, that every member on arriving at New Harmony, should have been at once an active and efficient co-operator. He should have required every one to sign a bond of union, giving power to the officers to expel refractory members. The grand cause of failure, in short, was a want of authority in the managers and of subordination in the members at large.

Owen himself, if judged by his public addresses,† bated not one jot of heart or hope: the tranquil obstinacy which had supported him as a child under unjust punishment by a father, sustained him now under the vexations inflicted by ignorant, unruly, selfish, un-

* *Co-operative Mag.* ii. 340.   † Ibid. 413, 445.

grateful men. He swallowed the bitter pill in private, and put on a placid countenance for the world. In the spring of 1827, he published a parting letter to the communistic societies, now amounting to ten, established on the estate of New Harmony. He here confesses that the town is merely a " receiving and probationary place;" and says that it is convenient for it to be so, until all the land destined for communities should be occupied : convenient because the town thus applied, was a useful place for receiving strangers desirous of inspecting the communities around, and had been in fact the centre from which the most valuable members had emanated. A cross-questioner might have inquired, whether the adoption of communism in the town itself, would have intercepted these advantages.

Owen acknowledged that experience had shown one thing: the necessity of great caution in selecting members. No societies with common property and equality, could prosper, if composed of persons unfit for their peculiar duties. In order to success it was needful to exclude the intemperate, the idle, the careless, the quarrelsome, the avaricious, the selfish; all in short, who were intent on advantages for themselves or their own communities, to the neglect of the interests and happiness of mankind at large. One wonders whether for a society so weeded, any peculiar organization would be necessary. It is just the selfish and the intemperate who constitute the difficulty of our present arrangements.

A few months later, on Sunday the 9th September,

1827, the members of the London Co-operative Society
had a breakfast in their rooms, 36, Red Lion Square; ·
Lady Elizabeth Dawson, Miss Rolland, and other ladies
being present.   Owen had lately arrived from America.
He made a speech, in which, according to the report
we have, he denied the truth of the rumours that New
Harmony was a failure; and asserted that the accounts
given in the American papers were "totally ground-
less, and the fabrications of the enemies of the system."
If Owen really said all this, which I much doubt, he
was guilty of considerable misrepresentation; because
there certainly had been several gross failures.   When
however, he added that he left ten co-operative communities on the lands of New Harmony, all going on
in the best spirit, and with every prospect of success, I
can believe that the afflatus of the projector convinced
him of the truth of what he asserted.

Owen on leaving New Harmony, did not belie the
character he had earned for munificence in the cause of
education.   His earnest desire was, that the children of
all the ten communities should receive the best possible
. training, and if it might be, without cost to the parents.
But deeply gratifying as such an arrangement would
have been, he hesitated about taking upon himself the
whole expense of the schools.   He had sunk a large
sum at New Harmony, and with the help of the
6,000*l.* or 7,000*l.* supplied by Maclure, had paid for the
property, real and personal, that he had purchased;
and he felt it doubtful whether his remaining income
would allow him to undertake to feed and clothe all

those children who were not provided for by Maclure. This much he would do for the current year: he would subscribe 600*l.* for this purpose; relying upon the members to contribute their surplus produce in aid. I must remark here, that though I have mentioned Maclure's contributions to the purchase of land, and to the provision for education, no allusion is made by Owen himself to that gentleman's liberality: an omission which I do not profess to understand.

At the end of another half-year, Owen was again at New Harmony, eagerly looking for the harvest of success which he had resolved to anticipate. On Sunday the 13th of April 1828, he delivered an address* to the inhabitants, and we may read in it what had been the course of events during his absence. He had hoped that fifty years of political liberty would have fitted the Americans for the adoption of his system: a strange notion: since history seems to inform us that the greater the political freedom of a nation, the stronger is its tendency to individualism; and that it is among the subjects of arbitrary governments that people combine together.

Of the ten communistic societies, two had bought their land from Owen: the other eight had taken 500 to 1,000 acres for a term of ten thousand years,† at the low rent of fifty cents, or a little more than two shillings an acre; subject to the condition that the land should be used for communistic purposes; and failing that, with a power to Owen to resume his grant.

---

* *Co-operative Mag.* iii. 127.   † Ibid. ii. 450.

This land was let to the last-formed associations; which consisted, as it will be remembered, of persons acquainted with each other's habits, and previously living in intimacy. Owen had anticipated that these small bodies, with consonance of manners and sentiments, and set down on an ample territory, let to them on the easiest terms, would have devoted themselves with earnestness and success to carrying out the social principles of their patron. But he had found to his grievous disappointment, that affairs had not gone on as he had expected. Communism, co-operation, socialism (call it as you will), had not made way. The abominable notions of old society had prevailed: each man had been thinking of himself and his own family: the good of the whole community had not been uppermost in every member's thoughts: the true interests of all the ten communities, the solid advantage of the nation and of the human race, had not taken the prominent place it deserved in all their proceedings: the land had been applied, contrary to agreement, to serve the interest of each occupier, and it must be given back again to Owen under the terms of the lease.

The conclusion from these last experiments was inevitable: that families trained in the ways of the ordinary world, could not be brought to live together with that mutual confidence, forbearance, and unselfishness, which were essential to carrying out true communism. There were other causes for regret: there had been monopoly: there had been individual misconduct. But what were these, when compared with the

17—2

utter breaking down of those plans, which fairly carried out, would have regenerated the world: what were they when set by the side of the grief felt by Owen at the disappointment of his long-cherished hopes, now blasted by the misconduct of others? Yet he would not indulge the folly of resentment: men were what circumstances had made them. "Shall I be angry and irritated with my fellow-beings, because they have been ignorant of their real interests? With the principles which I deem so true and valuable for the promotion of virtue and happiness, would this conduct be rational in me? I can only feel regret instead of anger."

But one thing was plain: communism must be abandoned. Unwillingly as this conviction might be received, it could no longer be resisted. It was vain to hope any more, that men habituated to the common pursuits and sentiments of the world, could throw off the character that had been impressed upon them, and could be fitted for a society in which the motives to action, the daily course of labour, the manners and mode of living, were all of them different, and in many respects the reverse, of those which commonly prevailed. Hard had been Owen's struggle, bitter was his grief. During a quarter of a century he had revolved his theories; he had made experiments and had succeeded to a miracle; the world had acknowledged his success; he had earned the undying hatred of the partisans of the old system; now, when the best half of his life was gone, he had spent several years and a vast sum of money, on a grand attempt, and it had broken down, and that so utterly, that even his obstinacy was conquered: his plans must be abandoned.   Here he was, loaded with a large tract of country, with a town built by the enthusiasm of the contemptible Rappites, of men grossly enslaved to the superstitions of mankind.   They in their folly, had done what he with his boasted wisdom had utterly failed in.

But what should he do with this heavy burden of land and buildings, which had swallowed up a fortune, and now remained profitless?   He would not even now abandon it to the common herd of men.   He would let it to those who were desirous of promoting the " Social System;" and they, if they pleased, should live in separate families ; either uniting their labour for common purposes, or carrying on the operations of life in the ordinary way, at their own pleasure.   A better day was at hand.   The children of the colonists should be educated and trained in the right way : they should be uncorrupted by the vain traditions of the world : and when they grew to manhood, the social and co-operative system should flourish on the lands of New Harmony. Thirty years have passed, and that better day has not yet arrived.   The lands remain in possession of Owen's family, but they are not the seat of a communistic society.

CHAPTER XXIII.

Two New Events—Mexico: Preliminaries — A Memorial sent to
Mexico—During Voyage: Religion—Legislative Labours—Friend
during Voyage—Free Negroes—Slaves: Happiness—Owen's Rashness—Epicureanism—Education—Fallacy in Reasoning—Journey
as far as Puebla—Love of Nature—Another Example—Mr. Exter
—The President: Favourable Reception—Conversation with—
The American Minister—Result of the Project.

My last chapter brought Owen's history down to April
1828. Soon afterwards, there occurred two events,*
both of which seemed to him of high importance: the
one, an agreement to meet the Rev. Alexander Campbell at Cincinnati in April 1829, for the discussion of
the principles of religion; the other, a negotiation with
the Mexican Government, for the grant of means to
try a communistic experiment within its territory. The
debate has lost its interest: the Mexican affair is necessary to this history, and is not unworthy of our
attention.

In the summer of 1828, not many months after the
breaking up of the experiments at New Harmony,
Owen met with what appeared another opportunity
of carrying his views into practice. The Mexican
Government had granted to certain persons, several

---

* *British Co-operator*, 71.

millions of acres of land in Texas; a province almost unknown at a time when the United States had not yet interfered with it. The grantees applied to Owen to assist them with a scheme of colonization. Notwithstanding the defeat he had just suffered, he entertained the proposal; and recommended them to attempt the establishment of "communities on the social system," like those which had been so vainly tried in Indiana.

Owen was at this time in England: and his advice having been accepted, application was at once made to the representatives in London of Mexico and other South American republics. The communication was favourably received: and Rocafuerte, the Mexican authority, requested Owen to furnish him with a memorial on the subject. This was done of course, with alacrity; and Owen's composition, containing his usual assertions and arguments, was translated into Spanish, and despatched by the October packet to Vera Cruz, with a favourable recommendation from Rocafuerte to the President of his republic. Owen, according to his usual prudent custom, had taken into his confidence the British prime minister and the United States' ambassador in London. He also resolved to follow his memorial across the Atlantic, in order to press it on the attention of the Mexican rulers. He had numerous copies of it made, and forwarded to all the governments of Europe and America. He obtained letters of introduction to the Mexican Government, from Rocafuerte; to Bolivar, from the Columbian minister in London; to the United States' ambassador in Mexico, from the American representative here; and from Lord Aberdeen and his friends, to consuls and vice-consuls.

On the 22nd November 1828, Owen embarked on the *Spey* at Falmouth, and sailed slowly towards South America. His time was fully and agreeably occupied during the voyage. He had become a dreamy enthusiast; and untaught by experience, still indulged hopes of changing the constitution of the world. But first, he had to prepare for the discussion with the Rev. Alexander Campbell in the following April: for Owen was not one of those who postpone preparation for lecture or discussion, until within a few days or hours of the appointed time; he always industriously worked up his notions into the best form he could give them. He now hoped, after all his experience of the obstinate beliefs and ingrained superstitions of men, that he should be able to put together such a statement, such a series of propositions, as should be decisive of the question at issue. After April 1829, every man, be he Christian, Jew, Mahometan, Hindoo, Buddhist, or follower of Confucius, should have no choice but to abandon his old faith, and adopt the tenets of Owen.

He also employed himself in a task,* which to any other man would have been one of extreme difficulty, requiring the long continued and laborious use of solitude, reading, and reflection; and quite incompatible with the nausea, noise, disturbance, and inconveniences, of a sea-voyage: he set himself to frame " a new code of laws in accordance with the laws of human nature; "

* *Co-operative Mag.* iii. 187.

and to develop "the outlines of a universal government, founded on those laws, and upon the experience of all nations and people up to the present period, as far as this experience is detailed in the English language." If Owen could accomplish this, in the absence of books, he must have had an astounding memory. Further, he had to prepare a code of laws for the expected administration of Texas.*

Owen had the good fortune, or rather the ability, to make friends wherever he found men. He was highly satisfied with the captain of the packet ship. He experienced warm sympathy from the only cabin passenger besides himself: Lieutenant Deare. This gentleman, far from ridiculing or slighting Owen's occupations, applied himself to study them: read the papers as they were written: and even incurred the labour of copying them with his own hand; so that if the originals should be lost, the world might not be without a duplicate.

The only notable thing recorded during the voyage, is Owen's opinion of the negroes whom he saw, when the packet touched at two or three ports. First, at St. Domingo, he went on shore at Jacquemel: and instead of a few huts and wretched inhabitants, as he had expected, there were commodious houses, a decent town, and a people better dressed, cleaner, more orderly, milder, more polite in manners, and freer from apparent anxiety, than the labouring populations of civilized

* *British Co-operator*, 71.

countries. These however, were a free people. At
Jamaica he spent several days among the slaves : and
if the liberated blacks of Hayti had amazed him, the
servile blacks of our islands utterly disturbed all his
previous convictions.

" Wherever* I go, I find philanthropy and religion
mere names to confound the understanding, and deceive
the very best intentioned individuals. If Thomas Clarkson, Mr. Wilberforce, William Allen, Fowell Buxton,
and other British philanthropists, could make an unpre-
judiced comparison between the present state of the
manufacturing and other labouring classes in the islands
of Great Britain and Ireland, and the slave population
of the West India colonies, they would discover that
they had a task equal to all their united powers of
body, mind, and means, to advance the former to the
same enjoyments that are now in the actual possession
of the latter."

Whatever the condition of the negroes might have
been in former times, Owen found the Jamaica slaves
" better dressed, more independent in look, person, and
manners, and greatly more free from corroding care
and anxiety, than a large portion of the working classes
in England, Scotland, and Ireland." He therefore requested with the greatest earnestness, that the "good
religious people of England" would not disturb the
happiness and independence which these slaves felt in
their actual condition. For as their animal wants were
fully satisfied, they had nothing to desire but humane

* British Co-operator, 93.

masters; and nearly all the masters now were, from a sense of interest, humane.

It would be useless now to pursue Owen's sentiments on this topic any further, but that his strange rhapsody throws much light on his character.   He spends a few days in the corner of a single island, and at once pronounces an opinion on the condition of the slave populations of all the colonies.   He is thrown into the society of a few slave-owners; humane men, who present the institution in its most favourable light: he converses with a slave coachman, who is rich enough to purchase his freedom, but forbears to do so, fearing that if he were free and should fall sick, there would be no one to take care of him.   From these few facts, without any verification, without any suspicion of the well-known distinction between domestic and field slaves, without any inquiries about the sale of negroes and the separation of families, or the inevitable corruption of the morals of the masters, or the thousand abominations that did and must occur in such a state of society, Owen leaped to the conclusion that slavery as it existed, ought not to be disturbed.

Besides this rashness in argumentation, we see in Owen's mind at this time, a low standard of social well-being.   Here are coloured people, well fed, handsomely dressed, sufficiently housed, exempt from anxiety, generally contented, protected by the law from gross outrages.   They cannot, it is true, choose their own masters; they must work at the bidding of another; their masters or mistresses may vent on them as much

ill-temper as they please and they have no redress; their
marriages are a farce; the honour of their women is not
safe; they are a degraded race, living under "the cold
shadow of an aristocracy" of colour.   But what are these
evils, when put by the side of plenty of food, of clothing,
and of shelter, together with absence of anxiety? Owen's
social philosophy looks to me, in this instance, material
and base.

One difficulty he did feel: he was the apostle of
education, and the slaves were ignorant.   True: but in
this case ignorance was happiness: for slavery and
knowledge could not long co-exist.   If indeed, wise
social arrangements could be introduced into our colonies; that is, if communistic societies could be established; such an arrangement would be superior to
slavery: but to set the blacks free, and to establish the relation of employer and free labourer as in Europe, would
be only to go from good to bad; from slavery with
abundance to liberty with destitution.   Better then, to
keep the negroes ignorant at present, lest with education discontent should appear.   For what, after all, was
the aim of education? Was it to give something that
was in itself valuable: was it to cultivate the faculties,
and so to fit men for the task to which nature destined
them: was it to raise them to the dignity of manhood,
and to instruct them how to fulfil their duties to each
other and to God? By no means. The aim of education,
as Owen understood it, was to train men for the new and
true social organization of which he was the prophet: to
lead them to abandon the vicious customs of the world

as it exists, to give up individual straining after success, the desire of rising in life, the competition of every man with his neighbour; and to devote themselves to promoting the well-being of the community to which they belong and of the world at large. If the negroes could have such an education as this, it would be in the highest degree beneficial: but as to such instruction as would make them discontented with their present condition, and as would at best, fit them to live as free labourers under capitalist employers, that would be nothing but evil.

I have pointed out the rashness of deciding on the condition of the slaves, after some days' residence among a very few of them in a corner of one island. Besides this, there appears a gross fallacy in the inference from the facts. Owen lands at Jacquemel, and is astonished to find the free blacks in the possession of an abundance of the means of living, and exhibiting much politeness of demeanour and refinement of manners: he lands at Kingston and meets among the slaves with the same plenty of the necessaries of life, and great apparent happiness. He concludes that slavery is for the present, favourable to the happiness of the negroes. Now if he had found the free blacks miserable, and the slaves happy, he might well have suspected that slavery was in the actual condition of things, advantageous. But seeing freemen and slaves equally happy, he would fairly have said that as far as the facts went, slavery and freedom had nothing to do with the matter; and that the happiness of both freemen and slaves must be caused by circumstances common to both; such as

climate, soil, abundance of land, sparseness of population, and original constitution of the race. Altogether,
Owen seems to have proved himself a superficial observer and an unsound reasoner.

Having concluded this digression on a matter which
seems to me very illustrative of Owen's character, I
proceed with his voyage to Mexico. At Port Royal,
Jamaica, he had met with an old neighbour, Admiral
Fleming, who was then in command on that station; by
whom he had been very cordially received; and who
had given him a letter to the Bishop of Puebla, the only
remaining bishop in Mexico. Having soon afterwards
sailed on to Vera Cruz, and travelled as far as Jalapa,
he had a cordial reception from Maclure, who had left
New Harmony, and was about to proceed to Mexico as
soon as the late revolution had subsided. At Perote he
met Santa Anna, who with fifteen hundred troops had
arrived just before him. He found the general "an
interesting and young looking man for the important
rank and station he had gained:" he was politely
received and had an escort promised for Puebla. On
arriving at that town, he presented Admiral Fleming's
letter to the bishop. This sole high dignitary of the
Mexican Church, conducted himself in a most agreeable manner; even going so far as to profess an agreement with Owen's views of society. An impartial
observer might have suspected, that the bishop's solitary condition suggested to him the prudence of adopting an appearance of liberality, quite foreign possibly,
to his internal convictions.

It may be remembered that while Owen was a mere child, a casual acquaintance with an Oxford undergraduate, to whom he acted as a guide among the walks about Newtown, inspired him with a certain fondness for natural scenery. On this long journey, fifty years later, the old taste was amply indulged. During the two days from Puebla to Mexico, " I was highly gratified, particularly when on horseback, with the grand plain and mountain scenery of this district. The exercise, the air at this elevation, and the magnificent plain and mountain scenery, created feelings of enjoyment not to be described. More than once, while contemplating at one view Popocatepetl, Izcacciahuatl, and Orizaba, three mountains each higher than any in Europe, I felt that I could willingly have made the voyage, run all the risk I encountered, and renewed all the fatigues of the journey, for the pleasure I experienced on these occasions."

Such an effusion is quite a relief to any one toiling through the monotonous repetitions of Owen's social philosophy; not commonly varied by elegancies of any kind. Another example occurs soon afterwards : " When we separated, I had to proceed to the great square in which Mr. Exter lived; and when I had advanced into the middle of it, the grand Cathedral of the Republic on one side, and on the other the truly magnificent palace, not an object of any kind moved, nor was the slightest sound heard. The air so exhilarating, that to breathe was to inhale pleasure. All around was calm and peaceful; where but a few days before, civil war raged, soldiers were killed, and citizens were plundered. The heavens, owing to the stillness and peculiar clearness of the atmosphere, were in their highest beauty. Every star seemed to send forth its extent of brilliant light upon the scene around. I stopped involuntarily, and enjoyed for some time the pleasure not to be described, which so new and singular a combination of circumstances was calculated to produce."

On Owen's arrival at the city of Mexico, he had the good fortune to be received into the house of Mr. Exter, a great English merchant, who was a large proprietor in Texas, and who was well acquainted with the members of the Government, and enjoyed their confidence. Mr. Exter devoted himself to the task of promoting Owen's views. He introduced him to Mr. Pakenham, the British Minister; who after reading the letters from Lord Aberdeen and Admiral Fleming, behaved with frankness and cordiality; and called with him upon the British Consul-General, and upon the representatives of Holland and the United States.

On the Sunday, a fête was held in honour of the recent election of the new President, General Guerrero; who in the evening was the great object of attraction at the theatre. The following day Owen was carried by Mr. Pakenham to an audience of the actual President Victoria; and Owen found him "a plain unassuming man, not trained in affairs of state, nor calculated to direct any crooked cabinet policy." Mr. Pakenham explained fully and clearly, Owen's measures during many years for the amelioration of society, and his object in visiting Mexico. The President replied that Rocafuerte's despatches from London had put him in possession of full information on those topics: that the Government had considered the subject; and that they were already prepared to make a grant to Owen of a district fifty leagues broad, along the whole line of the frontier between the republics of Mexico and of the United States; extending to the vast length of about thirteen degrees and a half of latitude: a territory large enough for a kingdom, though of an inconvenient form.

There was a revolutionary rapidity about this proceeding, which was really less encouraging than the formal delays of a settled government. Owen does not tell us whether this thought occurred to him. He expressed his thanks for the gracious treatment he had experienced; and inquiring how soon the legal grant would probably be made, was told, that it should be passed through Congress with all possible expedition. But this Congress: was it a shadow or a reality? Was it certain that no difficulties would arise? After this speedy transaction of business, a conversation of nearly two hours followed, lengthened of course by the interpreting of every speech. Many remarks were made upon the social improvements going on in Europe and the United States. Owen did not forget his favourite infant school: he mentioned that he had brought to South America, a set of apparatus for such a school; but that he had left it at Vera Cruz, and had now written to have it sent forward. The President appeared

18

interested, and accepted the apparatus on behalf of the Republic.

Owen found a warm friend and partisan, in the United States minister, Mr. Poinsett; who had heard the addresses at Washington in the Hall of Congress, and had since reflected upon them. His frankness encouraged Owen to put into his hands the papers written during the voyage, upon " all the religions, governments, codes of law, and present commercial estate of the world:" a library in truth, compressed into a few quires of paper. Mr. Poinsett read the manuscripts, and was so well pleased with them, that to promote the measures recommended, he would make any sacrifice in his power. Owen upon this, became still more confidential. He said that it was time for the British and American governments to adopt a new line of policy ; and ceasing to struggle for predominance as merchants and manufacturers, to study the real interests both of their own nations and of those to which they were accredited. Why should Mr. Pakenham and Mr. Poinsett, clutching emulously at a shadow, do injury to Great Britain and America, and at the same time retard the progress of the nascent Mexican Republic? When pressed to come to more particulars, Owen said, that he regarded Great Britain and the United States as the two most powerful countries in the world; (France seems to have been overlooked ;) and that if the British and the Americans would now adopt a decided policy, adjust at once all their little differences, and form a cordial alliance, they might secure the permanent peace of the world; and further, might give such a direction to the scientific and mechanical improvements that were going on, as should fairly distribute among all classes, the vastly increased products. After this there followed of course, a string of maxims and propositions containing Owen's peculiar views. That a deep impression was made on Mr. Poinsett, and through him on his friends at Washington, is tolerably clear.

After this, Owen was introduced to many influential people, and then took advantage of an escort to Vera Cruz; whence, by the kindness of Admiral Fleming, he got a passage in a royal vessel to the West Indies, on his way to the United States. The result of the voyage was very simple. Owen did not become governor of a vast province, " stretching like a pair of garters across the map of" America: he did not go through the feverish stages of projectors; hope, apparent success, a minute difficulty daily growing larger, fear, resolution not to be beaten, doubt, despair: he did not struggle again with the roughness of backwoodsmen, nor vainly try to stimulate the apathy of the Indian. All these annoyances were spared him, for the promised grant was not confirmed. Before leaving Mexico* he had had his doubts, because the existing law forbade the exercise of any religion but the Roman Catholic; and such a restriction was inconsistent with the fundamental principle of Owen's system of government. The President had told him indeed, that his administration had considered this difficulty and was prepared to overcome it.

* *New Moral World*, i. 378. 26th Sept. 1835.

18—2

There was a singular law which restrained the legislative discussion of religious matters for a certain number of years: but that term would expire in the following spring; and when the subject came in due form before the Congress, the Government would use its influence to obtain a law like that of the United States, putting all creeds on an equal footing. On this contingent expectation, Owen resolved that as soon as the necessary measure had passed through the Mexican Congress, he would bring colonists from Great Britain and the United States, and would found a government " on the principles of Truth, Charity, and Knowledge." He was spared, however, the mortification which, judging from his other attempts, we may say, would certainly have been the result. Before the spring and the new law on religion appeared, there was a change of Mexican administration : the liberal party fell from power: the new ministers cared nothing for Owen: the district never came into his hands. Thus ended the magnificent project.

CHAPTER XXIV.

Scotch Community: Account necessary—Orbiston: Situation, &c.
Constitution—Manufactories, Barrack—Reasons for letting to
Tenants—Socialism: not Communism—Combe's Reasons—De-
fended: Parisian Example—Abram Combe: Severe Training—Education—Tastes and Principles—Conversion to Owenism—Change
of Character—Combe and Hamilton's Zeal—Particulars to June,
1826—September, 1826—Change of Measures—Spring, 1827: Progress—Detailed Account—Continued—Fatal Misfortune—Combe's
Indiscretion: his Death—Fate of the Members—Explanation—
Fate of the Property—Conclusion.

In Chapter XX. I have related that a difference of
opinion had arisen, between Owen and those of his
friends who had resolved to found a communistic society
in Scotland. In consequence of this dissension, Owen
took no part in carrying out the project: and it may
be thought that for that reason it might be passed over
in this biography. But I think that such an omission
would leave my work incomplete: because the community in question was begun and carried on by Owen's
disciples, in a mode generally accordant with his principles, though with some variations in practice which
led him to stand aloof. We have seen how these new
notions looked, when reduced to practice in the latitude
of Indiana, by rough and independent settlers: our
pictures will be incomplete if we have not a view of
the same notions realized by the more sober-minded

inhabitants of Great Britain, and in a thickly peopled country.

This Scotch society was established about the time Owen first went to the United States: and the account on which I principally rely was printed in 1825.* The *Orbiston Company* was so called from being established on the Orbiston estate, of which it had purchased 291 statute acres: all excellent arable land, on a dry and healthy site. It was nine miles from Glasgow, thirty-five from Edinburgh,† and not far from Holytown. It was placed on the Clyde about two miles from Hamilton, and delightfully bounded on one side by the Calder; which river separated it from the lands of Motherwell, where a larger experiment was intended. It was proposed to accommodate two hundred families.

The scheme was in the hands of a company of capitalists, who subscribed the funds in 200 shares of 250*l.* each: making a sum of 50,000*l.*, the greater part of the shares being actually taken up. These gentlemen did not propose to sit down on the land themselves, and sacrifice the superfluities to which they had been accustomed, for the satisfaction of daily toil and rough companionship. But they were willing to risk a considerable sum of money, in order to give a chance of plenty and happiness to those who hitherto had suffered destitution and anxiety. They proposed to put the place into a habitable state, and furnish it with all the appliances required; and then to let it for a

* *Sphere of Joint-Stock Companies,* p. 58, &c., by Abram Combe.
† *Co-operative Mag.* i. 161; and ii. 317.

certain percentage on the outlay, to a company of tenants, composed of persons disposed to labour and live on the co-operative principle. The interest to be paid was moderate; being only three and a half per cent. for the first two years, and five per cent. after-wards: the law expenses being defrayed by the capi-talists.*

The community was to be neither purely agricul-tural, nor purely manufacturing, but a mixture of both. The capitalists undertook to build manufactories and workshops: and a fall in the river of eight feet, gave an excellent water-power. The members were to live, not in separate houses, but in portions of a huge build-ing, an eighth of a mile in length. This was to be placed more than a quarter of a mile from the Calder, and fifty yards above the level of the stream; with a slope towards the river, and a view at once extensive and beautiful. The private rooms were all to be of one size, sixteen feet by twelve: giving, after deducting what was taken up by bed and closet, twelve feet by eleven and a half of unoccupied space. The eating-room, fifty feet by forty, and nineteen feet high, was to be divided by partitions into boxes, each to hold eight persons. Besides these, there were to be lecture room, ball-room, drawing-room, and library.

It would be tedious to give a full description of the detailed arrangements. But the principle adopted is worth notice. It was originally proposed that the members of the community should buy the land, erect

* Private Letter from Mr. Hamilton to Mr. Pare, Sept. 24, 1831.

the buildings, and purchase the tools and machinery:
and that the capital raised by benevolent persons should
be lent to the members to enable them to do this. But
it was afterwards resolved, as I have mentioned, to
make all the purchases directly with the funds of
the capitalists, and then to let the land and plant to
the working community, or company of tenants. Two
reasons were assigned for this plan: that it would be .
both more simple and more secure than the other.
As to the latter, we see at once that the capitalists
were in the situation of a landlord: and we should be
much surprised if a country gentleman were to buy
an estate for a farmer, and stipulate to receive interest
on the purchase money, instead of buying the estate
for himself and letting it on rent for a term of years.
It is true that the capital was in this instance advanced
for philanthropic purposes, and not for the sake of an
income: but it was contended with justice, that though
this particular affair might be begun and carried out
at the expense of people who cared little about the
money they had advanced, the system of communism
could never become general unless it could be made
to pay those who found the money for it. If it could
be understood on 'Change, that funds laid out in constructing communistic villages, would pay six per cent.
with good security, the system would spread rapidly:
whereas, if the income were only two per cent., or if
the principal were insecure, nothing considerable would
ever be done.

This arrangement of the two bodies, of capitalists

and of tenants, was the work of Abram Combe, the author of the pamphlet to which I have referred. Another of his regulations caused much discussion among the friends of co-operation. He contended that however great would be the gain of combination in working and living, a community could not be successful, without each member felt the spur of individual advantage; and therefore, he insisted that every one's maintenance should be in proportion to the work he accomplished. This it is true, was giving up the principle of communism: and though I entirely agree with Mr. Combe, I cannot wonder that the advocates of that principle should be dissatisfied. The notion that a man's maintenance should depend on his labour, and be in proportion to it, was loudly denounced[*] as inconsistent with the communistic principle; and as being "the very germ of the competitive system: of that system, which has ever hitherto produced, and will ever while it lasts, continue to produce, such division of interests, such dissensions, animosities, insatiable desires, and consequent miseries."

Combe in reply to these and similar invectives, published his reasons in the *Orbiston Register:* and they are worthy of serious attention, as showing the grounds on which a practical and thoughtful man, found it necessary to disregard the notions of his best friends. He says[†] that before he had any *experience* of the subject, his views of " equal distribution " were the same with those advocated by the *Co-operative Magazine*

* *Co-operative Mag.* i. 339.   † Ibid. ii. 92.

and by William Thompson of Cork: but that an experiment of associating a dozen or a score of families,
a few years before, had altered his convictions. The
persons associated in this instance, were professed converts to the doctrine of equal distribution: and their
conduct furnished an irresistible proof of the impossibility of putting the doctrine in practice. When it
came to the test of every-day life, it was found that
the associates did not really approve of distributing
to all alike. Combe was grieved to find that this was
the case; for the theory had delighted him. However,
the conviction was forced upon him: and when he
could no longer resist it, he comforted himself with
the reflection, that the other advantages of co-operation
were independent of this. He made no pretensions to
dictate to the Orbiston people on the subject: he only
desired that no compulsion whatever should be used,
but that all should judge for themselves.

To most persons no proof is needed, of the absurdity
of the principle of equal distribution. That a powerful and laborious man should receive only the same
food and clothing with a slight or idle one; that a
raw youth, only half-acquainted with his business,
should draw the same rations with a mature man;
that a mere labourer, with little more mind than a
horse, should enjoy the same maintenance with a skilful mechanic, bred to a difficult handicraft; are pro-
posals so unjust as to be apparently out of the pale of
argument. Yet grave and thoughtful men have put
them forward, and therefore the argument from expe-

rience is valuable. The Parisian socialists of ten years ago attempted the practice of equal distribution: but they generally abandoned it, on the ground that it led to an inquisition not to be borne. Equal distribution by all means, they argued; but then we shall expect equal work. You shall have the same maintenance that I have, but you shall do as much work as I do. And so a tailor, sitting by his brother, counted his stitches, watched his wandering looks, and harassed him with a superintendence worse than the worst evils of competition. Then came the thought: equal distribution means, maintenance independent of work; but if for equal maintenance equal work is required, the principle is disregarded, and we may as well return to the old arrangement of unequal distribution, in proportion to labour accomplished. Justice in short, triumphed over the whims of closet philosophers: and Abram Combe's experience was more weighty than the fanciful notions of philanthropists.

The account of the Orbiston community would be incomplete, without some notice of the man who was its most active manager. Abram* Combe, a brother of George Combe the phrenologist, was born in Edinburgh in 1785. His father was a brewer, and a casual circumstance led the youth to adopt the business of a tanner. He was apprenticed in Edinburgh, but lived in his father's house. His training was of the severest kind: work six days in the week from seven in the morning till eight in the evening: and on Sundays that

* *Co-operative Mag.* ii. 518.

harsh course of compulsory godliness which prevails in
Scotland even more absurdly than in England ; under
which young Combe was taken twice to the parish
church, and for the rest of the day was confined within
the walls which enclosed his father's house, brewery,
and small garden; besides being required to learn by
heart the two catechisms, psalms, paraphrases, and
chapters.   Such discipline, if universal, is enough to
drive the nation into infidelity and profligacy : just as
English puritanism was followed by the dissoluteness of
the Restoration.

Combe was for some time at the High School, Edinburgh, at first under Mr. Luke Fraser, and afterwards
under Dr. Alexander Adam.   Mr. Fraser is described
as a severe master, absorbed in his classical pursuits,
and punishing inexorably every failure in a lesson :
while Dr. Adam by his gentle nature won the hearts of
his pupils.   Combe early adopted a utilitarian view of
knowledge ; and failing, like Gibbon, to see any advantage in classical literature, he shirked his lessons as far
as he could do so with safety.   Like Gibbon too, he
regretted his boyish years, but for a different reason :
the historian lamenting the opportunities for scholar-
ship he had thrown away, the tanner grieving in manhood, that even so small a portion of his life had been
applied to the barren acquisition of Latin.

Combe, to perfect his knowledge of his trade, went to
London.   He there learned for the first time, when
removed from the parental discipline, that it was possible to be at once good and happy ; and that a man

might enjoy life without infringing the laws of morality. Fortunately, the reaction was not so severe as it often is in such cases: he did not rush from asceticism into vice. On his return to Edinburgh, he devoted himself to mechanical inventions as an amusement, but with no great success. He also indulged a satirical vein by writing lampoons and epigrams, and was of course feared and shunned by many well-meaning persons. He was attentive to his business and had the reputation of being quite sufficiently alive to his own interests. If men were ever to be judged by their speculative opinions, Combe must be pronounced a man actuated by the lowest principles: for he asserted that self-interest is with every one the ruling motive; and that he himself felt a strong desire to do justice to the operative classes, not from any hostility to employers, to which class he belonged, nor from any spirit of discontent, but because he distinctly perceived that by doing so, he should advance his own comfort and that of his children.* I believe that Combe, in neglecting to mention benevolence as an immediate motive of his actions, did himself gross injustice.

Up to the year 1820, when he was thirty-five years old, he continued to be a keen, honest man of business, fond of amusement, possessing a hearty relish for enjoyment both of town and country life, and capable of making himself highly agreeable to his friends. In October 1820, a visit to New Lanark caused an entire change in his character and pursuits. He heard Owen

* *Sphere of Joint-Stock Companies*, pp. 26, 27.

explain his views as to the formation of character, the defective institutions of society, and the advantages of co-operation: he witnessed the effects of the New Lanark schools: he was deeply impressed with what he saw and heard; and contrasting the misery of the world around him, with the peace and happiness of the projected new world, he became an eager disciple of Owen.

His ardent character underwent a change so great, that his friends called it a conversion.* From being censorious and satirical, he became forbearing and forgiving: having learned to regard men as creatures of circumstances, and if debased and guilty, only the more worthy of compassion. He had been selfish and much addicted to the pursuit of gain: he was now sympathetic, and rather careless about his own interests. Many of his relatives who had avoided all intercourse with him, on account of his satirical temper, now found him kind and affectionate. Instead of writing epigrams, satires, and lampoons, he applied his powers to the promotion of "universal benevolence and justice." He gave up attendance at the theatre, being now disgusted at the "low motives and false maxims which abound in plays:" and he gave up the use of animal food and fermented liquors. In short, his strong and ardent character had found the means of development, denied it by the narrow training of his early years, and by the ignoble pursuits of his manhood.

This was the man who had devised the form of the

* _Co-operative Mag._ ii. 562, 563.

society at Orbiston: and who in conjunction with Mr. Hamilton of Dalzell, whom I have mentioned in a former chapter, devoted himself to carrying out the project. The zeal of both these gentlemen, was said to be almost romantic.* They were praised for having acted in the spirit of invaders, who burn their ships to make retreat impossible: for having at once erected substantial buildings, incapable of reconversion into money, instead of having in a cowardly temper, rented land and temporary habitations. There were of course, cooler and more censorious persons, who qualified their proceedings as hasty, and their zeal as rashness; and who thought that the funds expended on buildings, would have been better laid out in the production of the first necessaries of life.

The history of Orbiston, is just that of all the projects that grew out of Owen's teachings; New Lanark always excepted. We have hopes and fears, small successes and great difficulties, confessed disappointment and ultimate failure. The building was begun in March 1825; and in January 1826, some portions having been finished by the hundred workmen employed, a few weavers from Hamilton were enrolled as members on their spontaneous application. Combe † had intended to advertise for tenants, but he found reason for believing that without doing that, he would have far more applicants than could be admitted. In June 1826, a visitor stated that about twenty rooms were finished in a neat, comfortable, useful style: that

* *Co-operative Mag.* ii. 373.   † Ibid. i. 20.

the external appearance of the great building would be respectable, but plain and altogether devoid of ornament (much like a union workhouse I suppose): and that the boasted Calder, though a mere mill-stream, had banks of a very romantic character. At this time the few inmates were mostly laborious, cool, calculating Scotchmen; fit for a rough and ready life; and suitable companions for men who would work hard at a trade, or in the field, and for none others. The informant thought that co-operation, even in this incipient condition, was producing a cheapness of living, since a man's food need not cost more than a shilling a day: but a Scotch labourer, who under ordinary arrangements had to maintain a family on a shilling a day, would not boast of the frugality of spending all his wages on his own food. At this time a debtor and creditor account was kept with each member; his labour being reckoned as worth 12s. to 30s. a week, according to its value in the world he had left; against which was charged the cost of every article he consumed.

Between June and September 1826, much progress was made in completing the buildings, and the number of members had risen to nearly three hundred. To simplify the management, these had been divided into "squads" of ten to twenty families: one squad being engaged in erecting a foundry and workshops for machinery; another being intended for the garden, a third for the farm, and a fourth for the dairy. To stimulate industry and frugality, every person's savings

were to be doubled by the managers before any profit
should be claimed by the society. These modifications of
Owen's practice, appear to me to show the good sense of
the managers: but the consistent co-operators grumbled
at the abandonment of communism, and complained of
what they regarded as the slowness of progress. The
Orbiston Register, however, asserted that the prospects
were most satisfactory: that the appearance of the
growing crops of wheat, turnips, and carrots, proved
the excellence of the soil: that for gardening purposes,
the ground was as good as that let around Edinburgh
at 12*l.* to 14*l.* an acre; while the persons employed in
the different trades would furnish a market close at
hand: and that by the industry and skill of the different
squads, such comforts as gas-lighting would soon be
within reach of the community.

All the hopes were founded on the system of socialism, not on that of communism: that is, on the adoption
of the greatest possible amount of co-operation short
of community of property. But the reasonable proceedings in this respect of Combe and his supporters,
were jealously watched and constantly girded at by
the pure communists, who for ever harped on the
theme of the societies forming on the strictest principles, at Exeter and Cork. The members at Orbiston
were disturbed and discontented; and at length on the
25th September, 1826, resolved after an animated discussion, to disregard Combe's advice and thwart his
policy, by establishing a real community of property,
From this day the project was doomed. The indus-

19

trious, the strong, and the skilful, would not remain at Orbiston to receive the same maintenance with idle and incapable persons: and a community made up of the rags and shreds of the world, would not long hold together. Mr. Combe was absent from the meeting at which this resolution was adopted, being detained in Edinburgh by severe illness: another ground for alarm; since the loss of such a man's exertions would be a perilous drawback.

In the spring of 1827, the community put on a fair face before the world. Some difficulties were acknowledged.[*] Many of the members had proved to be idlers who had come in the hopes of living at the expense of the industrious, but these sluggards had been dismissed. Those who were really acquainted with the principles adopted, and who were friendly to them, still hoped that all would go well. It was believed that the produce of the labour of the community far exceeded its expenditure: but the estimate was made from conjecture and not from data furnished by actual accounts. The building was almost completed, and there was an appearance of regularity in the arrangements. Various occupations were carried on: twine-spinning, net-making, cotton and silk weaving, tailoring, shoemaking, iron casting, and of course field work. The *Orbiston Register* was still published, and the mildness and good sense of many of its articles were eulogized.

Another account of about the same date, was written

* *Co-operative Mag.* ii, 171.

by a person behind the scenes, and therefore gives more particulars. Great improvements are alleged to have taken place; particularly in the habits and demeanour of the members. One of the greatest trials to the Englishmen at Orbiston was "the general filth which pervades Scotland," and which in a barrack-like building, with scores of rooms in close proximity, became a nuisance which was not to be evaded by any amount of individual care. It was useless to keep your own room sweet, if stenches poured in on you from every side. Precept and example however, had very much mitigated this evil.

The farming operations were going on successfully. There were about forty acres of wheat, which looked promising; and for the sowing of the spring corn, most of the members had turned into the fields; where they would remain till all was finished; after which they would revert to their indoor employments until harvest time. It was stated that the mode of living and working in common, had produced admirable effects on the morals and manners of the members: that the superiority of their condition was felt and acknowledged: that some who had left had begged to be readmitted, but in vain: that the women found their husbands happier and more free from care than they had formerly been: and that drunkenness had much diminished.

But in the early autumn of 1827, a heavy calamity fell upon the society, in the death of Abram Combe. Illness had for some time prevented him from con-

tinuing his superintendence; and during his absence
there had been adopted the unhappy resolution of
attempting a community of property: but had he
recovered his health, that mistake might have been
corrected. Combe had not given up his tannery at
Edinburgh, but had taken two partners to assume
the active management: and he had removed with
his family to Orbiston. The labour, anxiety, and vexations, of this large experimental establishment, are supposed to have been too much for his constitution, which
probably was weakened by his abstinence from animal
food and spirituous liquors. The vegetarian system
is endurable by men who, like oxen, can lie down in
the shade and digest their bulky food; but active men
require their pabulum in a smaller compass. Combe's
restless energy should have had good feeding to support it.

He must have been totally ignorant of the common
laws of health: for his zeal in stimulating his brethren
to good works, led him without any previous training
for hard labour, to set himself the task of digging the
ground, and to continue this exertion for fourteen days.
Then came a rupture of a vessel of the lungs, followed
by the incredible folly of undertaking in that condition
the task of instruction, which involved the necessity of
talking nearly all day. When the mischief had reached
its climax, he had recourse to Edinburgh advice. He
was at this time past forty; and if we were to trust
" the wisdom of many and the wit of one," we must
pronounce that, as he was not a physician he was a fool.

But Combe was no fool: he was only an enthusiast; in whom a hot desire to hasten forward the business in hand, prevailed over all the whispers of discretion: he was an earnest philanthropist, ready to sacrifice his business, his time and his person, to the carrying out a project, destined as he hoped to regenerate humanity, but requiring at first the fostering care and the unsparing exertions, of those who had commenced it. In Edinburgh he learnt for the first time, something of the structure and use of his lungs; and then he stood aghast at his own folly. I cannot wonder at his wish, that of the five years he had devoted to the study of Latin, one month had been applied to instruction in anatomy. However, after giving his lungs perfect rest for a fortnight, he returned to Orbiston in comparative health: and he continued to improve till August, when continued exposure to a draught of wind brought on violent inflammation of the lungs, which left him in a weakly condition from which he never rallied. He looked death in the face with a stoical firmness, and though tried by pain and weakness, revolved his past life, and dictated his own epitaph to his son of thirteen in the following words :—

> His conduct in life met
> The approbation of his own mind at the
> Hour of death.

He said that the last five or six years, during which he had been actively engaged in promoting the welfare of his kind, had been a period of delight; whereas his earlier life, in which he had thought of himself alone,

had been dreary and barren : and he added that were
his life offered to him over again, he would gladly accept
those felicitous five or six years and decline the rest.
He died on the 27th August 1827, in the confirmed
belief of the superiority of Owen's new system, over
the old system that actually prevailed; and in an unshaken expectation of the success of socialism.   I do
not believe that if Combe had lived he could have
saved his darling community : but his death was the
death-blow of Orbiston.

The origin of a nation is commonly hidden from us
by thick clouds of myth and tradition : the conclusion
of an unsuccessful project is generally equally impenetrable.   But in this case, through the kindness of
Mr. Pare,* I am able to satisfy the curiosity of the
lovers of a *dénoûment*. During Abram Combe's long
illness, his brother William had acted as his substitute.
Abram died at the end of August, 1827.   Within a
month of this calamity, there appeared in the *Glasgow
Chronicle* a letter complaining of the management at
Orbiston : to which William Combe replied, that the
best answer to the invective, was the success of the
project.   But he must have either deceived himself, or
wilfully put too good a face on a sinking concern; possibly in the hope to resuscitate it by his boldness : for
within a month of the date of his letter, he gave the
whole of the population notice to quit, allowing them
only a few weeks to make their arrangements.   In
November accordingly, the date fixed by the notice,

---

* Owen's literary executor.

and only three months after Abram Combe's death, most of the co-operators left Orbiston and returned to the world without.

It will be remembered that by Abram Combe's arrangement, the land, buildings, and plant, were the property of a company, which let the whole to the co-operators as tenants, and it seems, as tenants at will. The working community, therefore, was liable to be turned out at any time; and the sudden displacement was a result that was always contingent. I cannot believe that the benevolent and theoretical persons who constituted the company of proprietors, would have acted in this harsh manner: but something has been said about a mortgage for 16,000*l.* which hung on the estate; and probably it was the mortgagees who, failing the payment of interest, seized on the security. This may explain William Combe's apparent inconsistency; because he may have overlooked this danger.

In the year 1828, the tenants having mostly departed, the standing crops were sold, the furniture and plant were put up to auction, and in the end the buildings, being utterly useless, were razed to the ground. This result was a strange comment on Abram Combe's assertion, that as far as the proprietors were concerned, failure was all but impossible. He said*
that joint-stock companies sometimes received no income for many years, or even altogether lost their capital: but that as to Orbiston, it was impossible to conceive any circumstances under which fertile land,

* *Sphere of Joint-Stock Companies,* p. 63.

commodious dwelling-houses, convenient workshops or manufactories, and the best machinery, could become of little or no value. Three years later, and though the land remained, the houses and factories were so valueless that they were pulled to pieces.

Mr. Pare has expressed, no doubt, the sense of the co-operative world, in saying that the experiment was "as wrongly begun, and ill conducted, as it was abruptly ended."*

* Mr. Pare refers to *New Moral World*, vol. iii., corroborated by much private information.

CHAPTER XXV.

Owen at Cincinnati—At Washington a National Peacemaker—In London: Mission continued—Activity in London—Anti-Sabbatarianism—Equitable Labour Exchange.

AT the conclusion of my twenty-third chapter, I left Owen embarking for the West Indies, on his way to the United States. Having reached New Orleans in safety, he proceeded up the Mississippi; and after spending five days at New Harmony, went on to Cincinnati, to fulfil the engagement he had made, to enter on a discussion with a Rev. Mr. Campbell. At the appointed time, April 1829, the joust took place. Owen, with his twelve propositions, concocted on the voyage from Falmouth to Vera Cruz, presented what he regarded as an impenetrable front: Campbell appealed to what his antagonist called the prejudices of his audience: each combatant stated his own opinions rather than controverted those of his 'antagonist: both sides claimed the victory.*

From Cincinnati Owen travelled to Washington, " to proceed with his mission of peace between Great Britain and the United States." His friend Mr. Poinsett, had not forgotten the promise given in Mexico, that he

* *New Moral World,* i. 50, Oct. 10, 1835.

would urge his Government to give Owen an attentive ear. Van Buren in 1829 was rising in power, and filled the office of Secretary of State under " Old Hickory." He was deeply impressed with Owen's views of international policy; and was so desirous of constant conversation that the two gentlemen almost lived together. At last, Van Buren professing himself a thorough convert, arranged that President Jackson should receive them both at dinner. Jackson was a taciturn person; but after a long disquisition from Owen, he professed that however much the British might regard him as their enemy, nothing would give him greater satisfaction than a cordial alliance between the two countries, for the promotion of rational liberty throughout the world. Such a declaration from a diplomatic person, was of little value; but the same cannot be said of the continued attention which Van Buren had exhibited. Still, there was Owen's usual extravagance of hope, when he indulged an expectation of " cementing a cordial, permanent, national friendship " between the two nations: as though the puny efforts of any one man, could turn the course of the streams of national interests, affections, hatreds, and prejudices. He immediately afterwards sailed for Europe, furnished with letters from Van Buren addressed to the new American ambassadors to England and France.

In London, Lord Aberdeen, then Foreign Secretary, granted Owen an interview; listened patiently to his extra-official recommendation of international 'policy;

and declared, with, I doubt not, perfect sincerity, that if President Jackson's new ambassador came furnished with pacific instructions, nothing should be wanting on the part of the British Government, to settle all the disputes between the two nations. Owen states that when this assurance was communicated to the new American ambassador on his arrival here, negotiations were at once commenced, and issued in the settlement of all existing disputes. When our grandsons see the publication of the state papers of thirty years ago, they will estimate the services rendered by Owen, more accurately than is possible for us: but we shall be safe in saying that this spontaneous negotiation of his, was highly honourable both to his good intentions and to his diplomatic skill. It confirms the opinion that he possessed a singular power of influencing men of high political station. His earnestness, his sincerity, his placidity of temper, won the confidence of excellent men like Lord Aberdeen, to whom his socialistic notions were abhorrent.

It was about this time that Owen's connection with New Lanark finally ceased. He was now looking forward to the repeal by the Mexican Congress, of the restrictive laws as to religion; and to the consequent confirmation of the Texan grant. Pending this, his exertions took the direction of public meetings and lectures: he was surprised to find that England had made a great advance during three years, as to liberality in religion and politics: and he was gratified with the assurance of intelligent men, that they were looking forward to a general change in the social system. This statement being interpreted into vulgar language, means I conceive, that Owen's partisans had increased in number. News arrived from Mexico, that a change of parties had destroyed his hopes of becoming governor of a principality: but he consoled himself with his extended influence in Great Britain, and with the reflection that the world would be far more affected by his success at home than by his success abroad.

Owen was now not very far from threescore years of age, but with activity unimpaired, and with his time much at his command: his partnership at New Lanark having determined; the mutilated society at New Harmony having ceased to be inviting; Orbiston having passed from his hands; and the magnificent Mexican project having proved an abortion. He resolved to devote himself to the instruction of the working classes of London, to prepare them for the mighty changes he still hoped to effect. He reflected that the only regular leisure of busy men was on Sunday. This day had hitherto been set apart for religious instruction, and he well knew that to seize on any part of it for other purposes, would excite the bitter animosity of the educated classes: but he looked upon this feeling as springing from prejudice of a kind most injurious to the welfare of men; and therefore, he without scruple, set himself against it in the prosecution of his scheme of instruction. He commenced a course of secular teaching at the Mechanics' Institute, Southampton Buildings. After a short time an opposition was stirred up; and of about 1,000 members 140 were induced to vote against a continuance of the Sunday lectures, while the remaining 860 forbore to take any part, fearing as Owen conjectured, to incur the anger of their employers: a notion which unsupported by any proof, has to me very little the appearance of truth. Owen then removed to the "Sans Souci Institution," Leicester Square: and afterwards bought a chapel in Burton Street, Burton Crescent, where he gave continual lectures to crowded audiences.

Among his disciples was one Bromley,* the possessor of large premises in Gray's Inn Road, called the Bazaar. Bromley pressed upon Owen the gratuitous use of his building; and the offer being with some hesitation accepted, an additional congregation was assembled there. Owen was struck with the suitability of the Bazaar, for a place in which there might be effected an equitable exchange of productions, on the principle of labour for labour. The notion of such barter he had already explained: it was understood and appreciated; and several places of exchange were established elsewhere. The congregation assembling at the Bazaar, finding themselves distanced in the noble race of social improvement; and urged by the not very prosperous condition of the times, together with a rather high price of bread; impatiently pressed Owen to let them also try the experiment. Relating the circumstances several years afterwards, he says that he represented to his clamorous friends, and to Bromley the most clamorous,

* *New Moral World,* i. 395. Oct. 10, 1835.

that there could be no hopes of success without considerable capital and much preparation. But the disciples would not wait, and the well-known " Equitable Labour Exchange in Gray's Inn Road" was begun.

CHAPTER XXVI.

THE few remarks which I made at the close of my last short chapter, on the subject of the "Equitable Labour Exchange," present that institution to us in a light very different from that in which it appeared to the public during the period of its existence. Nor do I conceive that this difference is any proof of inaccuracy, or of deceit, in either account: for every public transaction has its internal and its external face; and the publication of "private and confidential" despatches, commonly gives a new colour to affairs conducted even by the most honourable men.

I should notice also, that the events crowded into a few sentences in Chapter XXV., really occupied a considerable period. It was in 1829 that Owen returned from the United States, big with his laudable

project of international brotherhood: it was not till
June 1832 that equitable banks of exchange were introduced in London.

My principal authority for this period is the *Crisis;*
a penny, unstamped paper, on co-operative topics,
avowedly "edited by Robert Owen:" of which the
first number appeared on the 14th of April 1832.
The name was bestowed on the ground that a great
change in the condition of man was imminent: that a
momentous *crisis* was at hand.   The paper started with
excellent prospects; the subscription list, before going
to press with the first number, being for nearly 9,000
copies.   When indeed, we compare this sale of a
weekly journal, with the daily circulation by scores of
thousands, of the present ordinary newspapers at the
same price, we must feel that Owen's influence was very
limited, and was far from having such an extent as to
cause just alarm to the partisans of things as they were.
A really popular prophet, about to preach with success
the overthrow of existing institutions, should have
counted his friends by hundreds of thousands.

The policy of Owen and his followers at this time,
had undergone a considerable modification, though their
principles remained unchanged.   They confessed* that
without arrangements difficult to effect, agricultural
communities such as those that had been tried in the
United States, could not proceed long without fatal
dissensions: and they recommended for this reason the
founding of co-operative societies, in which working

* *Crisis*, i. 47, 3.

men should combine to buy the necessaries of life at wholesale prices, and undertake gratuitously the task of distributing the commodities among themselves. Every man his own shopkeeper! was the cry. It was hoped that the retailer's profit thus saved, would be set aside to form a fund, with which hereafter to found true communities. A great many of these co-operative stores were in fact established; and many of them had a continued existence. Nearly twenty years later, the *Christian Socialists* were surprised to find a great number of such institutions in England and Scotland. In many cases they were no doubt, useful; as leading to a combination for a beneficial purpose, and as tending to check the pernicious practice of buying from shops upon credit. But with a few exceptions, such as the eminent one of the "Rochdale Equitable Pioneers," even the primary object of buying at a cheaper rate, was not accomplished: the ignorance of the purchasers exposing them to be preyed upon by the London or Liverpool wholesale sellers. I say this, not from conjecture or inference, but from facts which I have found stated without contradiction, in the honest pages of the *Christian Socialists'* publications. As to the imagined funds to be raised by these means, for the purpose of founding communities, these never came into existence, except in the untutored imaginations of the writers in the *Crisis:* and it is really wonderful that men could be found to indulge such expectations.

On the 16th of June 1832, the *Crisis* brought out a new scheme, of " Equitable Banks of Exchange." The

arguments by which the scheme was supported, consisted
of a curious medley of the doctrines of the Attwood
school of paper currency, and of the declamations of
radical orators against machinery. It was confessed
that nothing could or ought to prevent the growth of
machinery; but it was alleged that as this increase
went on, the wages of labour must continually fall
lower and lower (a purely gratuitous statement): and
that poverty, vice, and misery would disorganize society.
But a partial remedy, and a very easy one, was at
hand, in the substitution of "a perfect medium of exchange to supersede the present imperfect and unjust
standard of value, in the form of gold and silver coin,
or in bank-notes representing such coin." By means of
Equitable Banks of Exchange, to be established in every
corner of the kingdom, this new medium could be established; and it was warranted to possess the excellent
qualities of increasing or diminishing in proportion to
the variations of commodities to be distributed, and of
being unchangeable in value.

· On the 30th of June 1832 appeared an account of a
public meeting held for carrying out, *inter alia*, this
project. It was then resolved to form an Association of
"the intelligent and well-disposed of the industrious
classes," together with enlightened and benevolent men
of all ranks and parties, in order to "employ beneficially
and educate usefully, all who are unemployed and uneducated in the British empire." Truly, a Herculean
task! Of the measures agreed to be pursued, the sixth
was, "to receive provisions, clothing, and other pro-

perty, and services of every description, to be exchanged on the equitable principle of *labour*, for *equal value of labour*, through the medium of *labour-notes*." But as these notes would not pass current in the market; and as therefore, a man with his pocket full of them, might be unable to buy a loaf of bread at an ordinary shop; it was resolved to establish a bank "in which to exchange the labour-notes for the currency of the country."

It must be remarked as to the former of these two resolutions, that it was not intended to exchange labour for an equal *quantity* of labour, but for an equal *value* of it: that is, a day's work at picking oakum was not to exchange for a day's work at watchmaking. If the watchmaker's day had a value twice as great as the oakum-picker's day, the labour-notes awarded would be in the same proportion. And when each of these men had exchanged his labour note at the proposed bank, for the currency of the realm, the watchmaker would go home with 5s. to the oakum-picker's 2s. 6d. How were the respective values to be estimated? Doubtless by the ordinary rates out of doors. And of what service was the labour rate? Why not pay the 5s. and the 2s. 6d. at once? It might be answered that within the small circle of the co-operators themselves, these notes would pass as currency, and the use of so much gold and silver would be saved. And this very small imitation of the economy of money effected by bankers' cheques and by the clearing-house, is the only possible advantage that I can see in the arrangement: an advantage of a minute kind, and scarcely in the contemplation of the projectors.

But there is one grand omission, which is at the bottom of all the errors of the socialists, and which would of itself vitiate this whole scheme: I mean the disregard of the claims of capital. All wealth, say the socialists, is the produce of labour: why should the capitalist come in and take toll? The answer is easy. All wealth is *not* the produce of labour. To produce wealth, self-denial as well as labour, is necessary: and the man who by restraining his appetites accumulates stock and applies it to production, is entitled to a part of the commodities which have come into existence by the help of this stock or capital. A savage who should spend a month in constructing a pitfall, and should allow another wild man to use it, might fairly require a portion of the game caught. If a manufacturer construct, or cause to be constructed, a machine by which cloth is made with less labour, he is entitled to a part of the cloth produced. He might have spent his own time in pleasure, and might have employed domestic servants instead of machine makers: his self-denial has accumulated a capital by which cloth is made more easily: shall not he enjoy part of the benefit? But the Equitable Labour project makes no mention of capital: labour is to be trucked for labour; and there is no place for self-denial. We might ask also, how were "services of every kind" to be exchanged? For how could services be rendered?

There is a frightful complexity about the whole

scheme. First a man's labour is to be valued, as it is among us the profane: then he is to receive, not money, but a labour note; which document he may, if he pleases, take to the Bank and exchange for money. But here is another opportunity for confusion, and one eagerly embraced. How shall the labour-note be drawn? Shall it acknowledge that Thomas Jones has effected labour to the value of 5s.? By no means: that would be a simple proceeding: and simplicity, as we all know, is the bane of business. It shall be stated in the note, that Thomas Jones has effected ten hours' labour. But when this note is presented at the bank, how shall the clerk cash it? He cannot pay in hours. No: but he is instructed to pay at the rate of 6d. an hour; and so Thomas Jones receives ten times 6d., or five shillings. Now here is Benjamin Smith, a skilled mechanic; who has worked only five hours; but then his time is twice as valuable as Thomas Jones's, and his half-day's work has to be remunerated as highly as Thomas Jones's whole day's. How then is Benjamin Smith's note to be drawn? If he takes to the bank a note for five hours, he will get only 2s. 6d., whereas he is entitled to 5s. The remedy is easy. He has only worked five hours, but give him a note for ten; and then at the bank he will get his 5s. The "hour" therefore, at the Equitable Labour Exchange, did not mean a real hour's labour: it meant a conventional hour. If I am again asked, why was not money put at once in the notes instead of hours, I can only reply once more that men of business dread simplicity.

One manifest difficulty was, the just valuation of the goods presented.   Any one might bring in anything whatever, and receive a labour-note for it.   A draper might send the goods remaining from the last season, refused by his customers for their hideousness: the iron-monger might send his hardware which had been super-seded by some new patent article: the lamp-maker might trundle in a cartload of argand and solar lamps, when camphine and moderators had displaced them: the baker might furnish bread as stale and dry as remain-der biscuit.   Who should set a value on the miscellaneous deposits?   Owen was guilty of strange sophistry when he said, that if the objection were raised, of too much being left to the honour of the depositor, "the same re-mark may be applied with equal justice to short weight and measure, when persons are desirous of committing a fraud."   In carrying on a business, however, a buyer does not trust to the honour of the seller as to weight and quantity, but tests his accuracy by scales and mea-sures; and this protection would no doubt, be resorted to by the managers of the Labour Exchange.   The gist of the objection was this: that there is no fixed standard, no aliquot part of the earth's circumference, no admea-surement of distilled water at a certain temperature, by which the worth of an article can be ascertained; and that therefore, there was room for dishonourable misre-presentation on the part of the depositor.   The difficulty soon exhibited itself in practice.

At first of course, the means of valuation would be very imperfect; and practically, much would be left to

the honour of depositors.   We cannot therefore wonder
at a caution given to all persons concerned.   These
were told that there was absolute necessity for integrity
in all their proceedings; "the success of the undertaking depending entirely upon the most pure faith and
honour:" and it was recommended that if any attempt at
deception should be made, the offending person "should
be made acquainted with the prejudicial effects of such
conduct, not only to himself, but to thousands who may
be receiving the benefits of the society; and that in case
of a second attempt by the same person, he should be
expelled:" a recommendation quite inconsistent with the
sophistical assertion I quoted above; since in matters of
weight and measure, so high a standard of morality is
not necessary, however desirable it may be.   In short,
a project, depending for success on the pure faith and
honour of the members generally, is at once destined
to fail.   There is in all classes of society, much kindness, much generosity, much sympathy : but unbending
integrity and high honour are rare in every class, and
are seldom found among illiterate, needy persons.

Owen however, could see no difficulty in the project,
or would not see any in presence of the public.   He
asserted * that "to men of business who are accustomed
to reflect, the whole operation will appear plain and
simple."   And he regarded the Equitable Labour
Exchange, as the first of a series of measures, to promote a rapid increase of wealth by facilitating exchanges
upon equitable principles.   Great were his expectations

* *Crisis*, i. 66, 2.

as to results: for he declared that as soon as the public
saw the plan carried out in one or two well-conducted
examples, they would rush into the adoption of it, to
the destruction of the existing modes of carrying on
business.   Owen's rashness of prophesying was marvellous and incurable.

Early in September 1832,[*] there appeared a long
"catalogue of rules and regulations" for the government
of the Exchange: announcing in the first place, that
the capital should be unlimited; then that the surplus
funds should be applied to furnishing employment and
education: afterwards giving instructions as to members,
trustees, treasurers, management, council, governor and
directors, nomination of officers, mode and time of balloting, and general meetings: an elaborate skeleton.

On the 3rd of September 1832, before this constitution was published, the Exchange was opened for the
reception of goods.   The report three weeks later was,
that deposits poured in, and that exchanges by means of
the labour-notes had been going on several days.   The
notes had been made at a great expense and in an
admirable manner, so as almost to defy forgery.   The
boast of the week was that the coin of the realm had
been refused in payment for goods, although at the same
time, any one might exchange coin for labour-notes, and
thus buy at pleasure.   The deposits had been so extensive, that on the Thursday evening it had been necessary to decline any more until the following Monday.
The first portion of the experiment was successful;

* _Crisis_, i. 105.

goods of one sort or other, were largely brought in:
the second and more difficult remained to be tried;
would the goods go out again into the hands of purchasers?

Let us pass on to the 13th of October. The number
of deposits is still large. On the previous Monday
morning, an impatient crowd had surrounded the doors
long before the hours of business; and it had been found
necessary to alter the arrangements, in order to relieve
the footpath of Gray's Inn Road from the obstructing
throng. A singular resolution had been adopted, probably from necessity. There had been a vast number
of trifling deposits, involving valuations, issues, and
entries innumerable: and so, to the vexation of the
needy class of people, it had been determined to receive
no article of less value than twenty shillings. A week
later this regulation was praised, though it had caused
great dissatisfaction: by the 10th of November it had
been repealed.

Difficulties of course, there were. Besides the satisfactory obstructions caused by the multitude of deposits,
there was grumbling about the valuations made. A
tailor wrote to the *Times*, stating that he was a poor
unemployed journeyman, and that he had been induced
to borrow 2*l.* to purchase materials, with which he had
made a coat and taken it to the "Bazaar." After waiting three days, he got labour-notes for 36*s.*: so that he
lost 4*s.* by the transaction, besides all his labour. The
reply given in the *Crisis* is this. All the goods deposited are valued below their price outside: and the

tailor in question is not injured by the transaction, since the goods he would take out of the Exchange for his labour-notes are valued at an equally low rate. This reply was disingenuous, and I might say absolutely false. If the labour-note reckoned at 6*d.* an hour, was really worth more than 6*d.* an hour, it would follow that outside the Exchange, the notes would be at a premium: and a note for twenty hours, reckoned at 10*s.* inside the walls, would fetch 11*s.* or 12*s.* outside. But it was never pretended that the notes were at a premium. Indeed it was confessed on the 3rd of November, that they were received by only some shopkeepers, and by them unwillingly, even at par:* and by the 3rd of January 1833, only four months after the first opening, the notes had fallen so much below par, that several associations of working men had been formed to correct the evil. The reply given to the tailor therefore, was untrue: and it would have been far better to investigate the case and correct the valuation if it proved false.

In the midst of all the hubbub of the Exchange, the question naturally occurs: what is effected beyond what is done by the ordinary mode of buying and selling? This question was asked and answered, by one who chose to see with his own eyes. On the 3rd of November 1832, it was announced in the *Crisis*, that Owen's time was so much engaged with the Labour Exchange, that he wanted time to perform his duties as editor; and that his eldest son Robert Dale Owen, who happened

* *Crisis*, i. 137, 2.

to be in London, had become his substitute. About two months later,* the new editor gave an answer to the question I have asked, and said that the Exchange principle, " abstractly considered," had three great advantages: first, that the producer obtained at once, without effecting a sale, an *immediate* representative of his produce; secondly, that the profit of dealers, or middlemen, was reduced from twenty, fifty, or a hundred per cent., to eight and one-third per cent.; thirdly, that the valuation was made by disinterested persons. These advantages might be great, but it is not easy to see that they are identical, or even equivalent, with what was proposed by the establishment of the Exchange: viz., that every man should obtain for his labour an equal value of labour. Much less do they seem identical with the first avowed aim of Owen, to substitute labour-notes, varying in quantity but unchangeable in value, for the imperfect medium of gold and silver, or their representatives. The principles in short, seem singularly perplexed and uncertain. I think I understand, though I do not approve, the fundamental notions of socialism, and the fundamental notions of communism: but as to those of the Equitable Labour Exchange, I am a good deal in the dark, and do not think it worth my while to grope my way to the light. Owen himself felt that the scheme had not proved to be what he intended. He said † that really in this its first stage, its infant and imperfect state, it was little better than a superior pawnbroking establishment; but that he hoped it was

* *Crisis*, ii. 5, 2. † Ibid. i. 174, 2.

proceeding to the second stage of a retail trade, and
that it would ultimately become a wholesale trade: a
great falling off from first expectations!

While this doubtful success was achieved in London,
Owen was cheered by a cordial reception elsewhere,
and especially in Birmingham. At this time the Reform Bill had not passed many months; and the Political
Union of Birmingham, which had occupied a very prominent place in the country during a protracted agitation, was not yet dissolved, although greatly weakened.
The minds of the men who boasted that they had
carried " The Bill," had not yet subsided into their
ordinary repose; but were eager for a repetition of the
stimulants they had enjoyed. When Owen appeared,
he was met by eight thousand people, as he thought:
the largest and most gratifying assembly he had ever
seen. It was resolved by all classes of the audience,
without a dissentient voice, that it was desirable to
establish Equitable Labour Exchanges on a grand
scale; with a central establishment in London, and
branches throughout Great Britain and Ireland: and
further, that the first branch should be at once set afoot
in Birmingham. Owen was induced to remain that he
might be present at a public dinner, in order to keep
alive the enthusiasm. All went swimmingly. The
branch was started, and more money was at once
raised for maintaining it, than had been raised altogether in London. I could show, if I were not afraid
of being tedious, that this branch was carried on with
much caution, the managers being instructed by the

experience of Gray's Inn Road, and being men of ability and accustomed to business. It ultimately broke down however, like all the other attempts.

In the meantime the London Exchange was going on, and a large amount of business was done; the weekly deposits by the end of December being at the rate of 50,000*l.* a year. But difficulties were at hand. According to Owen's account * already quoted, the scheme was forced into a premature existence by his followers, contrary to his wishes. This undue haste may account for the careless way in which the agreement was made about the premises where the Exchange was carried on. They belonged, it will be remembered, to Mr. Bromley, who offered them and even pressed them on Owen, for the promotion of co-operative projects. Owen understood that no charge was to be made for the use of them; but Bromley asserted that the gratuitous use of them was intended to be only temporary, and that after a few months a reasonable rent must be paid. Then came haggling about the amount: Bromley demanding at the very lowest, 1,400*l.* a year; adding to which 300*l.* a year for taxes, the Exchange would have to pay 1,700*l.* a year for premises only.

It was therefore determined to leave Gray's Inn Road, and to carry on the business at the Surrey Institution, Blackfriars. Various rumours reflecting on the Exchange were immediately afloat, but the confidence of depositors was unshaken. This was early in January

* *New Moral World,* i. 395.

1833. The removal however, was not to take place
without difficulty. A dispute arose between Bromley
and his tenants, about various matters ; but principally
about the fixtures, for which Bromley had received 700*l.*
out of Owen's private purse, and which were now claimed,
but as to some of them ineffectually : partly also about
ground-rent, which the company had paid for Bromley,
under fear of an execution from the landlord. So hot
was the quarrel, that Bromley resorted to violence to
prevent the removal of the property. As soon as the
Exchange was fairly off the premises, a bazaar was
opened on a similar principle, as a private speculation.

The removal to the Surrey Institution, Blackfriars,
was only intended for a temporary resource, until a more
suitable place could be found. Owen soon took other
premises in Charlotte Street, Fitzroy Square, with a
deposit office in John Street. Pending the opening, the
managers framed and adopted a new constitution, fitted,
as they thought, to correct the evils which experience had
brought to light. Persons were now invited to become
members of an association for carrying on the Exchange,
and none would be admitted without proof of good character: so that the idle, the fraudulent, and the utterly
destitute, would be excluded. Members were required
to pay in advance 1*s.* a quarter for their privilege.
Persons not members might tender deposits; but as the
receiver was at liberty to demand that a member's ticket
should be shown by the depositor, there was really a
power of refusal reserved. Members therefore, were
the only persons who could make an indefinite quantity

of deposits. And they had another privilege of far higher moment. From the first establishment, the depositors, generally persons of small means, sent their goods with the wish to take provisions in return, if not wholly, yet to a large extent. But it was difficult to get farmers, butchers, or millers, to deposit their commodities, as they naturally preferred selling them out of doors for cash. So early as November 1832, it was announced, as a thing worthy of notice, that a particular baker had agreed to send bread; but on condition that he should receive half cash in payment; and to make the arrangement possible, it was required that depositors who required provisions, should pay half cash for them. But under the new constitution, in March 1833, it was ordered that members should have the preference as to provisions, and that no stranger should take any provisions until every member who wanted them, was served.

The new constitution worked after a fashion until July 1833, a period of almost four months; and then difficulties were again confessed. These were said* to have arisen probably, from the "inefficient organization of the conductors, a matter, not of reproach, but as it were, a temporary inconvenience which ever attends the novelty of change in human affairs." The editor thought that it would now be easy for the working class, under Owen's sanction, to reconstruct the entire arrangements, and to establish confidence. But these perpetual changes boded no good. Besides this, the conductors took it ill that their efforts should be thus publicly

* *Crisis*, ii. 212, 221, 224.

censured; and they replied that the difficulties had really arisen from the niggard behaviour of those who had promised capital and withheld it; as well as from the unfortunate circumstances attending the removal, added of course to want of experience. Adversity too often leads to recriminations, and is not likely to be removed by them. The experiment was evidently drawing to a disastrous close.

Owen must have been deeply grieved at this failure. To add to his annoyances, he had to undergo the penalty of censure as the governor of the concern. His pecuniary sacrifices and his labours were forgotten; and at a meeting of "trades' delegates," a speaker, in his very presence, congratulated his friends on the fact that the working classes had wrested the management out of Owen's hands. They would now show the world and Mr. Owen what they could do.

Owen's loss was considerable. He had persuaded himself, as we have seen, that Mr. Bromley had offered the Gray's Inn Road premises to be used permanently, rent free; and he had not taken the common precaution of a promise in writing. But he had consented to act as governor of the institution, on the undertaking (verbal only I presume) of the persons engaged with him, that no expense or risk should fall on him. The sudden removal however, caused a considerable loss: some of the goods deposited altogether disappeared :* that part of the stock which was over-valued would remain, and would have to be sold at a loss; and in one way or

* *Crisis*, ii. 230, 2.

other there was a confessed deficiency of 2,500*l.* For this large sum, the committee of management was responsible. But it was represented to Owen that it was the prominence of his name which had caused many persons to come forward: that the loss would be distressing to all, and to some positively ruinous. He therefore himself paid the entire amount; and only regretted the draft upon him, as limiting his means of promoting the good cause, and of assisting many applicants for assistance.*

It is amusing to read the excuses of anonymous writers, for undoubted failures. In the *Crisis* of the 7th of June, 1834, not written however, nor edited, by either of the Owens, it is stated that the Exchange in its old capacity had ceased to be. But this fact is not spoken of with regret. On the contrary, it is regarded as a step in the onward direction. For, says the editor, there may be too much of unity as of anything else: and co-operation might go so far as to tie us together so that we could not move a step. The trades were about to act independently instead of being conglomerated into one mass. Nor did this imply competition: since the tailor is not the rival of the shoemaker, nor the shoemaker of the carpenter. It is better that each trade should manage its business. I must again remark, that we must not lay this good sense at Owen's door: for he would no doubt, have repudiated it with indignation. It was not his custom to change his mind, or to profit by experience.

* *New Moral World,* i. 401, 2, Oct. 17, 1835.

CHAPTER XXVII.

Trades' Unions: Owen's Sympathy—Erroneous Grounds—The Dor-
chester Labourers—Thoughtless Conduct of the Trades' Unions
—Owen takes a Part: soon retires—Lost Sight of by the Public—
Obscure Activity—Denounced by Bishop of Exeter—Owen's
Irregularities in Publishing—Book of New Moral World: Maxim
—Owen's Monotony—Imminence of Social Change—Paternal
Government: Holy Alliance—Contempt of Learning—Visionary
Character.

ABOUT the time when the Equitable Labour Exchange
was drawing to a close in its last habitation, trades'
unions were fast spreading through the country. The
repeal of the laws against combinations had produced
its effect; and the working classes now did openly
and legally, what they had before done in corners and
by unlawful means. Owen had a strong sympathy
with the movement, as one tending "to arrest the
continually increasing oppression of the unproductive
classes over the industrious."

This statement, that the working classes were daily
more and more trampled down under the heel of the
capitalists, was one which Owen undoubtingly believed
and constantly repeated, but of which he offered no
proof. Had he taken the pains to investigate the question, he would have found that as machinery had
increased and become more efficient, wages had steadily

risen; and not money wages merely, but real wages, by which I mean the command over the necessaries of life. The condition of the labourer, both in town and country, has unquestionably improved considerably since the seven years' war, since the American revolution, since the wars of Napoleon. Although it were much to be wished that it had improved more, it is utterly false to say that it has deteriorated. Owen was misled by his desire to paint the present condition of the world in the blackest colours, in order to raise his proposed form of society into bright relief. I am bound to say however, that I have the same sympathy with trades' unions, combinations, and strikes, which he had. I deeply lament the folly, exaggeration, and violence, of which the associated men are often guilty; but after long observation and reflection, I am convinced that in many of the largest trades, the workmen cannot, without combinations and strikes, succeed in keeping up wages.

Owen had hitherto held aloof from these unions, believing, as he tells us, that they " were too much in their infancy, and too much under the control of inexperienced guides " to be effective in their action. But his feelings were aroused by the case of the " Dorchester labourers," imprisoned and sentenced for having passed the narrow boundary which separates lawful from illegal combination. I imagine that the prosecution against these poor men was properly instituted; but that the sentence, and the enforcement of it, were a severe exercise of authority. The minds of the people how-

ever, had been profoundly disturbed by the continued
efforts which had carried the Reform Bill : great
changes in every department of society were anticipated : a revolutionary spirit in short, was raging in
England.   Earl Grey's government resolved to put an
end to this excitement, at whatever cost; and these unfortunate Dorchester labourers offered themselves as a
sacrifice.   The poor ignorant men had, no doubt,
broken the law : they had been regularly tried, con-
victed, and sentenced, by a competent tribunal.   The
hardship was not that of passing an *ex post facto* law,
nor that of stretching an existing law.   The question
was ; should the Crown exercise its privilege of pardon-
ing ?   I cannot in my conscience approve the answering
this question by an appeal to policy; because I think
that a Crown pardon ought to be as much a part of the
administration of justice, as a trial and conviction are.
But what statesman has ever yet dared to act on abstract
principles ?   What minister has had the audacity to
reduce to practice the superb maxim, *fiat justitia, ruat
cœlum ?*

I do not wonder then, that Owen's sympathy was
aroused.   He became a member of the unions, and
when they determined upon a petition in favour of the
Dorchester labourers, and upon a grand procession to
enforce it, he put himself in communication with the
Ministry, after his usual careful fashion.   Lord Melbourne held a conversation with him, and strongly
recommended that the grand procession should not
pass the Home Office.   Owen thought this advice

reasonable, and offered to hold himself responsible for the peace of the metropolis, if the military and police forbore from interference. He reported to the committee of the procession, the wishes of Lord Melbourne, and urged the acceding to them: but he was opposed by one of the members, a man whom he describes as inexperienced, and quite incompetent to understand the strong position which might, with the help of prudence, have been assumed. As usually happens in democratic assemblies, the noisiest advocate was the most successful: the committee slighted Owen's advice and set Lord Melbourne at nought: the procession with insolent bravado, filed past the Home Office; and the fate of the convicts was sealed.

Owen however, was not driven away by this defeat. He had become accustomed to the excitement and turmoil of a certain kind of public life; and was no doubt, unconsciously disposed by the failure of his own measures, to lend himself to this scheme of extended unions. There was something of grandeur about the names, and even about the real aims, of the associates. Owen was elected at once Grand Master of the Miscellaneous Lodge; and soon afterwards, one of the delegates of a trades' union congress. When this body commenced its sitting, he was made chairman, and continued to fill that post during the sixteen days of the session. After a long but calm discussion, the Congress agreed upon a constitution for the Grand National Consolidated Union: and Owen says that it comprised " laws, rules, and regulations, more advanced in real civilization than

any code which had previously been adopted by any
public assembly." This praise from a man of such
eccentric notions as Owen's, may convince us that the
constitution would be pronounced by most of us, eminently utopian and whimsical. Owen, no doubt, proved
himself an excellent chairman : for at the conclusion of
the Congress, he was solicited almost unanimously, to
accept the high-sounding office of Grand Master of the
National Consolidated Trades' Union. But still smart-
ing from the losses he had suffered as governor of the
Equitable Labour Exchange, he declined the post ; and
when it was pressed upon him, he accepted it indeed,
but soon found sufficient reasons for retiring.

From this date for nearly twenty years, Owen's proceedings have little to interest people generally. The
Co-operators, or Socialists, as they came to be called,
still looked to him as their prophet, and from time to
time assembled and did him honour. But the world
outside this rather small circle, heard little of him, and
gradually forgot his existence. For his writings, when
not directed to some practical object, were of an unpopular character : and he had exhausted his power of
exciting the enthusiasm of rich and powerful men.
Once he had been capable of stimulating, by precept
and generous example, to the sacrifice of tens of thousands of pounds. If we may believe a French writer,
M. Louis Reyband, he had himself spent 40,000*l.* on
his philanthropic projects. These had failed : according to his friends, through accident, through the interference of others, through over-haste on his part,

through anything, in short, but want of soundness in principle: and socialism, or communism, was none the less practicable, and certainly none the less useful, because one man had missed his aim. But the public verdict was final; the schemes had failed: and the public is much of the same mind with Cicero, when in his oration for Pompey, he recommends that great general partly in that he was capable, but equally in that he was fortunate. Owen may have been a great general in the war against social corruption; but from the time he left New Lanark he was remarkably unfortunate: and so the public put him aside and would have no more of him.

But Owen was still busy among his friends, and has left abundant proof of his activity with his pen. He was ever ready, also, for co-operative meetings in London, Cheltenham, Manchester, Reading, Birmingham, and a thousand other places. He crossed and recrossed the Atlantic, with as little appearance of repugnance as most persons exhibit to a land journey of a few hundred miles. But the knowledge of these activities, was confined to a narrow circle: for the leading newspapers took no note of his proceedings, and his publications were not to be seen on the counters of respectable newsvendors.

In 1840 however, people generally were made aware of his continued existence. He had always, as we have seen, been rather a favourite of people in power; and in 1840, Lord Melbourne presented him to her Majesty. The Bishop of Exeter took advantage of this step to

utter one of his bitter philippics:[*] and after blaming
the impudence of Lord Melbourne in bringing such a
man as Owen into the precincts of the Court, he seized
the opportunity of denouncing the tenets and practices
of the Socialists and of their great leader. Especially
did he inveigh against what he called their "loathsome"
notions about marriage; which, said he, were really too
bad to bear to be published. I suspect the rough-
tongued prelate of using an artifice here to cover his
own ignorance : and I believe that if he had been
required to say what the socialistic notions about
marriage really were, he would have been silenced.
Co-operation and socialism, by no means involve any
weakening of the marriage tie. Communism it is true,
has been declared incompatible with marriage, by some
zealous communists. But there was nothing about
Owen's opinions which any one need shrink from repeating : since all he desired was a greater freedom of
divorce, under tolerably stringent limitations. Indeed,
the bishop himself was constrained by the force of
truth to distinguish Owen from his followers, and to
speak of him, not as a voluptuary, or as a vicious
person, but as a man peacefully inclined, and as an
unhappy visionary, possessed with an ill-regulated
desire to benefit his kind.

During a part of this period, the co-operative periodical called the *New Moral World*, was regularly published : but Owen was not responsible for what it contained, as he neither edited it nor wrote regularly for it.

---

[*] *Mirror of Parliament*, 1840, i. 316.

There was another work of a similar title, which was really his: the *Book of the New Moral World.* This was written in parts, but it is not easy to say what were the dates of the original publication; since Owen had a habit of reprinting his writings from time to time, without numbering the editions or giving any information about them. Easy circumstances placed him, as they had placed Swedenborg long before, in a peculiar situation as to his books. Most authors are dependent upon a publisher for bringing their productions into print; and the publisher, having the fear of the public before his eyes, insists on regularity in form and dates. But Owen, having determined to devote a large fortune to the good cause, could afford to indulge strange whims: reprinting his essays, or his report to the county of Lanark, in the midst of recent disquisitions; so that a purchaser of his publications finds himself in possession of several copies of the essays and other early compositions. The same licence has introduced the confusion of dates I have mentioned.

The *Book of the New Moral World,* as I have it, re-published in 1849, "complete in seven parts," has on its title-page the maxim, " truth, without mystery, mixture of error, or fear of man, can alone emancipate the human race from sin and misery." Owen's antagonists may fairly say, that on his own showing, the human race never will be emancipated from sin and misery; for that the searchers after truth, though they may aspire to freedom from mystery and fear of man, cannot even hope to be without mixture of error.

Whatever faults we may charge upon Owen, we must at any rate forbear from charging him with inconsistency. Indeed the uniformity of his teaching is painful to the reader; and in its want of relief and variety, resembles those vast prairies over which the young and buoyant Captain Head galloped five-and-thirty years ago, and which are so nearly on a dead level, that it requires long experience to detect the existence of any deviation. Such are Owen's publications: repetitions of each other so precisely alike, that when the dates are wanting, it would invite a tedious logomachy to decide which was of his youth, which of his old age.

At every period of time, the great change is imminent: the decisive experiment is about to be made: the *elixir vitæ* of society is all but found: let people beware how they commit themselves to the existing order of things, since the *New Moral World* is just bursting into being. In the dedication of this book to His Majesty William IV., Owen says that the old system with all its evil consequences, was about to pass away; and that there was on the verge of inauguration, a new system, " founded on self-evident truths, and insuring happiness to all." As a consequence, the names of His Majesty and of all who governed the nations of the world, would be "recorded as prominent actors, in a period the most important that has ever occurred in the history of mankind." Notwithstanding the scepticism of men, "the great circumstances of nature, and the existing state of human affairs, were ripe for the change."

Still also, was there the hankering after paternal

government, under which everything should be done for the people and nothing by them: under which all circumstances should be so exactly arranged, so nicely balanced, so precisely fitted into each other, that men, women, and children, must of necessity be wise, good, and happy; free from drunkenness and vice, contented, dutiful, and healthy in body and mind. So far did this go, that Owen had no scruple in praising the Holy Alliance, the bugbear of all liberal men. He said that at the close of the late war, " of what are called the civilized nations," an alliance was formed by the leading governments, to protect each other from national revolutions; *and it was a wise measure* to prevent premature changes in each state—changes desired by the people before they had acquired wisdom to give such changes a right direction."

Nor had the lapse of time corrected in Owen's mind, the false notion dear to him, as to most self-taught men, that the severe training of scholastic education is useless or even worse. Oxford and Cambridge, as well as the public schools, make it their especial business to teach the " languages, customs, habits, and ideas, *of barbarians.*" The Greeks and Romans barbarians! Homer and Horace, Demosthenes and Cicero, Alexander and Cæsar, Pericles and Pompey, Pythagoras, Plato, Aristotle, Brutus and Cato, all of them barbarians! Lycurgus indeed is excepted. He, in Owen's opinion, made a nearer approach than any other lawgiver, statesman, or philosopher, to the discovery of the true principle, that men are formed by circumstances, and may be trained to anything you please. "But excepting Lycurgus, no one appears to have had a conception of this first of all sciences; a science destined, and ere long, to ensure the permanent well-being and happiness of the human race."

The *Book of the New Moral World,* was written when Owen was fast approaching the commonly-assigned boundary of human life: and it seems that as an elderly, or old, man, he was the same unhesitating schemer, the same builder of new worlds, the same visionary enthusiast, that he had been in the maturity of his years. Now, as then, he pursued impossible projects, by impracticable means.

CHAPTER XXVIII.

Startling Passages: Spirits—Address from Spirits—Singular Senti-
ments—Spirits not Infallible—Compliment to Owen—Departed
Friends : Certainty of the Facts—Spirits of Parents: Religious
Truths—Special Providence—Yet denounces all Religions—Spirit
of Duke of Kent—Of others: Trivial Communications—How
Owen was converted—Table-turning—Owen's Disciples : his
Inconsistency—Apology—Was Owen in his Dotage ?—Owen's
Grounds of Belief—Stated by Himself—Actual Facts—The Table
Rapping—Extraordinary Replies to Unknown Questions—Owen's
Obstinacy—The Imposture Unveiled.

In reading Owen's *Autobiography*, a man of the coolest
temperament is startled by some passages. Thus at
the very onset,* in a fictitious dialogue between Owen
and " Inquisitor," answering a question : " What makes
you so confident of ultimate success ?" Owen says,
" The daily aid which I receive from superior spirits,
who promise effective assistance until success shall be
secured." Spirits! and Robert Owen! a man,

> " So wise
> And wary held, he scarce received
> For gospel, what the Church believed.

Yet when the respondent suggests that all this may be
a delusion, he replies, that other persons may think so ;
but that facts which he has witnessed, and which
thousands of others are daily witnessing, constitute

* Introduction xxxii.

evidence too strong to be upset by "inexperienced negations."

In the next page we are astonished at the systematic form of this spiritual world. Owen had received on the very day when he was writing, a communication from superior spirits in the United States, headed, "An Address to the world;" containing principles and practical instructions greatly in advance of the most advanced liberals of the day. We cannot wonder that Owen tenders his best thanks to the spiritual senders.

The address would be the more acceptable because the sentiments of its angelic authors are very much those of Owen himself; and because even the favourite expression of "the surroundings" of men is adopted. But to the uninitiated it is rather surprising to find angelic persons talking of "the crack of doom;" and still more so to see the juxtaposition of "the love of a Jesus, the boldness of a Paul,—the morals of a Socrates,—the eloquence of a Brougham, and the religion of a Madame Guyon."

Owen, however, though possessed with a deep reverence for these spiritual visitants, denies their infallibility, and states plainly that in one respect he differs from them. They seem to have been infected with the democratic tendencies of the country from which they addressed him; and accordingly they deny that there is reason to expect from governments any help in passing from a false system of society to a true one. I have remarked in several places, that Owen was much addicted to securing the sympathy and assistance of ministers of state : that he successfully cultivated the good opinion of personages of the highest rank : and that his principles of government were rather paternal than democratic. On this occasion he held fast to his opinions, and refused to receive the *ipse dixit* even of an angel.

The address, which covers six octavo pages, concludes with a gratifying compliment. The spirit world looked to Owen in the task of regenerating society : it knew his untiring fidelity : it rejoiced in his having reached a ripe old age : it saw him busily arranging his papers, and preparing his departure to a higher and diviner state : it felt confidence in his judgment and his fidelity, and was conscious of his desire to aid man as man.

But these communications did not come from the general spirit world merely; not only from beings in whom we feel a simply speculative interest : most gratifying and delightful manifestations also were given by departed friends and relatives. As to doubting their truth that was out of the question.* No one of sound judgment, possessed of a sincere desire to discover the truth, and who fully and fairly investigated the subject, could hesitate to believe that these messages of love and instruction were what they professed to be. Owen himself was "compelled by the evidence of his senses to know that spirits occupy spaces, by them called spheres; and that they communicate with their

* *Autobiog.* i. 199.

friends here on earth, in their natural character, except that they are not visible as when living."

One of the most interesting and important visitations to Owen was from his parents. He confesses that until this startling event happened, he had been quite un-aware of the necessity of good spiritual conditions for forming the character of men. The physical, the intellectual, the moral, and the practical conditions, he had understood, and had known how to provide for; but the spiritual he had overlooked. Yet this, as he now saw, was the most important of all in the future development of the human race. If he had neglected this formerly, it was because he had not enjoyed a sufficiency of divine light, until like Paul he was called to his work. He owed his conversion to the spirits of his father and mother, who kindly, and as it seemed most anxiously desired that he should see and know the truth of our future existence, "and the unimaginable glories and happiness of a never-ending, progressing, immortality." For once, Owen was found to confess himself mistaken in his early opinions.[*]

The language he uses in describing this manifesta-tion, and in commenting upon it, is strikingly different, both from that of his earlier days, and from that of his age when he speaks of religion generally. He says here,[†] that in looking back on his past life, " I can trace the finger of God, directing my steps, preserving my life under imminent dangers, and compelling me onward on many occasions." It was under the imme-

---

[*] *New Existence*, i. 15.   [†] Ibid. i. 16.

diate guidance of the Spirit of God, that during the inexperience of his youth he accomplished much good for the world. The preservation of his life from the peculiar dangers of his childhood, was owing to this inspiring Spirit. To this superior invisible aid he owed his appointment at the age of seven years, to be usher in a school, before the monitory system of teaching was thought of: to this he must ascribe his migration from an inaccessible Welsh county to London and then to Stamford, and his ability to maintain himself without assistance from his friends. So he goes on recounting all the events of his life great and small, and attributing them to the special providence of God.

Yet it must not be supposed that Owen had joined any particular sect, nor even that he had become a Christian. Within a year of his death, he used the strongest language in denouncing the existing theological systems.[*] He desired to declare in a voice of thunder, that "religion has ever been the bane of humanity, and the cause of all its crimes, irrationalities, absurdities, and sufferings; and that until these deadening superstitions, based solely on the irrational notion that man can do good to God, shall be removed root and branch from humanity, man will remain an insane fanatic and bigot; madly destroying, unconsciously, his own happiness and the happiness of his fellows." And again he says,[†] that all the time and money employed about religion are wasted, and evince gross ignorance on the part of those who spend them. But

* Autobiog. 1 a. iv.   † Ibid. 1 a. viii.

this apparent inconsistency was not caused by any second change of opinion: for a few pages later * he tells us, that " the wise and good Creator " has destined man to pass through the evils of the present system, no doubt, to fit him for a much higher and superior state of existence.

So much for the communications from Owen's father and mother. Next to these, the most interesting to him were what he received from the Duke of Kent. In the *Autobiography* we find mention of the " unspeakable gratification and happiness of being visited by the spirit of his Royal Highness;" who addressed † him in precisely the manner and phraseology of his life-time; speaking of his domestic relations, and giving valuable information about *the spiritual spheres,* and as to past events and personages. Owen was made aware ‡ that the duke, since his departure, has exercised a watchful fatherly care over her Majesty, his daughter, and her family, as well as over the interests of the British people: and that he has felt an affectionate brotherly sympathy with the King of the Belgians. We learn also,§ that the duke, living in spiritual spheres where titles are unknown, had a most anxious desire to benefit, not a class or sect or party, and not even a particular country, but the whole human race through all futurity. His conduct in these communications ‖ was entirely consistent with that of his lifetime—affectionate, considerate, and

* *Autobiog.* 1 a. xxv. † Ibid. 194. ‡ Ibid. i. 198.
§ Ibid. i. 199. ‖ Ibid. i. 229.

friendly: with appointments duly made of day, hour, and minute, and these punctually kept.

On many occasions, the duke's spirit manifested itself in company with that of President Jefferson, whom Owen surprisingly designates as his disciple as well as friend; and of the celebrated Dr. Franklin. These three furnished knowledge of great moment, together with notices of persons who when living were dear to them; and they never indulged in any trivialities. In one instance there was a gathering of these three, with Dr. Channing, Dr. Chalmers, Shelley, Lord Byron, and what is more astonishing, several of the old prophets; besides eight of Owen's own deceased relatives. One would expect some grand and various expositions from such high intellects and noble hearts: but to our disappointment, there is only the same uniform tale, of a desire to reform the world, and to unite the population as one family or as one man. Doubtless a great and worthy object: but it would have been more pleasing to us, if we had heard something of the sagacious understanding of Franklin, of the multitudinous eloquence of Chalmers, of the imaginative and wild beauty of Shelley, of the Greek enthusiasm of Byron, of the moral grandeur of the rapt seers of Israel. It is even painful to see what very small matters were disclosed through this great machinery. For example:* on the 12th of October, 1853, Owen was informed by the spirit of one Grace Fletcher, a kindhearted creature, what was the best way to cure a cold

* *The Future of the Human Race*, 19.

under which he was suffering: he was to have some beef-tea and go to bed; to put a bottle of hot water to his feet; to forbear from going out in the damp; above all not to forget the beef-tea and the warm wrappings.

In the year 1855, Owen published an account of the manner of his becoming a believer in these revelations.[*] He had called, two years before, at the house of a Mr. Hayden (afterwards Dr. Hayden), to buy a book explaining the spiritual manifestations in America: the author being the Rev. A. Ballou, a gentleman " universally known and esteemed throughout the United States, of high standing for ability, truthfulness, integrity, and a sound, calm, cautious judgment." Mr. Hayden having produced the book, said, while he was receiving the money for it, that his wife having heard much of Owen, was very desirous of seeing him. Now Mrs. Hayden was " a medium." Owen was shown into a room with a large dining-table and a good fire; and took the opportunity while he was alone, to satisfy himself that there was no machinery under the table or elsewhere in the room.

After a time Mrs. Hayden came in, and seated herself, as did her guest, near the fire and several feet from the table. Some conversation followed about common friends; when unexpectedly, there came some raps on the table, which were repeated with much urgency, as if to attract attention. Owen up to this time was not a believer, and had said nothing about

* *Address on Spiritual Manifestations,* 9.

spirits; but at last, when the uproar became so great as to interrupt the conversation, he asked what it meant. The imperturbable Mrs. Hayden, accustomed to the society of the invisible, and no more alarmed than is a grave-digger by churchyard ghosts, replied that certain spirits were bent on making a communication. Owen was astonished, because, as he says, he had not come for the purpose of spiritual intercourse. The raps continuing, he became anxious to know who were the authors of them; and the medium having kindly undertaken to inquire, found that they were "friends of Mr. Owen." "Most extraordinary!" replied Owen; and I confess to a participation in his surprise. Still the clatter went on, until he desired to know who these importunate people were, and consented to take the alphabet and ask their names.

"The spirits," said Mrs. Hayden, "will rap at particular letters, which you will take down, and see what word or name they will make." The first name was Robert Owen. What Robert Owen?—Your father. Are any other spirits present?—Your mother is with me. Give me her maiden name.—Anne Williams. Several other questions: when did each of them die? where? and other such puzzling matters. All being answered with perfect accuracy, Owen began to believe that there were in the universe things not dreamt of in his philosophy. He went home, studied Mr. Ballou's book, and found it full of well-attested facts backed by sober reasoning; and determining, very wisely, to investigate the subject further, visited the medium twenty to thirty times.

Owen found Mrs. Hayden "always truthful and simple minded," and her *séances* uniformly interesting and satisfactory. He visited other mediums, and one even more developed than Mrs. Hayden; who, as he learnt, ultimately arrived at such a stage of spiritualism, as to be able "in her normal state," to see and converse with her ghostly visitants. In short he became a zealous disciple of the new faith.

The belief extended itself to table-turning of course: and he indignantly censured "the absurd statements attempting to account for moving of tables and other ponderable materials, by imperceptible muscular power, or by the random conjectures of non-investigators, and of course unbelievers." The subject is too well worn to allow me to give more than two or three examples. On one occasion, after Owen had long been in company with fourteen superior spirits, while he and his friend in the body were near the door conversing together, "a large round heavy mahogany table," several feet distant from them, moved along the carpet towards them. At another meeting, when a third person was present, the table again moved; and "the medium" stated, and Owen implicitly believed, that "the spirits had often lifted that table several feet up from the floor." * In England at another time, Owen had his hand shaken by the warm fingers of a lady lately deceased; and a good many other strange unmeaning pranks were played.

This conversion to the faith and practice of the

* *Address on Spiritual Manifestations*, ii. 12.

extravagant spiritualists, was very unpleasing to his friends and disciples. The inconsistency was gross. In former days, Owen had been an unbeliever of the coarsest type: he had denounced (and indeed he continued to denounce) all the religions of the world, as unfounded and mischievous: he had dissuaded men from spending their time and efforts in preparing for the next life, when they might be labouring successfully to make this world a paradise: he had declared it absurd to offer to God services which could not possibly benefit Him: he had even spoken with great hesitation of the Power to which we owed our existence, as doubting the being of any personal divinity. These notions he had not kept within his own mind, or confined to the small circle of the initiated; but had blazoned ostentatiously abroad, and had published with as much zeal as most men employ in concealing sentiments so unpopular. His disciples had followed in the same track, and had become notorious for setting at nought the most cherished opinions of the world. And now Owen had become a believer in the land of spirits, in a future existence, in a glorious immortality; and not contented to wait for death as the portal to the world of shadows, employed himself in conversations with the tenants of Elysium.

The Owenites looked on with shame, at this defection of their prophet: much as the Israelites would have looked, if they had beheld Moses bowing down before the golden calf; or as the Arabs, if Mahomet had been seen carving an image of the Most High. They spoke of this folly as a passing cloud, which obscured for a time the brightness of their luminary; and they were willing to believe that fourscore years of age formed a sufficient apology.

It would indeed, be most unfair to judge Owen by this vagary when he was more than eighty years old: a time of life in which few men's intellects are unimpaired. Yet he certainly retained his powers of mind longer than most men; and up to the last, five or six years later than the date of his conversion, there is nothing in his writings to indicate absolute dotage, though there is an exaggeration of that want of order and precision which always characterized him. As late as 1851, when he was eighty, we have an impartial testimony to his state of mind and body. Mr. Horace Greely, a well-known American philanthropist, but not a disciple of Owen, stated * publicly, that " Owen has scarcely looked younger or heartier at any time these ten years; he did not seem a shade older than when I last before met him, at least three years ago. And not many young men are more buoyant in spirit, more sanguine as to the immediate future, more genial in temper, more unconquerable in resolution, than he is." That Owen was fresh, sanguine, and buoyant in 1851, is, I confess, no absolute proof that his mind was unimpaired in 1853. One other sentence in Horace Greely's letter is curious. He says that he cannot agree in many respects, with a man who is " stone blind on the side of faith in the Invisible;" on which

* *R. Owen's Journal,* ii. 80.

the editor of the *Journal* asks, whether it is really a defect to be blind to what is invisible: only two years later, however, Owen's friends had to apologize, not for his blindness, but for his childish credulity.

What were the grounds on which his faith rested? It would be an incomplete biography which failed to assign them. In September 1853, there appeared in the *Quarterly Review* an article, on " Electro-Biology and Mesmerism ;" in which " spiritual manifestations " were also discussed. Owen had intended* to publish a reply ; but he found that the writer was guided by " *dominant ideas* so far wide of the subject," and evincing so total an ignorance of the facts, that he abandoned this notion, and contented himself with stating certain propositions, under a conviction that the spirits themselves would in the end, clear the public mind for the reception of them. There were seven heads.

1st fact. The media† are the electric telegraphs used by the spirits, and are unconscious how they become such.

2nd. The media have no control over the spirits, but the spirits control them.

3rd. The media know not whether any spirit will come when they ask for one; or if one should come whether it will come immediately or after much delay.

4th. When a spirit comes, the media do not know what spirit it is, until, if to a rapping medium, it gives its own name by the alphabet.

* *The Future of the Human Race*, 16.   † Mrs. Hayden and others.

5th. When the name is given, the media have no knowledge what the spirit will say of its own accord, without any questions being asked—or, if questions are asked, what the replies will be.

6th. The media do not know how long any spirits will remain with them after the spirits have announced their presence.

7th. The spirits express themselves very much in accordance with their character when living upon the earth in the flesh.

It would not be fair to say that there is a begging of the question in every one of these seven statements: for it is not pretended that they constitute an answer to objectors.   Owen himself was satisfied of the truth; and he was indifferent to the disbelief of other persons, because he was certain that the spirits in their own time would convince the world.   A man who rests on the preternatural, is negligent of the weapons of reason and argument.

If Owen had desired to bring men to his new faith, he would have stated the mode of his own conversion. He went to Mr. Hayden's an unbeliever: his unsought interview with Mrs. Hayden startled him: he returned again and again, and was more convinced every time, of the absence of imposture and of the genuineness of the alleged miracles.   What was there in the proceedings, which accounts for this result?

It will be remembered that at the first visit, Owen had time, before the medium made her appearance, to examine the table and the room for concealed machinery, and that his inquisition convinced him of the absence of such a thing. When therefore, during the subsequent conversation, there came a reiterated and clamorous knocking, as of one claiming an audience, he was nearly persuaded, that there was something in presence, not to be accounted for by any known agency: the preternatural had at once, all but gained a convert. Had Owen ever seen a conjuror: a professor of natural magic? If he had, was there a single one of his tricks, which at first sight he could explain? Yet surely there was nothing in the mere fact of a noisy clatter on a table, half so marvellous as a common wizard's exhibition; a thing which no one imagines to be preternatural. Take Houdin's performances in Algeria.* He told one of the marabouts, or native wizards, that he should find a franc in his hand, close it as tight as he pleased. At a signal the marabout opened his hand, and the franc was not there. "Ah!" said Houdin, "I see I used too much force, and passed the franc through your hand into your girdle." The franc was found in the girdle. Houdin was fired at and caught the bullet in his teeth; and then discharging a gun, the wall was bespattered with blood. These and a hundred other feats, a man may see any day for a shilling: and yet Owen stood agape because there was a knocking on the table by an invisible agent.

It is true that another part of the performance was far more specious, and was really difficult of explanation. Owen asked questions about things which could

* *Westminster Review*, July, 1859.

scarcely be within Mrs. Hayden's cognizance. She might happen to know that the father at Newtown was named Robert, and that the mother was by birth a Williams: but it is acknowledged that other replies were often given such as could not have resulted from previous knowledge. Owen notices that the Duke of Kent's spiritual answers had the exact ring of his manner during his lifetime; though this taken alone, might perhaps have been attributed to the credulous fancy of the listener. On the whole, however, it is not disputed that there were frequent revelations of things, with which the medium could not have become acquainted in the natural course of events.

But there was another peculiarity in the case, which unexplained, might well stagger the wholesome scepticism of any but a very well-trained mind. Mrs. Hayden and the other mediums, did not even know what questions were put. When Owen asked what was his father's name, he did not speak this inquiry: he did not necessarily put it into words; he only thought the inquiry. How then, could the medium furnish the reply? How could Mrs. Hayden, by what exercise soever of ingenuity, tell Owen that his mother's maiden name was Williams, when she did not know that he was thinking about his mother? I do not wonder that Owen was imposed upon: I regard it as no sign of dotage that a man of imperfect early training, and possessed with a notion that the world and its beliefs were out of joint, should be impressed with so specious an exhibition.

But though I can excuse Owen's conversion, I cannot say so much for his continuance in belief after the jugglery was exposed. Wonderful as was the feat performed, it was but a trick after all. The discovery of the contrivance was due to Mr. G. H. Lewes; a gentleman to whom the world is much indebted, whatever may be thought of his philosophical opinions, for having, at a period when grave discussion is quite out of favour, devoted much labour to the study and abridged exposition of metaphysical questions. Clear however, as was the explanation of the deceit, Owen refused to be convinced.

The spiritual replies to the questions thought, were given thus:—The visitor was placed with an alphabet before him, and a pointer in his hand: and as he drew this along the letters, a rap from time to time told him at which to stop. All the letters thus noted, being put together, constituted the answer. Owen said to himself;—what was my mother's maiden name? With his pointer, he ran over the alphabet till he came to W; then came a knock: the second time of going over he was stopped at I: then at L: and so on till he had got all the letters of the name Williams. Mr. Lewes revolving the matter, felt certain that the medium derived the necessary information from the visitor. But how? Did the visitor, knowing what letter ought to be selected, involuntarily stop on coming to it, so as to give the spirit a chance? The suspicion was worth following out. Mrs. Hayden had come to London: Mr. Lewes visited her: he agreed with a friend on certain questions to be mentally asked, and on the answers to be obtained: he went and thought the questions: he paused with his pointer on the letters that would form the concerted answers: he received a rap at each pause: the letters so selected, when put together, formed answers indeed, but answers of so absurd a character, that the spiritual world must stand absolved from having given them.   The truth was out and the imposture was exposed; the mediums were clever conjurors, and tricksters to boot.   But Owen refused to have his eyes opened: he had made up his mind after careful investigation, to believe in the spiritual world, and in Mrs. Hayden as its interpreter: who was Mr. Lewes with his metaphysical learning; who was the editor of the *Quarterly* with his presumptuous affectation of superiority; that they should presume to dictate laws to old Robert Owen! He had passed from the extreme of disbelief to the extreme of credulity; and who should gainsay him!

CHAPTER XXIX.

Contents of Chapter—The World a Lunatic Asylum—The Dean of York and Sir R. Peel—The *Athenæum*, 19th July, 1851—Owen not neglected—Petition to House of Lords—Presentation of it: other Petitions—Tracts for the World's Fair—The Christian Socialists—Letters: one to Prince Albert—To the Earl of Derby and to others—Wishes to become M.P. for Oldham—For any Constituency—Would he have succeeded as an M.P.?

THE last chapter contains an account of the most remarkable circumstance of Owen's old age. In the present chapter I will mention a few facts which, though they are less interesting, it is yet necessary to relate. Some of these occurred before the conversion to the spiritualist faith.

In November 1850, when Owen was in his eightieth year, he began the publication of his *Journal;* a weekly paper devoted to the ordinary task of promoting new views of society. Among the usual miscellaneous matter, and the ever renewed histories and eulogies of New Lanark, appears an elaborate attempt to prove that the world is a great lunatic asylum. "To change* this lunatic asylum into a rational world, will be the work to be accomplished by this *Journal*." It is really a relief, in dragging one's eyes over the monotonous, dreary waste of Owen's writings, to find so much novelty

* *Journal,* i. 4, 1.

as appears in this title of an article: but the pleasure
is short-lived; for on looking at the alleged "proofs" of
the universal lunacy, we soon find this tiresome repro-
duction of the old tale: "These proofs are to be found
in the principles and practices of all nations, emanating
from the lunatic idea, opposed to all facts, *that men form
their own character*, or mind and conduct." This is the
crambe repetita with a vengeance! What reader could
go any farther? As to the alleged universal frenzy of
humanity, we may fairly apply to Owen the well-known
anecdote of the madman, who in a half-lucid interval
said, "The world is pleased to say that I am deranged:
I assert that the world is deranged: unhappily, the
world has the majority."

On the 1st of February, 1851, appeared an amusing
letter to the Dean of York.* The Dean had written,
in Colburn's *New Monthly*, some memoirs of the late
Sir Robert Peel; and had headed one chapter: "Owen
of Lanark and his visit to Drayton—Peel an example
of true piety." Unfortunately, he had half supposed,
as many other persons did, that Owen was dead: and
he aggravated this impertinence by asserting that the
first Sir Robert had once declined to receive Owen at
Drayton. This had been done, he said, at the instance
of Mr. Peel (*the* Sir Robert): who remonstrated with
his father on the impropriety of countenancing a man,
whose great object was that of Voltaire, to overturn the
Christian religion. Sir Robert, as the Dean says,
questioned Owen upon the subject, and received such

* *Journal*, i. 105.

a reply as led him to decline to co-operate with him in pressing on the Factory Act, and to request him to leave Drayton, where he was staying. A few days later, however, Owen again came to Drayton; but Sir Robert, who had received a third remonstrance from his son, declined to receive him. Owen's reply was, first, that he was unquestionably alive; a reply that settled the Dean's doubts: and secondly, that he was not aware of having been at any time treated uncivilly by the first baronet. The Dean may have been right as to the fact; but the discussion may have been so politely conducted as not to have hurt Owen's feelings.

In July of the same year, 1851, there appeared* a notice of Owen, in a paper little addicted to such topics as social science. The *Athenæum* of the 19th of July, said: "We are reminded by the printed petitions of the Houses of Parliament, of the continued existence and activity of Mr. Robert Owen." The writer went on in a kindly strain, to remind his readers of the success of the New Lanark experiment; and of the " flattering caresses from princes and statesmen lavished on the manager of the Scotch cotton-mills." He added that Owen's notions had been fully discussed, and that his plans had had ample trials in various places, " with the universal result of failure; but that, nevertheless, the world was greatly indebted to him for the present system of infant training, and for the humane and reasonable modes of teaching generally." Owen replied, in a letter to the editor of the *Athenæum,* published in

* *Journal,* ii. 145.

23

that paper, that it was a mistake to speak of his plans as ever having been fairly tried, since the capital necessary for the purpose had never been raised.

The article had also stated that of the benefactors of mankind, few, perhaps, have suffered greater neglect in old age than had fallen to Owen's share. This assertion also was repudiated. "Another, but a very natural mistake, you have made. Because my name does not figure among those in the fashionable world who attract the notice of the public, you imagine I am neglected. Never was there a greater misconception. I only wish my fellow-creatures were half as well taken care of in their old age as I have been; or as comfortable, contented, and in the enjoyment of as much personal happiness as I experience. I would not exchange my unpopularity with minds filled with the prejudices of the old world, the kindness of so many sincere friends, and the undisturbed quietness of my present enjoyments, for the patronage of all the authorities of the world. I have seen too much of the annoyance and discomforts attending popularity, to have any desire for the slightest portion of it—at my time of life especially." It is very pleasing to find in old age, an absence of the querulousness which sometimes distinguishes it, and the substitution of a placid contentment.

Owen was at all times fond of petitioning Parliament; and it was a petition which caused the *Athenæum* article. In the *Journal* * will be found the one to

* Robert Owen's *Journal*, ii. 92.

which the editor probably alluded. It is very short, and contains the old song in unusually pithy language. It begins thus: " That your Petitioner has devoted a long life, under most favourable opportunities, to investigate the causes which produce, and through succeeding ages reproduce, the miseries of the human race." It goes on to say that the petitioner has discovered the causes of these evils; and that, therefore, the longer continuance, or cessation, of them, must depend upon " the will of the authorities who possess the direction of the physical and mental powers of society." After adding that the petitioner was fully prepared to develop his theories into practice, it declares that " there is nothing wild, visionary, or impracticable, in any part of the statement now made." Finally, a select committee of investigation was demanded.

This petition was presented to the House of Lords on the 3rd of July, 1851, by Lord Brougham; who said that it emanated from a very celebrated man, and a great public benefactor. Mr. Owen held peculiar opinions; but he was a great public benefactor, for he was the founder of infant schools. His lordship thought that the petitioner ought to have an opportunity of appearing before a select committee of their lordships' House. The late illustrious Duke of Kent, the father of her Majesty, had been a patron of Mr. Owen's plan; and a man more religious, or more attached to the Church, than his late Royal Highness the Duke of Kent, it would be difficult to find. Lord Brougham then eulogized Owen, as being of all men, the most moderate, the most tolerant, and the most accessible to reason. He moved that the petition should be read by the clerk at the table; and this was done. The Marquis of Lansdowne, however, opposed the appointment of a committee, as irregular and useless; and the matter dropped. Lord Brougham is to be praised for his desire to support an old friend of public life: yet no one probably was less distressed by the failure of his motion. Within about a fortnight, another petition was tendered to the House of Lords, by the indefatigable, but importunate old man; this time on the topic of education: and Mr. Thomas Duncombe presented to the House of Commons, something like a duplicate of the one I have already mentioned.

In the same year, 1851, but a little earlier, Owen had written a number of tracts, for the enlightenment of the visitors to the Great Exhibition in Hyde Park:[*] and he got them translated into French and German for distribution among foreigners. The object proposed was, "to make known and explain to the people of all nations, through the visitors to the world's fair, the great and glorious changes which are on the eve of accomplishment for all people, through the progress of knowledge; and especially through the attainment of the practical knowledge of the causes of good and evil to man, and of the means of removing the evil and permanently attaining the good." The heading of the second tract may be taken as a sample of the whole.

" Universal and everlasting peace and good will among all nations and peoples."

By this time, the Christian Socialists, headed by Professor Maurice and Mr. Kingsley, together with Messrs. T. Hughes (Tom Brown), Ludlow, and Vansittart Neale, had attracted considerable attention. The old co-operatives and their prophet, were of course often alluded to ; and Owen at last thought fit to correct some of the statements made about him. Christians, and most sincere Christians, as these men were, they were received with all cordiality by the old, and equally sincere, unbeliever. " Friends and brothers in the cause of truth," began Owen ; and then proceeded to his usual exposition of his grand discovery of the overwhelming influence of circumstances, of the science of their proper direction, and of the rational system of society founded upon it. The Christian socialists had a strong sympathy with Owen in his desire to reconstruct society, to banish competition, to form associations in which all possessions should be held in common. But they complained that the Owenites were apathetic in action, though fond of lecturing and listening: that with their tongues they were lively and decisive, yet that from all practical measures they drew back with alarm. The complainants did not make sufficient allowance for thirty years of trials and disappointments. If a new sect of co-operators were now to spring up, and to ask the Christian socialists to join them, they might perhaps clap the new converts on the back and advise them to go in and win, while they themselves shrunk from further efforts. Disappointment will do its work on the energies of man.

I do not pretend to catalogue Owen's doings or his writings: I pass on to another publication;* Vol. I. of the *Rational Quarterly*, printed in January 1853. There appears here, a renewed proof of Owen's industry, in the form of a long series of letters of the previous year, addressed to personages of high rank. First there is one to H.R.H. Prince Albert, in which reference is made to former communications, as a fitting preparation for the present one. Owen tells the Prince, that judged by his public speeches, he must be pronounced far in advance of his class in every part of the world; and therefore he will express himself to the Prince as man to man. Owen was in his eighty-second year; his life therefore was precarious; and there was danger that his practical knowledge of social science should die with him. Columbus during eighteen years, had solicited different governments, to be allowed to discover a new continent for them: Owen during thirty years, had unsuccessfully prayed the governments of Europe and America to permit him to organize for them " a new world of goodness, wisdom and happiness; " a world that would advance steadily through all ages. The social discovery would as far transcend the material one, as the full blaze of day transcends the early dawn.

By the same post Owen wrote to the Earl of Derby, then prime minister: reminding him of the respon-

* R. Owen's *Rational Quarterly*, vol. i. 44, &c.

sibility of his position; and telling him that a British Prime Minister, possessed of wisdom and energy, could give a beneficial direction to the governments of the world. To the Marquis of Lansdowne, at the same time, he wrote that " circumstances have arisen through a long life to compel me to become an agent of nature to make the most valuable and important discovery for the permanent advantage of the human race, that man has yet been permitted to find out and unfold to his species." What that discovery was I need not repeat. The Marquis was requested to support the prayer of a petition which the Earl of Derby had been asked to present. Mr. Disraeli and Lord John Russell were favoured with similar communications expressed in somewhat different language.

Owen in his best days had been nearly elected member of Parliament for a Scotch constituency: and from time to time he felt a renewed desire to sit in the House of Commons. As a man of eighty he offered himself for Oldham, and in his address to the electors, condescended, in the opening at least, to lay aside the language which had become by frequent repetition a mere jargon. " I claim your suffrages for the following reasons:—1st. Because I made the Bill for the relief of children and others in cotton-mills, &c., &c. 2nd. Because I was the first who introduced into cotton-mills systematic order, &c., &c. 3rd. Because I invented and introduced rational infant schools, &c., &c." The fourth item might probably tell well in the district for which the address was intended. " 4th.

Because I introduced the first fine cotton-spinning by machinery; extending the highest numbers previously attained, 120, and of inferior quality, to upwards of 300, and of superior quality: thereby opening an immense new branch of the cotton manufacture." After reciting many other claims, the address concludes thus : " It is true that I am old : but I am not yet past good and substantial public service. If, however, you have a younger candidate, that can effect more for the good of the people,—elect him by all means. Your friend, Robert Owen.—Seven Oaks, Kent, Aug. 2, 1852."

More than three years later, there appeared in a small tract, the following unmeaning notice to the world generally :—

" If the constituency of any county, city, or borough, will elect me, free of all trouble and expense, to a seat in the House of Commons, I will in that assembly advocate the system of society which is in accordance with all nature, and which will lead to the permanent happiness of the human race. I will also endeavour through the same public medium of information, to induce the civilized world to change their practice of continually creating causes of evil to the human race, for the practice of creating causes which will produce good to all, and overcome all evil."*

Whether Owen even in his best days would have advanced his reputation by becoming a member of the House of Commons ; whether he would have been listened to, after curiosity had been sated by a first

* *New Existence*, viii. 27.

speech; whether he would have made such an impression, as to induce the House to consent to the introduction of any bill of his, or to appoint a select committee; whether in the committees of the House he would have been useful in eliciting information or constructing a report;—is, I think, very doubtful. As a mere speaker he would have met with small encouragement: as a man of one idea he would have been regarded, I fear, as an intolerable bore. Talking, laughter, bucolic imitations, would have perpetually greeted him. It was better for him that he was not elected.

CHAPTER XXX.

IN my chapter on Spiritual Manifestations, I have expressed no opinion as to the soundness of Owen's mind
at the time of his conversion. The "Notice" which I
have quoted at the end of the last chapter, may cause
a suspicion that in December 1855, there were some
appearances of dotage. But on the other hand, it must
be remembered that he had now been living between
two and three years, under ghostly influences; and that
persons who pass half their time in spirit-land, contract
a contempt for mundane opinions and human logic.

Though Owen's notions generally were stereotyped,
and with the exception of the case of the spiritualists,
scarcely ever broken up to be recast, he nevertheless
indulged his followers occasionally with a new nomen-
clature. Thus at the end of 1854, he called a " great
preliminary meeting" for the 1st January 1855, as the

commencement of " the true millennial state of human existence." This was a blending of the new rational society, with the spiritualist influence.

On New Year's Day accordingly, the lecture-room in St. Martin's Hall was crowded. People on entering,* were surprised to see a theatrical arrangement of drop-scenes and side-scenes, painted to exhibit to the eye " different combinations of *good conditions*, which Mr. Owen, Mr. Pemberton, Mr. Buckingham, and Mr. Atkins, proposed for the rising generation of the human race." For the side-scenes, Mr. Atkins had painted eight columns, " to exhibit an epitome of the creation of the world from its commencement, step by step, through all its gradations to the present time, . . . showing with how much ease, by adopting Mr. Owen's and Mr. Pemberton's principles of education from birth by the eye and ear, all useful and real knowledge may be now given to all who shall be placed within these new rational conditions." The reporter of the proceedings must have been either an enthusiast, or a person well paid to enact that character. We may believe that the spectators were surprised to see a lecture-room turned into a theatre: but it is our turn to be astonished when we hear that " the audience seemed at first stunned and then electrified with these extraordinary representations, opening the first glimpse of the *new existence of man upon the earth.*" The spectators perhaps, expected a dramatic representation, with Mr. Owen, it might be, as the old man; Mr.

---

* *Robert Owen's Great Preliminary Meeting*, 3rd Edit. xi.

Buckingham as an Hindoo wizard; and the spirits of the Duke of Kent, of Tom Paine, of Byron, Channing, and Chalmers, hovering around or whispering behind the scenes. Owen however, appeared in his ordinary costume: Buckingham was too ill to be present: guardian angels there were none.

Another meeting was held on the 1st of May, when Mr. Owen, Mr. Pemberton, and Mr. Atkins, were once more on the platform, but without the accessories of theatrical scenery. This meeting again was only preliminary: but on the 14th May, Owen's eighty-fifth birthday, " a great convention of delegates of the human race," was held in the same place, for the purpose of hearing the old man " inaugurate the commencement of the millennium." The convention had been called by " a *proclamation*, dated London, 25th November, 1854." The proceedings consisted of speeches by Mr. Owen and his friends; after which the meeting separated. The millennium, the new existence of man upon the earth, was, we must suppose, inaugurated.

Stimulated by the popularity of the two gatherings in May, Owen called a third meeting for the 30th of July, in the same year, 1855. As nothing occurs in the report of it, about crowds or enthusiasm, I presume that there was a flatness in the proceedings. I have done injustice to the assembly of the 14th of May, by omitting to state that it agreed upon petitions to be presented to Parliament. On the present occasion, Owen read a fictitious examination of himself, by the committee which ought to have been appointed but was not. The haziness of the invention reminds one of the good fortune of the traveller in the East, who was shown the ladder which Jacob dreamed that he saw.

Most men are unwilling to parade their own want of success; and Owen was backward in talking of New Harmony, of Orbiston, of Queenwood, and other failures; while New Lanark and the Factory Act were often at the tip of his pen. But in this examination he states plainly, that for fifty years he had been petitioning Parliament, and without success, to investigate the subject of subjects. But why, asks the fictitious committee, had he so long persevered in this course? Because he had hesitated to bring the subject before a public unprepared to receive it; and because he regarded the British Parliament as the fittest channel of communication. I cannot quarrel with a veteran of 85: a younger man would have here laid himself open to flat contradiction, and a charge of careless misstatement. After a series of questions and answers, Owen concluded the examination in a highly satisfactory manner, by putting into the mouth of the committee, this final statement: " You have made out your case, and you have overcome all our objections, and removed all our difficulties." Owen, after reading this document aloud, put to the meeting a string of resolutions which were carried unanimously. The small success of this meeting did not encourage him to call a fourth; but for three years after this date, and indeed till the year of his death, he published his

Millennial Gazette; consisting of a series of tracts on the subjects indicated by the title.

I will now pass on to the year 1857, when the old man exhibited an activity that could not have been looked for. First, he published a volume of his *Auto-biography*. Portions of this had been written at previous times, but other portions were fresh from his pen. There is an introduction in two parts, of different dates: the first, of December 1856, being a dialogue between himself and an old friend whom he calls Inquisitor; the second, of 16th October 1856, a spiritual "Address to the World" from the United States, which I have mentioned in a former chapter. In the former of these parts, the old friend urges the task of writing his own life, as a matter of high import to the whole race of man. Owen replies that he is always desirous of gratifying his friends or faithful disciples; and that if he has hitherto neglected their solicitations, it has only been in consequence of his devotion to the mission he has been engaged in through a long life; and as to the success of which he is more sanguine the longer he lives, notwithstanding the gloomy prognostications of his followers. Truly, it must have been in anticipation of him that the poet sang, " Hope springs eternal in the human breast."

A second volume was published in the following year, and was numbered, not volume " two," as by any other person, but " one A." There is a reason for using this unusual ordinal: that the second volume is an appendix to the first; having indeed, an introduction, but consisting mainly of reprints of documents, such as the essays on the formation of character, and the original factory bill.

The style of writing in these volumes, where they are not reprints of former publications, is singularly loose and wandering; and the arrangement is almost as defective as the style. I have made considerable use of the facts stated; and therefore I have asked myself with some anxiety, whether I have justly confided in their accuracy. On the affirmative side, I remember, that even very old persons, with a failing memory, will recollect the incidents of early life: and to such a degree that a man unquestionably in his dotage, who cannot recall what he has heard five minutes before, will nevertheless, run over in exact order a series of names, or of facts, with which he was familiar in his boyhood. We might therefore, have considerable reliance on Owen's account of his earlier years. Fortunately, we have other grounds to rest upon: for the *Autobiography* was to a large extent written long before 1856, and printed piecemeal in various publications.

In this same year, 1857, Owen called a meeting, to be held, like the gatherings of 1855, in St. Martin's Hall, Long Acre. A pamphlet afterwards appeared, bearing the title of *Report of the Meetings of the Congress of the Advanced Minds of the World*, convened by R. Owen. This congress sat day by day, from the 12th to the 25th of May 1857; and discussed or maundered over, the old topics, including of course the doctrine of circumstances, socialism, and spiritualism.

About the same time, Owen appeared in a different place, where though he was treated with decency, he was certainly not listened to.   On the 22nd to the 24th of June 1857, a conference was held in Willis's Rooms, under the presidency of the Prince Consort, for an inquiry into the causes of " the early age at which children are taken from school," and to suggest remedies for the evil.   Any one who looks over the papers read in the various sections, will find that the proposed object was not strictly adhered to, but that many topics were introduced.   An educational conference would more properly describe the affair as it turned out.   It was whispered however, among the initiated, that the particular form was of little consequence: for that, though the bringing together the friends of education, and the eliciting and comparing of information, were objects sincerely proposed, yet the thing principally aimed at was to prepare the public to receive with equanimity, the intended proposal of Government to largely augment the annual educational grant.   A few years before, 100,000*l.*, had been grudgingly voted: at present a million is said to be expended directly and indirectly. Whatever other good followed, the conference unquestionably strengthened the hands of the administration in this important matter.

It occurred to Owen that he had some right to be heard on such an occasion.   More than sixty years before, when the importance of education was not generally understood; when men of information and social importance argued, that if knowledge was power, ignorance in the masses was necessary to their subordination; when the American revolt and the French revolution had disposed statesmen to keep subjects down with a firm hand, rather than to train them for freedom; at this period, Owen had devoted one-third of his laborious savings to the promotion of the Lancaster and Bell schemes. Afterwards, in mature age, he had spent uncounted time and money, in the training of the young people within his reach. Surely, he above all men, had a claim to be heard.

On the last morning of the conference, in the great room at Willis's, Owen made his appearance, and secured a place, not exactly among the actors in the drama, but on the platform outside the circle. Listening with patient attention, and as well as his confirmed deafness would allow, he thought he discovered an opening for what he had to say. His long and hard experience must have told him that he would not be listened to; but the presence on the platform of his old friend Lord Brougham, and of the veteran Marquis of Lansdowne, was a guarantee that he would suffer no insult. In the absence of Prince Albert, Lord Granville presided: he was unwilling to hurt the old man's feelings, but dreaded probably an unnecessary prolongation of the morning's proceedings; for who should say to what length Owen might run on? who could foresee whether he would not commence the reading of the ever dear essays, or the report to the county of Lanark? There were a few sentences uttered: a gentle remonstrance from the noble chairman: some whispered conversation: a suggestion of being out of order, and a recommendation to take another opportunity: the business went on, the conclusion was huddled up, and Owen was left to empty benches. It is easy in such a case, to moralize on the ingratitude of mankind: but Owen had wilfully placed himself where he knew that he should be slighted and shunned.

At the close of this year 1857, Owen again showed the visionary condition of his mind, by printing a letter, addressed * to " the potentates of the earth; in whom the happiness and misery of the human race are now invested." Especially it was intended for " Austria, France, Great Britain, Prussia, Russia, Sardinia, Turkey, and the United States of North America," on the ground that these powers were at peace with each other, " and could without war, easily induce all the other governments and people to unite with them in practical measures for the general good of all through futurity."

Owen's intercourse with the spheres of spirits, had failed to alter his opinions as to free-will and necessity. In this letter he states, almost more strongly than ever, his dogma as to the irresponsibility of man; and reiterates his assertion that it forms the true foundation of society. A sincere but astounding conviction! that to tell men:—you are not responsible for your actions, and to reward or punish you for them is absurd—is the true mode of securing a well-conducted and happy world. I quote the very words of the letter.†

* *Autobiog.* 1 a. x.   † Ibid. 1 a. xi.

" That the maker of anything, gives to the made, all its made qualities and powers.

" That the Great Creating Power of the universe gives to all things created, the created qualities and powers which they possess.

" That the Maker and the Creator, being the sole authors of these qualities and powers, are alone responsible for them and their actions during their existence.

*　　　　*　　　　*　　　　*

" That the Creator not only gives, but forces on the created, all the qualities and powers which it possesses or can acquire."

Having laid down these propositions, as the ground on which the " surroundings " of society ought to be based, Owen modestly begged of the potentates to hold a congress in London ; and promised that, health permitting, he would be present with them, and instruct them in their duties. He suggested that the meeting should not be held till the following May, that the authorities of China, Japan, and Burmah, might be invited.

About the time of the Educational Conference, it was determined by a few friends of social advancement, to attempt the formation of an " Association for the Promotion of Social Science." Some gentlemen from Birmingham having taken a leading part in the preliminary arrangements, the first meeting was fixed to be held in that town : and from the 12th to the 16th of October, 1857, there was a constant reading of papers, with making of speeches and self-glorification, according to the established forms of such gatherings. Hitherto the association has prospered: as to the future it would be rash to prophesy. Some persons make much of the case of the British Association for the Advancement of Science; and argue that since that has succeeded, and has enjoyed a long existence, there is no reason why the Social Science Association should not succeed also. To this it may be replied, that many affairs fail when there is no apparent reason why they should not be successful: they fail through ill fortune, or through the incapacity and negligence of the conductors. And there is as much difference between the British Association and that of which I am speaking, as there is between the undisputed certainty of the truths of physical science, and the uncertainty of the maxims of moral and social science. The British Association can banish quackery from its sections, a task which the Social Science Association will find vast difficulty in accomplishing. Few people imagine themselves acquainted with the laws of nature, without much study and reflection: nearly every man who can read and write, believes himself capable of putting the social machine to right; and pronounces dogmatically on plans of legislation and penal reform.

Owen was not troubled with reflections of this sort. He hailed the formation of the society, as the daybreak of a new era. "What* a glorious commencement to this happy period, has been the late meeting in Bir-

* *Autobiog.* 1 a. i.

mingham of the National Association (of all parties) for the Promotion of Social Science !

" For the first time in the history of man, the door has been wide opened to admit of truth unrestricted by power and prejudice, on subjects of the deepest interest to all humanity.

" Long will that meeting, its founder, and its leaders, be held in remembrance by the human race."

Owen read a paper* in the section on punishment and reformation. It was entitled, *The Human Race Governed without Punishment.* A very short epitome is given in the *Transactions;* the great number of communications making it necessary to compress the less important papers. It reads so much like a sketch of one of Owen's earlier effusions, that it carries one back forty years, to a period when he was in his glory.

This being the last of his productions to which I shall call attention, I will copy the epitome; as exhibiting the old man in his monotonous consistency :—

" In this paper, the writer supported the proposition, that in a society based on its true foundation—' that the Creator gives all the qualities and powers to and possessed by the created '—the punishment of man by man will be unnecessary :—

" By the aid of this principle the writer stated that he had governed a population, originally very inferior, of between 2,000 and 3,000, for upwards of a quarter of a century, without punishment; and that they were by public consent allowed to be for that period, the

* *Transactions,* 1857, 280.

best and the happiest working population ever known
to exist in any country.   And all the children of this
population were so trained, educated, and placed, from
one year old, that vice, crime, or evil passions, or unkind conduct to each other, were unknown; and the
strongest affection between them and their teachers,
was strikingly manifest at all times to all who witnessed
their proceedings.

" Mr. Owen expressed his conviction, that the time
would surely come, when the population of the world
would be governed solely under the influence of universal love and charity: and divine as those principles
were, they were yet the principles of common sense,
for governing mankind, and forming the character from
birth to death."

If Owen said all that was here attributed to him, it
must be confessed that his own exploits were magnified
in his eyes by being seen through the mists of years.
As I have shown already, it is not true that there was
no vice at New Lanark: for illegitimacy, though not
frequent, was by no means unknown; and the practice of drinking to excess, however diminished, continued to a late date.   Nor was punishment dispensed
with: since illegitimacy was fined; and the custom of
drinking in the new year was heavily fined.   These
facts we know, and probably a great many more of the
same sort have escaped us.

During the following year, Owen's constitution began
to give way under the load of eighty-six years; though
he still felt an ambition to be examined by both Houses

of Parliament, either at the bar, or in committee. In October, 1858, was held in Liverpool the second meeting of the Social Science Association. Owen's failing health quite unfitted him for travelling: but his old restlessness was upon him: the opportunity of attending such a conference was an irresistible temptation: perhaps the words "social science," appeared to him, as they did to Louis Blanc, equivalent to socialistic science: at any rate to Liverpool he would go.* At the end of his journey he took to his bed. But on one of the days of the meeting, after two hours spent in dressing, he was seated in a sedan chair, carried to St. George's Hall, and placed on the platform. Lord Brougham, true to his friendship for him, took the veteran by the arm, led him forward, and obtained him a hearing. "Then Mr. Owen," says his admirer, Mr. Holyoake, "in his grand manner, proclaimed his ancient message of science, competence, and good-will to the world." He was unable to complete his first period: Lord Brougham supplied the clause wanting, clapped his hands, and uttered words of encouragement; suggesting in an undertone that he should be carried back to bed.

He was carried back, under the care of his faithful attendant Rigby, and lay in bed an hour, unconscious. Reviving, he asked what he had said on the platform; and his words being read over to him, he expressed his sense of their importance. Again he fell into unconsciousness. "That scene on the Liverpool platform

* G. J. Holyoake's *Life and Last Days*, &c.

will not soon die out of recollection. Lord Brougham
and Mr. Owen, the two marvellous men who stood
there, were a sight not soon to behold again. Lord
Brougham's vivacity at eighty, was as wonderful as Mr.
Owen's undying ardour at eighty-nine." *

During a fortnight, Owen was confined to his bed
at the Victoria hotel: many inquiries about his health
being made by Mr. Rathbone, Mr. William Browne,
M. P., and others. One morning, however, he told
Rigby to pack up that he might go. "Go, sir? where?
To London?" "To my native place: I will lay my
bones where they came from." Natural sentiment was
prevailing even over the ruling passion. He was got
to the Mersey; ferried across (another ferryman was
soon to carry him), and conveyed by the railroad to
Shrewsbury; from which place he had to go thirty
miles in a carriage. Coming after an absence of
seventy years, to the border line of England and Wales,
he knew it, and raising himself up gave a cheer. He
attempted to persuade Rigby that the atmosphere of
his native land was sensibly different from that of
England. "What scenes had the wanderer passed
through since last he gazed upon the mountains!
Manufacturing days, crowning success, philanthropic
experiments, public meetings at the London Tavern,
continental travel, interviews with kings,† Mississippi
valleys, Indiana forests, journeys, labours, agitations,
honours, calumnies, hopes, and never-ceasing toil; what

* Eighty-seven was Owen's real age.
† Princes would have been a safer word.

a world, what an age had intervened, since last he passed his native border!"*

Passing an estate he had known, he proposed to drive up and ask if Dr. Johns were at home. Dr. Johns had died twenty years before. But his daughter was there, and rejoiced to show him hospitality. He asked for flummery, the dish which had accidentally ruined his digestion as a child; and it was almost the only thing he ate. Arriving at Newtown, his native place, he and his attendant adopted fictitious names; and stopping at the house where he was born, gratified their curiosity by finding that the particular room of his birth was well known. His real name was made out by the owner of the house, Mr. David Thomas, whose guest he afterwards offered to become, that he might give an important message to the inhabitants. A whim again seized him, and he returned through Shrewsbury to Liverpool.

Again from Liverpool he went to Shrewsbury, and on to Newtown. He travelled with difficulty, but pointed out the objects he passed. His courtesy prevented him from becoming as an invalid the guest of Mr. David Thomas. He went to an hotel, and there he died. His medical attendant ordered him stimulants, but he wilfully refused them, though they might perhaps have restored him for a time. The rector of the place calling, Owen declined to see him as a clergyman, but afterwards suggested to him some visionary plans for the regeneration of Newtown, and requested

* Holyoake, 8.

him to confer with the magistrates and other authorities on the subject. Up to this time he had no immediate expectation of death, though he took some pains to learn, for future use, the exact spot where his father was buried. His eldest son arrived from London in time to receive his farewell, and to witness his placid departure.

The following letter from the son, the Hon. R. D. Owen, appeared in some of the papers:—

"*Newtown, Montgomeryshire, Nov.* 17, 1858.

"MY DEAR SIR,—It is all over. My dear father passed away this morning, at a quarter before seven; and passed away as gently and quietly as if he had been falling asleep. There was not the least struggle, not a contraction of a limb or a muscle; not an expression of pain on his face. His breathing gradually became slower and slower, until at last it ceased so imperceptibly, that even as I held his hand, I could scarcely tell the moment when he no longer breathed. His last words, distinctly pronounced about twenty minutes before his death, were *relief has come.* About half an hour before, he said, *very easy and comfortable.*"

The body was removed into the house where it was born, and was treated with funeral honours. But the burial, in accordance with Owen's own tastes and opinions, was simple and frugal. Mr. Holyoake, Mr. Truelove, Mr. Law, and Mr. Rigby arrived in one party from London to take a part in it; as did Mr. Pare from Dublin, Colonel Clinton from Royston; besides

Mr. Robert Cooper, Mr. W. H. Ashurst, Mr. and Mrs. Francis Pears, Mr. Thomas Allsop, and Mr. W. Cox. The little town of course suspended all business and amusement, to witness the interment of its distinguished son. Clergymen and medical men, gentlemen and men of business, joined in the procession. The body was carried first to the New Church, where the affecting service of the Church of England was read to many unwilling listeners; and then the procession moved on to the ruins of St. Mary's, an ancient Saxon structure, where the body was laid in the grave of its parents. The Co-operators, or Socialists, who were present, regretted that they could not dispense with the Christian forms, and that they were debarred from pronouncing an oration over the grave: but they found nothing to complain of in the simple and graceful conduct of the officiating clergyman.

Thus was Robert Owen buried by his own wish, which was held sacred by his friends, in ground consecrated by the Church; with the formalities of a religion which he contemned; attended by mourners who for the most part had no sympathy with his opinions; in an ancient graveyard hallowed by historical associations which to him when living had little meaning. The bones of the prophet of innovation lie among the picturesque ruins of mediæval orthodoxy.

END OF THE LIFE.

PART II.

———◇———

CHAPTER XXXI.

Reflections on Owen — How he became what he was — Nature —
Circumstances — He was self-educated — Self-education considered
— Its alleged Advantages and real Disadvantages.

IN the previous chapters of this volume, I have tried
to confine myself to the immediate duty of a biographer;
I have narrated the incidents of Owen's life; adding
some account of the works he wrote and of the opinions
he held; and abstaining from lengthened comments and
statements of my own views. I propose now to indem-
nify myself for this forbearance, by devoting a few
pages, to such reflections on Owen's character and philosophy, as have occurred to me in wading through his
numerous publications.

I shall be acting in entire accordance with his sentiments as well as my own, in asking first, how the man
came to be what he was. I answer, as he himself might
without inconsistency have answered, that his peculiarities were much owing to nature; and that in few
cases might be more truly applied the maxim, that the
child is the parent of the man. At ten years old, as at
forty and as at eighty, there were amiability of temper,
rectitude of principle, firmness carried to obstinacy,
restlessness of temperament, and a reflective habit of

mind. But though nature did much, it was far from doing all which determined Owen's character.

It will be remembered that he received some rudiments of instruction at a village school: that his progress there was such as to cause him, at his master's request, to be made a monitor, or pupil teacher, or usher, while he was a mere child, fit only for a female preparatory school: that his precocious fondness for reading was gratified by the use of the private libraries of his little town: that the influence of some serious maiden ladies dragged him into the perplexing meshes of controversy: that in his first situation at Stamford, the worthy people with whom he lived had risen from the rank of pedlars or packmen, and were of course very imperfectly instructed: that after that time until he was twenty years old, he did not associate with persons of education: and that till he was a mature man, he spoke an uncouth jargon, and was unable to write English with propriety.

It is true that he had read many standard authors; and that at Stamford he had so much leisure as allowed him to enjoy his book for hours every day, frequently under the noble trees of the neighbourhood. He says himself that during twenty years he spent five hours a day in reading. Such continued application was quite enough, as far as time was concerned, to make him a highly accomplished man: a good linguist, and an adept in science. Yet, in fact, he knew nothing of Greek or Latin, was ignorant of French and German, and was entirely uninstructed in exact science. He was ac-

quainted with only one language, and that was English:
he was innocent of mathematics and philosophy. Owen
in short, had not received even the elements of a liberal
education at school or at home: he was strictly a self-
educated man. Now many self-educated men rise to
eminence: they are often remarkable for a certain greatness of purpose: in some instances they distinguish
themselves in a particular branch of science: they have
pith and strength in their faculties. But commonly
they have a peculiarity which marks them out from
persons who have gone through the regulation drill of
the schools: they may be better or worse than these
persons, but they are not the same.

What is this singularity? One man becomes an
authority on chemistry or geology; and in his particular department is thoughtful, cautious, sensible; but
lead him out of that and you find him shallow, dogmatical, sceptical as to the conclusions of others, rash
in forming his own, and, above all, glorying in his
licentious freedom of mind. Another, with no special
topic of his own, but with a great fund of knowledge,
always adopts that view of a question which is held
by the minority: he is in political economy an anti-
Malthusian; in politics an ultra-democrat with a bitter
antipathy however, to Jews or Roman Catholics; in religion a Brownist or a Swedenborgian. A third, deeply
read in English literature, with an elegance of taste
and discrimination in authorship, runs utterly wild when
grave opinions are to be discussed: and in trying to
explain his own notions, pours forth such a profusion of

language without order or precision, as to make it impossible to judge what notions he really has, or on what ground he rests them.   The characteristic of these men is that they are whimsical, crotchety, intellectually eccentric, deficient in that balance of mental power which results from early training.

I am no admirer of mere learning: I do not worship

"The bookful blockhead ignorantly read,
With loads of learned lumber in his head."

I am far from calling that a good education, which crams the memory without developing the understanding: which turns a youth into a walking lexicon, without a power of thinking for himself. But, on the other hand, I believe that the worst of our great schools produces some good results ; and I am convinced that a boy who has had an ordinary education till sixteen or seventeen, is far more likely in after-life to reason accurately and judge soundly, than another who has been under the necessity of teaching himself in the intervals of business.

A plausible argument may be advanced on the other side.   Granted that for most people a regular education is of great value ; because without it they will neither read nor reflect.   But for uncommon minds, such as Owen's, which have strength enough to force their own way without assistance, and which do really advance to knowledge without the stimulus of the birch, and the allurements of commendations and prizes, is not the absence of formal instruction a positive gain ?   Because the severe efforts necessary in their case for the acquisition of knowledge, the sharp combat with difficulties, the need of working out every elementary problem for themselves, should give a thoroughness to their knowledge; and above all, should secure a hardihood of intellect, not to be attained by those whose path is smoothed for them at every step. The mountaineer is more robust than the inhabitant of the temperate plain : the child of the peasant, if he survive the hardships and perils of infancy, acquires a finer constitution, and is more capable of bearing cold and hunger than the carefully-nurtured offspring of the gentleman. Severe training is needful for hardy frames and for great minds : and self-education is the severest of training.

This reasoning is specious but, as I believe, one-sided. I will not stop to inquire whether the illustration is accurate : whether severity of regimen in infancy is favourable to bodily development : whether the peasant boy is hardier and stronger than the gentleman's son brought up in the country, and afterwards at Harrow and Cambridge. Whatever may be the apparent appositeness of the illustration, I believe it to be inapplicable; because I dispute the truth of the assertion, that the minds of such men as Owen, are more severely trained than the minds of regularly educated persons. It is true that the self-taught geologist will probably be deeply versed in his science; that the self-taught chemist will most likely be an adept in the mysteries of analysis and equivalents; that the self-taught philosopher will be better armed for defence within the circle of his thought, than another who has derived his knowledge from books alone. But shall we say of a man who is a geologist and little more; of a man who is a mere chemist and ignorant of most other things; of a man whose philosophy is confined to a few maxims and to meditation upon these;—shall we say of any one of such men, that his mind is duly trained? We do not predicate of a mechanic that his body is trained, because long habit has given him great strength and activity of hand, while his arms and back have not been properly developed: nor of a groom that he is thoroughly trained as a man, if his legs for want of use are mere spindles, however dexterous may be his horsemanship. In the same way, I cannot call that a mental training, which brings out in great force, two or three faculties, such as those of observation and comparison, while it utterly neglects all the rest.

Self-educated men in short, are one-sided: they are lame in their minds. They have that fault which would result from the mode of education recommended by some innovators. These persons declaim against the present system as absurd, because it treats all boys alike, instead of studying the particular bent of the genius of each, and acting in accordance with it. If a boy has no memory for words, why lose his time and sour his temper, by forcing him to study Latin, Greek, French, and German? The same boy has perhaps, a natural superiority in mathematical powers, or may even have a fine memory for dates, facts, and ideas: why not cultivate this fertile soil, instead of ineffectually labouring at the barren one? By varying your instruction according to the peculiarity of each pupil's mind,

25

you will produce many able youths instead of as at present, attaining a uniformity of dulness. If I were writing a treatise on education, I should stop here to controvert this proposed alteration, by pointing out the inaccuracy of its base: since I believe that in fact, an overwhelming majority of boys are capable of successfully learning what is commonly taught in schools; and that they are rare instances in which boys of great general powers are deficient in a particular faculty such as that of verbal memory.

But suppose it were otherwise: let us imagine a society in which one-third of the children were deficient in a memory for words; another third, while acquiring languages with facility, had great difficulty in remembering the facts and inferences of history; and the remainder readily understood the demonstrations of mathematics, and solved problems with facility, but revolted from all instruction which required an exercise of memory. According to the educational notions I have alluded to, the first division might be made historians; the second, linguists; the third, mathematicians. This arrangement would tend no doubt, to make good historians, good linguists, and good mathematicians: but would it produce great men? or useful men? or such men as would make the world worth living in?

Let us take a parallel case. In a particular community, a number of children have weak arms; others have deficient legs; a third class want strength in their backs. Now if these unfortunates belonged to the middle or upper classes, their parents would not make it their business to further develop the already strong legs of those who had weak arms, but would direct their efforts to exercising and thus strengthening the arms. So the weak legs and frail backs would be carefully developed. Should not the education of the mind follow the same rule? If a boy have a treacherous memory for words, it is surely the more important to cultivate the weak faculty, as far as it can be done without causing disgust. If another has a facility in language, but an incapacity for close reasoning, that is the very reason he should be cajoled into mastering Euclid.

I know the inevitable objection: that by this course you will make poor linguists and feeble mathematicians: and that if all the Cambridge wranglers consisted of men with a natural incapacity for reasoning, while the classical tripos was filled with others of naturally bad memories and defective taste, the university would be a laughing-stock. I reply that I am not recommending masters to teach any boy only one class of subjects: still less am I supposing that education, regarded as a training of the mind, is to go on through life. There is a general education and there is a special education: the former to draw out and strengthen the faculties; the latter to fit a man for a certain pursuit. The education of boys should be general, that of young men, partly at least, special.

Now to apply this to the case in hand: does the self-educated man commonly put himself through such a mental training as to develop his faculties generally and his weakest faculties in particular? Or does he usually devote himself with ardour to a single pursuit, by which his strongest powers are brought out, while others are utterly neglected? The latter is notoriously the case. And this seems to explain why such persons are apt to be whimsical on every topic but one. They have obtained a superiority in a certain direction; and this they think, gives them a right to lay down the law on all subjects. On matters respecting which they know nothing, they preach and dispute and dogmatize, without any consciousness of their own ignorance. Owen with no language but his native tongue, expressed supreme contempt for the learning of Oxford and Cambridge, as to the merits of which he could not possibly form any opinion. On the currency question he talked *ex cathedrâ*; though apparently, he knew just as much about it as he did of the theory of the tides. He had in short, all the weaknesses of a self-educated, and therefore ill-trained, understanding.

I feel convinced then, that if we regard mental training as the process by which the faculties of the mind generally are developed, self-educated men are very ill trained, because they have only a few faculties well exercised, while the others are much neglected. But it may still be held that such men will be superior to others as to those faculties which they have laboriously brought out. Even here however, there is room to hang a doubt.

My opponent may first appeal to facts: he may say that if in a company of gentlemen taken at hazard, there is one self-educated man, you may expect to find him the cleverest person present on the topic with which he is familiar. I may grant this, and yet deny the inference implied.

The proposition may be put in this form: Self-educated men are far cleverer than the average of other men. I grant this unreservedly: I am fully convinced that such men belong to nature's nobility: I appreciate the strength of character which enables them to force themselves upwards through the superincumbent load of difficulties; which makes them shun delights and live laborious days; which under the pressure of daily toil, and in the face of corroding care, still urges them forward in the course of unrewarded study.

But then I ask: what would these men have been if they had received a regular education? Would they have been less resolute, less laborious, less intellectual, less bent on attaining to superiority? If the tendency of regular instruction be to make men vacillating, idle, apathetic, then I can understand that these men were better without it.

I have supposed a self-educated man in a promiscuous company of gentlemen: but let us now place him in the society of those higher minds to whom he naturally belongs; let us imagine him among the cabinet ministers, or the judges, or the fellows of Trinity College, Cambridge, or the fellows of Christ Church, Oxford, or the fellows of the Royal Society: will any one be mad enough to assert that the absence of a regular education will give him a superiority here?

The truth therefore, seems to be this: that a self-educated man is usually a person of resolute will and of excellent powers; that he is far superior by nature and by exercise to the ordinary men around him: but that the want of regular instruction has kept him from rising to that eminent place which is naturally his due.

May we not go one step farther; and say that even in the particular study which he may have chosen, we have no reason to suppose him more severely trained, than regularly educated men who have devoted themselves to the same study? Suppose that Sir Isaac Newton had not enjoyed the advantages of a learned education; and that in his ignorance of what had been done before him, he had spent his life in the invention of a system of geometry, similar to that which bears the name of Euclid. If in fifty years he had struck out a series of propositions substantially the same as those of Euclid's four first books, he would have wrought a marvellous work. In the performance of it, his mind would have been severely exercised, and his faculties would have been developed to the utmost. But instead of devoting himself to this useless labour, in what Robert Hall would have called an arena and no field, he fortunately learnt first, all that his predecessors had done, and then bent all his energies to creating a new method of analysis, and a new system of astronomy. Now in this useful, noble, glorious, undertaking, was his mind less severely exercised, were his faculties less fully developed than they would have been if his time had been expended in the bootless enterprise of inventing

Euclid anew? Self-educated men are constantly employed in re-discovering things well known: while regularly educated men of the same powers, devote themselves to the finding of new truths. Both classes task their powers to the utmost, and both obtain the same severe training.

These considerations suggest a doubt, whether the very term, self-educated, is not inaccurate: whether it does not convey to the hearer a false notion. When we say that Owen was self-educated, we mean only that he had no education but what he gave himself. But Newton, who had the advantage of a university course, we do not speak of as self-educated, although in truth, his labours as a man, as much constituted self-education as Owen's labours did. By self-education, then, we mean self-education only: we mean the absence of all other education. But if this definition were present to men's minds, they would not argue, as I have been supposing them to argue, in favour of self-education. They would not say, Owen had no scholastic education, therefore his mind was strong: Newton had a scholastic education, therefore his mind ought to have been weak.

One difficulty still remains. Owen had by nature, a mind capable of vigorous thought, as was shown by his early addiction to reasoning on the great problems of humanity: for twenty years he applied himself to reading during as many hours a day as would satisfy a reasonably severe student: how can we believe that such a mind, so nourished, should be uncultivated? I reply that mere reading, though it has its value, is an imperfect instrument of education. Let a boy merely read a history of England from Alfred to Victoria; and at the end of the year which may have passed during the perusal, he will be found quite unable to give a precise answer to a question about the Henrys and the Edwards. Let a man previously ignorant of French history toil through the *Annals* of Sismondi, and as many memoirs as you please of the reigns of Henry IV., Louis XIII., Louis XIV., and Louis XV.: and it will be a mercy if he does not confound Cardinal Richelieu with Cardinal Fleury; La belle Gabrielle with La Vallière; Madame de Maintenon with Madame de Pompadour. Inattentive reading leaves a general notion of the persons and facts described; as a drive through a new country, without a guide-book, enables you to say whether it was a champain or a hilly region, well wooded or barren, dry or abounding in streams; but nothing more. It is this tendency of the mind to lose itself in generalities and to drop particulars, which confers a high value on examinations. Give a series of lectures on chemistry, with abundant experimental illustrations: at the end of your course your pupils will have no distinct apprehension of half a dozen facts. But if you commence each day with a written examination on the topics of the previous lecture, adding an occasional examination on all that has preceded, you will have the satisfaction of finding yourself at the end of your course, with a really instructed class.

Reading or listening, without something to fix the attention, is of little value, though I am far from saying of no value. It happens to a mere reader, as it does to most of us with regard to the facts that occur before our eyes: the pages of the book, and the daily occurrences, though not forgotten, are remembered in an indistinct and disorderly manner. Most Englishmen are something of politicians. Yet if you were to take the first hundred educated men you meet, and require them to name the different prime ministers England has had since the Reform Bill, with the year in which each has acceded to power, the principal measures of his administration, and the cause of his leaving office, you would probably not find one of the hundred examinees who could give satisfactory replies. Some motive is required to induce a man to make such an effort as will impress facts on the mind. The same singularity is observable as regards verbal memory: we do not without an effort remember the ordinary words we hear. A large number of persons listen to the church service at least once every week. Take a man of thirty who has heard it fifty times a year during twenty years of the most observant and impressible period of his life: offer him a thousand pounds if he will repeat the service word for word: you will be none the poorer for fulfilling your contract. Nay; offer a bishopric to a clergyman on the same condition; and though he may have read the service ten thousand times, he will not arrive at the *nolo episcopari.*

Shall we then burn our books? Not at all: not any more than we ought to give up reading our newspaper. Though we cannot pass an examination as to the political facts we have witnessed, we really know a great deal more about them than we know about those events of the Plantagenets which we can describe with perfect accuracy. We know a vast deal negatively: we cannot be seriously imposed upon. We are certain that Lord John Russell did not carry the Reform Bill by heading the train-bands of London, or by arming the Birmingham Political Union: that Lord Melbourne did not counsel his royal mistress to dispense with Parliament and levy ship-money: that Sir Robert Peel did not treacherously conspire with the Czar against the liberties of Turkey. So, as to the results of our reading: we are rendered quite safe from any outrageous hoax. No one will persuade us, unfit as we may be for examination, that Saint Louis lived in our time: that Henry the Fourth was a coward: that Louis XIV. was a rustic, Louis XV. an anchorite, or Louis XVI. a tyrant.

Owen's reading, therefore, had its value no doubt. But we need not wonder that its results were small, when we remember that it was carried on by a solitary student, with a mind ill prepared to receive new truths, with no definite aim proposed, with no one to examine him from time to time as to the progress he was making. He read, like other self-educated persons, under the greatest difficulties, and with the least advantage possible.

CHAPTER XXXII.

Owen a man of Ability—Why did he in the end sink so low?—Immaturity of mind—Comparison with Malthus—Excellent Qualities—Constancy, Earnestness, Industry (perhaps excessive), Munificence (though a careful man), Veracity, Placidity, Domestic Excellence, Temperance—But Want of Humility.

SUCCESS is no certain test of a man's powers; still less is success in many vocations, a test of a man's intellectual powers: yet Owen's success was such, that it would be an unreasonable scepticism which would dispute his claim to be regarded as a man of considerable intellectual power. Very early in life he conceived certain notions, true or false: he nursed them through his youth: he developed them in his manhood: in his middle life he introduced his offspring to the world. And what a sensation they caused when they appeared! Make what allowance you please for the clever management in their bringing out; for the quackery of spending thousands of pounds in feeing the newspapers: there must have been some strength of understanding in the self-taught man, who could stand boldly before the world and win an attentive hearing, from great politicians such as Bentham and Brougham; from great ministers such as Liverpool and Aberdeen; from great democrats such as Jefferson and Van Buren; from great princes such as the King of Prussia and the Duke of Kent. The man was a man in intellect, as any one may know by reading his Glasgow-Lancaster speech, or his *Essays on the Formation of Character.*

But how was it that having risen so high, he afterwards fell so low in the estimation of mankind? I reply that he wanted that due balance of mental powers which we commonly call judgment: that from the absence of early training, and of early association with instructed persons, he grew up without any ripeness of faculties. It seems at first sight, a matter of astonishment, that the same person should be distinguished in youth for his infidelity, and in his old age for his credulity: but to me it appears that the two things naturally followed each other, and that both sprang from the same root. We are not speaking here of a man who, like David Hume, was really, and in the proper sense, a sceptic: of one whose habit of mind was that of doubt and indecision; who after searching into his own microcosm, and examining the external world, failed to find a basis for faith to stand upon; and whose delight was in subtle and abstruse speculations. Owen had not arrived at infidelity either by a long groping among the facts of his own internal experience, or by continued observation of the world without, or by reading the arguments of refining thinkers before him. But while he was a mere child, he had found impressed upon him, the notion that all religions were equally false. This opinion he adopted without scruple: in mature age he did not think of reconsidering it: it went with him through life: and in his disbelief he died. This was not the course of a sceptical, hesitating, doubtful mind: it was not the course of a rational mind, which requires verification of all facts, and of all opinions positive or negative, and which refuses to hold the faith of others until a sufficient ground for belief has been shown. Owen's hasty adoption of *disbelief* of revelation, seems to me quite consistent with his unfounded credulity in old age as to the world of spirits. Rash disbelief and rash credulity, are fruits of the same ill-conditioned intellect.

The same deficiency of sound reasoning power, of judgment, of common sense, is apparent in his own view of what he accomplished in early and middle life. The world gave him credit for having successfully devoted himself to the improvement of the condition of the factory hands, and to the promotion of education; and he was congratulated on having accomplished his aims. You misunderstand me, was his answer. What I have done at Manchester and at New Lanark, I regard as experimental: as a means of testing the truth of my dogma, that man is the creature of circumstances. My aim is infinitely higher than you imagine. I am not contented with having benefited a particular class of people, and with having introduced a new and valuable element into education: my intention is to reconstruct the world. He might just as well have proposed, with the philosopher in *Rasselas*, to govern the winds. As Malthus, aiming to overthrow the French doctrine, popularized in this country by Godwin, of the indefinite perfectibility of humanity and of society, happened in his enthusiasm to stumble upon the theory of population, which, though exaggerated, had a substratum of truth; so Owen, bent upon revolutionizing society in accordance with his doctrine of circumstances, impressed upon the world a conviction of the importance of improving the condition of the manufacturing population, and of instructing poor children even in their infancy. Malthus and Owen both had aims which they failed to reach. But Malthus, a man of education and of solid sense, was willing to learn from his opponents, and to correct his errors. In his later editions he expunged certain fanatical passages, which had justly given offence to humane and thoughtful men; and was content in the maturity of age to temper the ebullitions of inexperience. Had Owen possessed the same sobriety of mind, he might have been equally prudent and equally fortunate: but his self-taught and ill-balanced understanding, was incapable of estimating the strength of the arguments urged against him, and even of learning the very obvious lessons deducible from his own unsuccessful exertions. For forty years he went on preaching the same discourse, in nearly the same words: and labouring, as occasion served, to try the same experiments after a desultory and unsatisfactory fashion. Gradually therefore, he fell in the estimation of men, as those who are continually unsuccessful always do fall: lower and lower still at each purposeless and ill-directed exertion.

And the ill qualities which weighed upon Owen and prevented his ultimate success, must have been considerable; since he had many excellent qualities which tended to help him onward.

He had a constancy of purpose which no disappointment could disturb. What man but he, would have persevered forty years in a uniformly unfortunate struggle to reconstruct society? Who would have crossed the Atlantic eight times, and recrossed it as many: not in the pursuit of gain, or science, or pleasure; but that he might somewhere found a community whose example should banish want and unhappiness from the world? Sanguine to the last, he still believed that the dawn of the millennium was at hand: not indeed the millennium of the Christian fanatic, but the reign of material prosperity, of peace and universal charity.

High were his expectations of the results which would follow from the adoption of his schemes. The conferences or congresses of advanced minds, which he invited to assemble, were of far greater moment than any œcumenical council, or any Long Parliament, or any Revolutionary Congress, or any Constituent Assembly, which the world ever saw. Such parliaments, congresses, assemblies, could only change the political condition of a people: but by means of his congresses the people themselves would be regenerated. His great fundamental truth which he burned to establish, " would ultimately confound the learned, arouse the population of the world from its dream of error, change the entire system of society from its foundation through all its ramifications, and make man a new being;

so that he shall appear to be born again, with a new
heart, a new mind, new spirit, new feelings, and new
conduct."

Such enthusiasm should have heralded success. But
this was only one of his qualifications: he had also
untiring industry, and unfailing activity. In youth,
when he undertook the management of Mr. Drinkwater's mill, in a state of entire ignorance of the duties
devolved upon him, he saved himself from disgrace by
being first in the morning, and last at night, of all who
entered and left. At a later period of life, while during
a large part of two days, he was a solitary prisoner,
awaiting the decision of Sturges Bourne's Committee
as to allowing him to be heard before them, he employed himself in his ordinary occupation of writing.
Still later, in his voyage to Mexico, in despite of storms
and stenches and the qualms of a land-lubber, he composed an elaborate series of propositions, intended to
stop the mouth of a theological antagonist; and constructed constitutions for the reformation of society. In
short he was always at work.

It is not clear to me however, that this industry is to
be regarded as altogether favourable to success. Louis
Philippe, it is said, never allowed himself to be unemployed. Madame de Genlis, I suppose, in her remarkable education of him, had strongly impressed on his
mind the maxim, that idleness is the parent of vice:
and so the old citizen-king would be folding paper into
envelopes, rather than sit unoccupied. Was this unremitting industry favourable to his character as a

monarch? Was the same habit in Owen conducive to his success as a reformer? I have watched the progress of unusually industrious men: some have attained prosperity; some have fallen into adverse circumstances: and I have not yet satisfied myself that the uncommon industry was chargeable with either fortune. There is no disputing the fact that industry is favourable to happiness: that it closes many avenues through which dark and doleful thoughts enter and disquiet the mind. The reflective man, who sits idly in his chair, or perambulates his room, or lies awake counting the hours, and pondering on the mysteries of nature or the hard problems of the world, lays himself open to the attacks of feverish and morbid thoughts; of regrets for hours mis-spent and friends that are gone; of anticipations of possible misfortune for himself and his kindred. Castles in the air are pretty toys for hopeful youth, but age paints them in dismal colours.

Yet granting that the industrious man is the happy man, it does not follow that his activity is favourable to greatness. He whose waking hours are fully employed, and whose wearied body enjoys at night unbroken rest, is at a great disadvantage in all pursuits which require meditation. For you cannot say, such an hour I will devote to reflection, and then I will think out the intellectual and moral problems which perplex me. The really valuable thoughts are those that come unbidden, and are welcomed and cherished whenever they appear. Tell them to call again when you are at leisure and you lose them for ever.

When Owen was waiting hour after hour, for the decision of Sturges Bourne's Committee, he was little disturbed, because he applied himself to his usual occupation: he wrote in a strange room instead of by his own fireside. If he had been less industrious, the unbroken solitude and the anxious expectation, would have annoyed and distressed him. But would not many wholesome thoughts have presented themselves? Would it not have occurred to him, that though he was a great manufacturer, he was profoundly ignorant of statesmanship? that the management of a village with two thousand persons, was a very different matter from the administration of an empire? that clear as his peculiar notions were to himself, they might after all be unfounded? that if bold men had lived before Agamemnon, great thinkers had lived before Robert Owen? Such thoughts must, I suppose, have knocked at the door; but with his busy fingers he closed the portals of his mind against them. If he had been less active and industrious, if he had allowed himself more time for reflection, he might have escaped much unnecessary toil and many bootless sacrifices.

I say that Owen had many qualities favourable to success; and among them I have ranked industry. To this I may add his disinterestedness in money matters, his liberality, his munificence. I need scarcely recapitulate examples: his magnificent donations of one-third of his little fortune, to Lancaster and Bell; his expenditure at New Lanark in times of distress, to supply the wants of the workpeople deprived of their wages; his noble subscriptions to every attempt at carrying out his schemes; his immense outlay at New Harmony; his payment of the losses incurred by the Equitable Labour Exchange, for which he was not liable in court of justice or court of honour; his ungrudging expense in journeys and publishing. One fact I have not yet mentioned. When he gave up the management of New Lanark, and devoted himself to the prosecution of his ill-considered communistic projects: fearing that he might be led into such sacrifices as would leave his family without any provision; he adopted the wise precaution of making a small settlement on each of his children: and after this he felt himself at liberty to devote all the remainder of his means to what he regarded as the good cause.* The result justified his providence. Before the close of his protracted life, all his property in this country at least, had disappeared; but his family took care that a 300*l.* a-year, gathered ostensibly, perhaps really, from the New Harmony Estate, should be sent over for his use: and so, living with a friendly family at Seven Oaks, with an attendant of that class called by barristers a clerk, he had the means of indulging his garrulity in print. Thus, the man who in manufacturing and commercial ability was the equal of the Arkwrights and Peels, who might have extended his business indefinitely and enjoyed a vast income, who might have died a millionnaire, and left his sons as the first Peel left his, prominent members of the landed aristocracy;—this

* *New Moral World,* i. 401.

man preferred, with his eyes wide open, to enter on a course which, as he foresaw, would not improbably leave him penniless. Such disinterestedness was worthy of success.

And it must be remembered that this unsparing expenditure was not the careless profusion of a spend-thrift, ignorant of the worth of money. Owen had earned his property by steady and long-continued application to business: he had shown himself a proficient in frugality; having from ten years old succeeded in making his income, however slender, sufficient for his wants. We may remember the lines of Taylor:

> " Only frugal men
> Are truly liberal: and for like cause
> Will he who husbands time, have time to spare."

When the busy man spares you his time, or the frugal man gives you his cash, you have no doubt of the sincerity of his devotion.

Another characteristic highly favourable to success, was Owen's truthfulness. The best proof that he was a veracious man, is the unvarying consistency of his writings. A liar would have been much more amusing, but the uniformity of Owen's publications, however tiresome it may be, at least commands our respect. I once had an acquaintance who told me an unimportant anecdote three times in one week, and with an increase of number and quantity on the second and third occasions, almost rivalling the rapid growth of Falstaff's men in buckram. How could I trust such a man, good-natured as he was? Who would have confided money or business to the jolly Falstaff? But Owen's veracity and uprightness invited trust.

Then again, there was his singular gentleness of temper : there was a world of advantage in that placidity of his. He was one whom a man of the world, and no disciple, might speak of as " dear Robert Owen." He won all hearts by his sweetness : he had a charity which it was hard to resist. He was apt to attribute his own forbearance to the force of his doctrine of circumstances : how could he be angry with persons whose character was formed for them and not by themselves? But he was mistaken in thus assigning it : for other men imbued with the same doctrine, were just as cross-grained as the rest of the world. No man of a savage and morose temper, would have ever invented a theory so condemnatory of his own vindictiveness. So cool was Owen's temper that it was said of him by an opponent, that in arguing with him, you could not put him in a passion nor keep yourself out of one : and it must be confessed that a placid antagonist is the most provoking of men. Sometimes however, he got angry with the public for its stupidity in not receiving his mission : but then came the thought that the people are what they have been made; and this recollection was an excuse for quieting himself and smoothing his ruffled feathers. When he was on his deathbed, he was asked by a clergyman, whether he did not regret having spent his life on fruitless efforts and unaccepted schemes. Owen would not confess any regret : nor would he blame the world for refusing to accept one who was in advance of his time. David Hume said that a cheerful disposition was better than an estate of ten thousand a-year. If Owen's happy temperament failed to accomplish success, it doubtless secured him a high degree of content.

Benjamin Franklin said that George the Third's domestic virtues saved him from the fate of the Stuarts. In England no doubt, we are slow to believe any ill of a man who marries early, lives on good terms with his wife, and brings up a numerous family. If this prepossession is exaggerated, it is at least well founded. Owen had the full advantage of it: for he was irreproachable in private life. His public career provoked a scrutiny into his moral character: his denunciation of religion inevitably raised a suspicion that goodness was distasteful to him: the grave instructors of the nation were justified in asking what was his conduct in his own neighbourhood: the great manufacturers, provoked by his labours to secure the interposition of the Government between them and their workmen, sent a deputation to New Lanark to collect scandal; but Owen came unscathed from the ordeal: his worst enemies could find nothing against him. In his great meeting at the Rotunda in Dublin, a Rev. Mr. Singer stood up to oppose his propositions; but he thought it necessary to commence his remarks by declaring his belief in Owen's private worth. Long afterwards, the Bishop of Exeter, in a speech against the Socialists, denouncing their doctrine as loathsome, and urging the Government to put the law in force against them, could yet find nothing worse to say of their old leader, than that he was a weak visionary. What an advantage had Owen as a popular leader, when compared with a gambler like Fox, a spendthrift like Sheridan, or a debauchee like Wilkes!

If the inquisitors who visited New Lanark, had penetrated into the interior of his family, they would have found nothing to serve their purpose. Those who knew Owen well, represent him as a man of strong domestic affections. From the little mention made of his wife, I conclude that her mental qualifications were not such as to give her much influence over her husband, though she was an amiable and kind-hearted woman. Owen during his many absences, wrote constantly to her. His strong anti-religious convictions, must have given her great pain: but, as we have already seen, he consulted her feelings and those of his neighbours, so far as to attend public worship: and in his own house he scrupulously abstained from such remarks about religion as could hurt the feelings of any one present.

After reading Owen's works, and in the absence of any private information, I might have suspected, that like many men of amiable temper and of popular manners, he had no great depth of sentiment. There is little trace of regret for lost friends; nothing of that bitterness of recollection which the venerable Franklin felt, when anything reminded him of a grandchild who had died; no allusions to any wounds of the heart which often disturb the life of prosperous men. Yet this perhaps, shows rather the absence of a morbid

temper, than the want of an affectionate disposition:
and I cannot for a moment allow it to weigh in the
scale against the direct testimony I have received. We
may remember too, that in old age, some of the first
spirits he called up from their repose, were those of his
parents.

Though Owen, in his publications which I have
read, makes few allusions to his wife, either while living
or after her death, he expatiates on the merits and
successes of his family.* He mentions that his eldest
son, Robert Dale Owen, after writing much that was
excellent, was twice elected a member of Congress, and
carried the bill for establishing the Smithsonian Institution in Washington; a measure that John Quincey
Adams and another, had attempted in vain:† that his
second son, David Dale Owen, was professor of chemistry, mineralogy, and geology; and had been employed by successive American governments as their
accredited geologist: that his third son, Major Richard
Owen, was professor in a Kentucky Military College, of
chemistry, mineralogy, German, Spanish, and French
(a plurality of profession more creditable to the omni-
science of the gallant major, than to the resources of
the college): and that his only daughter living in 1851,
was the widow of a distinguished American officer.
The eldest son, now the Hon. R. D. Owen, was at one
time unfortunately distinguished by his public expres-

* Robert Owen's *Journal*, i. 114, 115; and ii. 23, 45, 53, 54, 61, 121.
† Had he lived longer, he would have added that this son had since
become the United States Minister at Naples.

sions of bitterness against Great Britain. He was elected a member of the Convention in Indiana which sits once in twenty years to revise the State Constitution; and in this capacity carried a law giving to married women a right to property distinct from that of their husbands. The anti-religious sentiments, which he shared with his father, had created a strong feeling against him; but the ladies of Indiana, in consideration of his services on their behalf, consented to forget this dark shade on his reputation, and presented him with a testimonial of their gratitude. Owen sums up the matter in language common to parents happy at home, by saying that his children were such as few persons were blessed with.

One other cause of Owen's success as a young man, was his undeviating temperance, and careful manner of living. He himself attributed his self-denying habits to the accidental injury of his digestive powers in childhood: but I should regard this as the occasion rather than the cause of his sobriety. Other people, young and old, know that gluttony and intemperance hurt their health; that protracted dinners and heavy suppers, that strong ale and ardent spirits, give them headache and nausea, gout and gravel: yet they " resolve and re-resolve, then die the same." Their resolutions made in " all the magnanimity of thought," avail them nothing. Owen had great firmness and self-command: and in those days, a temperate foreman or manager, was a jewel of price: so that when the blushing youth could convince Mr. Drinkwater that he might rely on his never being guilty of drinking, he had won the employer's confidence.

One moral virtue however, I cannot assign to Owen: I cannot say that he was a humble-minded man. Franklin (whom I have mentioned several times because he too rose from the ranks, with a flight indeed higher than Owen's in proportion to the superiority of his mind)—Franklin pronounced himself greatly wanting in humility. At one time he kept a diary of his faults, and succeeded in correcting many of them; but when he seemed for a time to have checked his pride, he found himself proud of his humility. Franklin was at least conscious of his weakness: Owen was unconscious of his. He publicly talked of himself indeed, as an illiterate person, and wondered that men of rank and learning should condescend to listen to him: but behind the scenes he made faces at Oxford and Cambridge, and poured contempt on the ignorantly-learned. He believed that his own philosophy was of higher value a thousand times, than that taught during all ages, from Pythagoras to Hume: that Plato and Aristotle, More and Harrington, Helvétius and Godwin, were fools when compared to him in the science of society: that great men could not arise in the present order of things: and he whispered, pointing to himself, that if one great man had arisen, he must be regarded as belonging to the new order about to be established. Just as a backwoodsman despises the man who cannot hit a dollar at a hundred yards: as an Indian looks down with contempt on the white man who dwells in a house and cannot follow a trail; as the stagecoachman of old would hardly converse with a passenger who could not distinguish between a near-leader and an off-wheeler, a pole and a splinter-bar; so did Owen in the narrowness of his acquirements, contemn all those whom the world called well-informed and accomplished. Columbus was a great man, for he discovered a new world: but what was his feat compared with the invention of a new *moral* world?[*] Owen would unwillingly depreciate the merits of the distinguished Genoese; and yet he could not help seeing that the addition of an entirely new moral world, was of more importance to the knowledge and happiness of our race, than was the addition of a material hemisphere.

This excessive self-esteem, this undervaluing of other men, may have been the fault of the understanding rather than of the heart. Owen's acquirements, with all his reading, were very limited: his entire ignorance of the learned languages, and even of French, cutting him off from worlds of knowledge, with which all educated men have some acquaintance: and making it impossible for him to weigh the merit and advantages of other theorists. We most of us think slightingly, while we acknowledge in general terms the excellence, of pursuits which we have never shared. The mathematician is apt to regard the study of language as a trifling occupation, compared with his own manly and robust pursuit: the classical scholar denies to the

* *New Existence*, v. 14.

mathematician the character of an educated person:
the modern linguist acknowledges the importance of
Hebrew, but feels not the slightest sympathy with a
Tyrwhitt scholar, and will not read a new translation
of the book of Job. We have no community of feeling
with the professors of knowledge entirely foreign to us;
and I am willing to believe that Owen's apparent conceit is partly to be accounted for in this way.

Thus it was that Owen's narrowness of views and
ignorance of other men's greatness, obscured his judgment, and prevented him from reaping the reward due
to him, for his consistency and firmness of purpose,
his enthusiastic devotion to his schemes of regeneration,
his veracity, his domestic excellence, his unremitting
industry, and his grand munificence: qualities which
would have made men pardon even his irreligion, if
sound sense had sat at the helm of his vessel.

CHAPTER XXXIII.

Owen's Writings—No Literary Merit—His Glasgow Speech—Merits as a Speaker—As a Chairman—Political Notions—Love of Paternal Government—No Popularity Hunter—Excessive Self-esteem —Dissatisfaction of Friends—Praised by Malthus, Southey, and the *Quarterly*—Praises explained.

OWEN'S writings have no pretension to literary merit: they are merely the vehicle by which he brought before the world a certain set of opinions. It is surprising that so great a reader should have failed as he did, to appropriate and assimilate any of the thoughts of the authors he perused. You may go through his various books, and never be compelled to recollect that Shakspeare or Milton, Bacon or Hume, Butler or Paley, Jeremy Taylor or Chalmers, Pepys or Boswell, ever wrote. Part of this singularity may be explained by his statement, that even as a child he read poetry and romances, not for the pleasure they afforded him, but with the predominant desire to know how much truth they contained. From this want of literary allusion, and from the carelessness and bareness of [style, Owen's writings are singularly unreadable. Then as to wit or humour, grave irony or pungent satire, there is [none of this; but a dead level of dull repetition and ill-constructed sentences. He was like Mirabeau the elder, whose fancy and fun all deserted him the moment he began to write for publication.

The arrangement of the matter was latterly as bad as the style : and even in the beginning of his career as a public man, there was only one composition that I am acquainted with, which was thoroughly pithy and terse. I mean the speech delivered at Glasgow in honour of Joseph Lancaster, in 1812. As it occupies only a few pages, and as it contains the germ of Owen's opinions, I give it here as it was published in 1826 in the *New Harmony Gazette :* no doubt in an amended condition.

" GENTLEMEN,

" In rising to address you on this occasion, I feel how very inadequate I am to the task which I wish to perform. The situation is altogether new to me. I am unaccustomed to public speaking ; and nothing but a strong sense of duty, added to Mr. Lancaster's particular request, should have induced me to accept the chair. I beg therefore, to entreat the utmost stretch of your indulgence to what I shall attempt to say.

" The principal object of this meeting is, to promote the cause of giving a good and proper education to those who would otherwise receive a bad and improper one. By education I now mean, the instruction of all kinds which we receive from our earliest infancy, until our characters are generally fixed and established.

" It is however, necessary, that the *value* of this object should be considered, as well as the means of putting it into execution.

" Much has been said and written in relation to

education; but few persons are yet aware of its real importance in society: and certainly it has not acquired that prominent rank in our estimation which it deserves: for, when duly investigated, it will be found to be, *so far at least as depends on our operations*, the primary source of all the good and evil, misery and happiness, which exist in the world.

" In proof of which, let us in imagination, cast our eyes over the surface of the earth, and observe the different appearances bodily and mental, which the inhabitants of the various regions present.

" From whence do these general bodily and mental differences proceed? Are they inherent in our nature, or do they arise from the respective soils on which we are born?

" Evidently, from neither. They are wholly and solely the effects of that education which I have described. Man becomes a wild, ferocious, savage, a cannibal, or a highly civilized and benevolent being, according to the circumstances in which he may be placed from his birth.

" It is an important point then, for us to consider, whether we have any influence over these circumstances; if we can command any of them; and if we can, to what extent.

" Let us then suppose, that wishing to try the experiment, we were to convey a number of infants, so soon as they were born, from this country into distant regions, deliver them to the natives of those countries, and allow them to remain among them. Can we suppose the result to be uncertain? No; they would become one and all, like unto those natives, whatever their characters might be.

"In the same manner, were an exchange of any given number of children to be made at their birth, between the Society of Friends, of which our worthy guest, Joseph Lancaster, is a member, and the loose fraternity which inhabit St. Giles's in London, the children of the former would grow up like the members of the latter, prepared for every degree of crime, while those of the latter would become the same temperate, good, moral, characters as the former.

" If such were to be the consequences (and surely no one will doubt them), then we can materially command those circumstances which influence character; and if we proceed on this principle, keeping it steadily in view, much more may be yet accomplished for the improvement of society, than has hitherto been ever attempted.

" We now come to the immediate application of the principle.

" There are in this city and suburbs, many thousand children, who from their situation, must generally be trained to vicious habits and to poverty; unless you, gentlemen, and our fellow-citizens, step forth to prevent the evil.

" I do not hesitate to say, the remedy is now in your power. You possess the means, and I trust you will not withhold them.

" The object is no less, than to remove gross ignorance and extreme poverty, with their attendant misery, from your population; and to make it rational, well-disposed, and well-behaved.

" You may ask;—how have we the means now in our power? I reply, our friend here, Joseph Lancaster, has prepared them ready to our hands: his important improvements and discoveries in education, when properly applied, will enable us easily, cheaply, and effectually, to accomplish it.

" And it is on this ground, and this alone, we can effect a speedy and radical improvement in society; for until we begin with that class in the community from whence servants and operatives are usually obtained, it is in vain to expect correct habits and sentiments in any other class. It is from close and minute observations particularly directed to the subject, I state, that the characters of children in almost every family, are materially influenced through life by those with whom they early associate, and particularly by servants. These impress their sentiments and opinions upon the young mind at a time when an almost indelible impression is made, which is scarcely ever afterwards wholly effaced.

" Here is the radical evil; and our first object should be to destroy it.

" Give but a rational education, now easily to be accomplished, to all those in the lower walks of life, and the character of the whole community will rise many degrees; and while none can suffer by this measure, all must be essentially benefited.

" But this cannot be effected by individual exertion. It requires our collective force to accomplish it; and fortunately this will be found equal to its attainment.

" Let us then, take every means in our power, to interest all those who have any weight or influence in the city, to enter heartily into the support and extension of the Lancasterian system of education for the poor, until every child of that class shall find a place in one of the schools.

" There, in a manner peculiar to the system, they must learn the habits of obedience, order, regularity, industry, and constant attention; which are to them of more importance than merely learning to read, write, and account; although we all know and feel the advantages which these have given to each of us.

" By attaining this object, we shall secure the well-being of the rising generation, and we shall also secure much more.

" The schools which will contain the younger children in the daytime, will likewise serve for evening and Sunday schools; and at which times those who may be past the proper age for the first, and strangers who come among us, may be instructed.

" The consequences of such a combined system of discipline and education among the poorer classes, will be, as I have previously stated, most beneficial throughout the community; but unless it can be made general, a comparatively small part of the intended good will be attained.

" It will be almost in vain to well-educate the few, if

they are to spend the greater part of their time among the ignorant and the vicious many. The manners and habits of the latter will continually counteract our good intentions to the former.

" What I now recommend is no fanciful theory : it is easily reducible into practice. You now have, or with a little exertion you may have, all the funds which are necessary : there are individuals ready and willing to undertake the task of management : and I think I may engage, with your countenance and assistance, that the whole shall speedily be put into execution.

" But we must not longer lose sight of the primary cause of this meeting.

" Without our friend here, Joseph Lancaster—this extraordinary man, whom Providence seems to have created for this great and good purpose—all our attempts would have been useless. Indeed, such a work as the one under consideration, without his aid would have appeared so impracticable, that it would not have had a beginning.

" I therefore refrain from attempting to express to him our feelings, in words ; this I am sure would be impossible. His health we cannot drink—it would not be in unison with the tenets of the very respectable religious community of which he is a member : but I beg leave to propose that we offer him our sincere thanks and gratitude, by general acclamation."

This little essay, even in its corrected form, has some inaccuracies of expression ; and it contains the fallacy of first defining education to be, the instruction of all

kinds we receive from our earliest infancy, and afterwards asserting that a good education may be easily,
cheaply, and effectually given to all classes: thus con-
founding the training at home by parents and play-
fellows, with the instruction communicated at school.
There is no insuperable difficulty in furnishing school
instruction: but to amend and perfect the home training, must be the work of generations or centuries.
Notwithstanding these drawbacks, the composition is certainly a very good one, and creditable to the speaker
or writer. If all his publications had been as brief
and full of thought, they would have been read with
pleasure instead of fatigue.

Even his disciples confessed their master's defect of
manner. Mr. Holyoake says, " Mr. Owen's speeches
had vivacity and humour. His writings have little of
either. His best book, and the one that made his
reputation—his *Essays on the Formation of Character—*
Francis Place revised for him. Mr. Owen ought always
to have put his manuscripts into the hands of others.
He had noble thoughts, but when he took his pen in
hand, he fell into principle-spinning, which is always
duller reading than the Fifth Book of Euclid. It is
very true and very important, but it bores you. However, his life of himself—his last work, and most
interesting of all—contains more personal facts of
interest and importance, than any political biography
which has appeared in our time."

I have heard Owen called a heavy speaker: and no
doubt, his placid temper was ill adapted to the utterance

of fierce invective, and to call forth by the blaze of oratory, the thunders of the multitude. But the same impartial authority who condemns his written compositions, gives him credit for power as a speaker:—

"He had personally an air of natural nobility about him. He had, as the *Daily News* says, 'an instinct to rule and command.' I only knew him late in life, when age had impressed measure upon his steps and deliberateness on his speech. When he had the vivacity of youth and middle age, he must have been an actor on the political stage, of no mean mark. He always spoke 'as one having authority.' He had a voice of great compass, thorough self-possession, and becoming action. Like many other men, he spoke much better than he wrote. Only two or three years ago, at a private dinner, arranged that Mr. Joseph Barker might be introduced to him, there were several university men, and authors of some note, present. Mr. Owen's conversation was the most brilliant of all the company. The last occasion on which he presided in public was when he made the presentation of a purse to his faithful attendant, Mr. Rigby. The patrician manner in which he spoke of his old friend, the dignity without haughtiness, the kindness without condescension, I never saw equalled. It was a relic of the old manner, which I have seen alleged in romance, as the characteristic of the princely employer, but which I never witnessed before. The meeting was like a reception by Talleyrand."

That measured and deliberate manner which is here attributed to Owen's advanced age, was at all times, I imagine, characteristic of him. When he first entered into public life, he was accustomed to write his addresses and read them fairly out; as for instance, at the Rotunda in Dublin, he kept an impatient Irish assembly three hours, listening, while he read an essay to them: and at a much later period he would produce a written paper to a meeting, and read it, interspersing it however, with remarks that occurred to him at the moment.

The best speakers do not make the most effective chairmen: and there is no doubt that many brilliant orators were inferior to Owen in the management of a public meeting. I have before me an account,[*] written professedly by "A Stranger," of a meeting at the City of London Tavern; and it gives a good notion of Owen's mode of procedure.

When the writer entered, the large room was nearly filled, with a mixed assemblage of well-dressed people and of the working classes. As Owen was a little behind his time, a bitter opponent proposed that some one else should take the chair: but this motion was not carried. Owen soon appeared, and the same proposition was again made by the same person, but the meeting would not listen to him. Owen's rectitude of intention and suavity of manner prevailed.

Owen *read* a paper, explaining his views:—" Little of novelty, much of expansion—it was long, very long. I confess that towards the close, I endeavoured frequently to count the number of the still unperused pages

[*] *British Co-operator*, 29.

of his manuscript. Yet in this crowded meeting no
expression of impatience was perceptible. I have been
in Houses of Commons, of course the best educated
portion of the community: I have been in the chapels
of universities, of course the most learned and the most
religious: and if any member of the one continued to
speak, or of the other to preach, for two hours and a half,
on the details of a plan for bettering the condition of
their fellow-creatures, I know what would be the result. .   .   .   .

"The address at length terminated: but how? By
asking the meeting to adopt it? No such thing. Mr.
Owen called on them to petition Parliament, to inquire
into the principles and plans it developed, in order to
determine upon their practicability and expediency.
Hitherto all was quiet; but as soon as he had sat down,
the spirit which had been so long smouldering, burst out
in all its fury.

"Among those who wished to be heard, was the notorious Robert Taylor; but there was a great clamour
against him. Among the most energetic of the advocates
of the meek and humble religion of the Gospel, was one
lady—yes, I must call her so—who was placed a few
seats behind me. Those about her, remonstrated.
Speak to a Christian! Speak to a whirlwind. .   .   .
'Turn him out—that's the infidel Taylor—no, no, no, he
shall not speak—he must not speak—I'll not let him
speak. Turn him out—turn him out.'"

After this came the Radical Hunt, "standing on a
chair near the centre of the room, with head erect; his

short white hair mantling over his florid countenance, his coat thrown open, and his right hand fixed on his side, in the resolute attitude of determined self-possession. . . . He was old England personified, and his very figure spoke him to English hearts." . . . There was a great clamour, and Hunt was told to go up into the gallery. He would not go up, for he had made one attempt to do so, and had been turned down again. Mr. Owen apologized to him, explained the cause of the mistake, and requested him to go up. "No! I am not one of your puppets, to be moved up and down at your pleasure." Owen was as determined as Hunt, but more urbane. "Mr. Hunt, I do not hear well, and as I should be sorry to lose anything of what you say, whether it be for or against my propositions, you will oblige me by coming up." Who could resist such amiability? Hunt went up; and prefaced a radical speech by hearty praises of Owen. The result of all was that after a long meeting, Owen obtained pretty nearly what he wanted.

In the prosecution of his schemes, Owen, as we have seen, was always most desirous of securing the goodwill and assistance of the ruling powers. He sent copies of his publications to all civilized governments: he communicated his intention of holding meetings in London, to our administration: he carefully guarded himself against the suspicion of wishing to create popular disaffection: he went to Aix-la-Chapelle to try to influence the assembled sovereigns: he carefully got introduced to the great leaders of the United States, and to the

President of Mexico. And this conduct was quite in accordance with his political views, which looked to a paternal rather than a popular government: that is, to a power which would rapidly alter the external circumstances of a population, rather than to the people themselves, who, until those circumstances were altered, could hardly be brought to make any efforts for their own improvement.

Owen's friends said that he was no popularity-hunter; and when we remember his conduct in denouncing religion in 1817, we must concede that he rather sought martyrdom than popularity. He certainly had exalted notions of himself and his prophetic mission, and looked to posterity, rather than to his own generation, for a due appreciation of his merits.

He had many hearty disciples; men who regarded him as their prophet. But his excessive self-esteem gave offence to some of the leading co-operators; and the annoyance found occasional vent. Thus, in December, 1827, a rather bitter attack was made upon him in the organ of his own party.*

The writer, after praising his zeal, unshaken firmness, perseverance, and constancy, his placidity and gentleness of temper, his devotedness and munificence, proceeds with some harshness :—

"But every point of his theory, or everything which he connects with our system, and thinks necessary to it, we have not adopted; nor do we think every part of his practice the most judicious. Indeed, on the con-

* *Co-operative Mag.* ii. 533.

trary, some of his practice we imagine very prejudicial to the advancement of our system. We think his always setting himself up as the author, the Alpha and Omega of the system, when he could bring forward in support of it so many great names, looked up to by every eye as among the lights of the first magnitude and brilliancy of the mental firmament : his charging all mankind, past and present, without exception of any but himself and those who have caught up the rays of his irradiation, with being buried in the most gross ignorance, in Cimmerian darkness, when he has not put forth one notion or one idea which has not often been expressed and promulgated before him ; his never (at least of late) adducing any instance of the former existence of the system or any part of it, notwithstanding his continued assertion of his basing his plan on facts and experience, when he could readily have found many such instances ; his religio-phobia, when he could easily prove that the Christian religion most expressly commands, and most continually inculcates, as the first thing necessary, the practice of our system. . . . All these inconsistencies, we think, have raised up many obstacles to the cause which he so strenuously exerts himself to promote, and have much retarded its advancement."

It is not at all surprising to find jealousies and misunderstandings among friends ; and such a want of success as that which attended most of the co-operative schemes of Owen's followers, is the very thing to give rise to quarrels. Attacks like that I have quoted, would no doubt have been frequent, but for a long purse and unfailing liberality.

We are more startled on reading the praises given in unexpected quarters. Malthus spoke with great respect of Owen; but this was in the early part of the career of the great communist, and had reference to his efforts in favour of factory children. The *Quarterly Review*,[*] however, long afterwards, had an article exhibiting a strong leaning to communistic experiments. Southey, in more than one place, spoke out decidedly in favour of Owen. Thus, in his *Colloquies*, he says:—

" If I were his countryman, I would class him in a triad as one of the three men who have in this generation given an impulse to the moral world. Clarkson and Dr. Bell are the other two. They have seen the first-fruits of their harvest. So, I think, would Owen ere this, if he had not alarmed the better part of the nation, by proclaiming on the most momentous of all subjects, opinions which are alike fatal to individual happiness and to the general good. Yet I admire the man; and readily admit that his charity is a better plank than the faith of an intolerant and bitter-minded bigot, who, as Warburton says, *counterworks* his Creator, makes God after man's image, and chooses the worst model he can find—himself."

And again, Southey makes Sir Thomas More ask:—

" But why do you think that the Owenite scheme is likely to be carried into effect by sectarian agency?"— " Because a degree of generous and virtuous excite-

* No. 82.

ment is required for overcoming the first difficulties, which nothing but a religious feeling can call forth. With all Owen's efforts . . . . he has not been able in ten years to raise funds for his experiments. Had he connected his scheme with any system of belief, though it had been as visionary as Swedenborgism, as fabulous as Popery, the money would have been forthcoming."

A little reflection shows why it was that men of the Tory party sympathized with Owen. He was not a Whig; he was not a Democrat; he was not a Political Economist. He was a loyal subject, the friend of system and order, bent on inducing the Government to undertake the employment and maintenance of the people: he was censured by the Radicals, as desiring to reduce the working classes to a state of serfdom or slavery: he denounced machinery as being, under actual social institutions, the labouring man's worst enemy: he hated the political economists, as men without sympathy or compassion. Therefore did Southey and the *Quarterly Review* more than half forgive his irreligion, and positively applaud his schemes.

Thus, notwithstanding a want of literary excellence, and a feebleness of oratorical power, his earnestness, his sincerity, and his suavity, gave him great influence as a public man; while he was not wanting in friends even among that Tory party to which the name of Socialist has since become abhorrent.

CHAPTER XXXIV.

Owen's Philosophy — Nature of Truth — Freewill — Rewards and Punishments condemned—Argument from Induction—Whence comes the Will?—Attempt at Refutation—Opinions on Marriage —Socialistic Error in disallowing the Claims of Capital—Machinery—Population—What Owen might have accomplished— Conclusion.

OF Owen's philosophy it is unnecessary to say much. If singularity be a merit, then is that philosophy deserving of study.

His first dogma he invented when he was a mere child, and his mature understanding held it fast. Truth, he said, is that which is always consistent with itself and with all facts, known or to be known. This, taken in one sense, is a mere truism: but if as I suppose, it was meant as a *practical test* of truth, the dogma is absurd; since a man must spend his life in running about after facts, before he can be sure that the opinions he holds are consistent with all known facts, to say nothing of those that are unknown. And as to truth being consistent with itself, no doubt absolute truth is so: but with regard to that approximation to truth with which our defective powers are forced to remain content, it is impossible to say that it is consistent with itself. The great difficulty a reflective mind has to contend with is, that by intuition, or else by an effort of the understanding, it arrives at a certain belief: by another similar process it arrives at another belief: and these two beliefs, though not directly in opposition to each other, are quite inconsistent. Whatever may be your philosophy, you must be content with imperfection. The only resource is to say that to arrive at absolute truth is impossible.

But Owen was no sceptic in philosophy: he believed that truth was to be found, and that he had found it. Another of his immature opinions, to which he afterwards adhered, had reference to the topic of free-will and moral necessity. He said without circumlocution or qualification, that the character of man is formed *for* him and *not by* himself:* that " as are the natural qualities of each one at birth, and as are the surroundings in which he is placed, so will the individual be."

In his system therefore, moral responsibility had no place: if men did wrong, it was because they were irresistibly impelled to it by " nature and surroundings : " punishment was unjust and inexpedient. If a man brutally attacked his wife, and nearly killed her, she was much to be pitied no doubt, for she was the victim of circumstances: but he also was an object of profound compassion, for nature and surroundings, and not himself, had made him what he was, and being what he was, he could not act otherwise than he did act. To punish such a man, to hang him if his wife died, was as absurd as it was inexpedient: the only suitable treat-

* *New Existence,* v. 6.   *Life,* I. xiii. xv.

ment was to put him into a reformatory: a moral hospital.

Praise and reward for good actions, were equally misplaced. Owen himself did many noble things: he spent great sums of money on education; he devoted years and a large share of property, to improving the condition of work-people: but he had no merit in these actions: nature and surroundings had made him what he was; he was irresistibly impelled to do the good he had accomplished.

A man of a wider view, or of a more timid character, than Owen's, would have shrunk from the consequences of this doctrine; and would have dreaded its application to practice. He would have stood aghast at the inference, that the sepoy traitor and murderer was as much to be pitied as the English officer he assassinated: that Napoleon was as much to be pitied as the Duc d'Enghien whom he shot in defiance of law: that the brutal Thurtell was as much to be pitied as his victim Weare: that Rush was as much to be pitied as Mr. Jermy: that Paul and Strahan were as much to be pitied as those whose money they misapplied. But Owen shrank from no consequences. He might have said that punishment was expedient, though it was not called for by justice; exactly as it was formerly maintained by high authority, that it is sometimes expedient to punish a madman, whose deranged faculties are incapable of distinguishing right from wrong. But Owen said no such thing: he was content to say that rewards and punishments ought to be abolished.

It would seem a reasonable inference from the doctrine of moral necessity, that there is no such thing as
right or wrong; and that all actions, like events, are
merely fortunate or unfortunate. To be born to rank
or riches is not right or wrong; it is good fortune: to
enjoy robust health is not right or wrong; it is good
fortune. In the same way, as it seems to me, Owen
should have said that a man whose nature was so excellent, and whose surroundings were so happy, as to
make him kind, benevolent, public-spirited, was simply
a fortunate man; and no more entitled to the distinction
of moral goodness than the man of rank or riches was.
Owen however, did not say this: he talked of right
and wrong in the same sense in which those words are
used by other men: he made the same distinction which
we make, between right and fortunate, between wrong
and unfortunate. Though he denounced rewards and
punishments, he himself sometimes praised, and often
blamed, his fellow-men.

The common sense, the general consent, of mankind,
is undoubtedly against Owen's doctrine: on what ground
then, did he rest it? He did not often trouble himself
to explain this: and as, after once adopting an opinion,
it did not occur to him to doubt it, he was not naturally
led to weigh anything adduced against it, or to seek
new arguments in its favour. But I imagine that he
relied principally on the facts brought forward in his
Glasgow speech, though he did not there venture to
draw the inference of moral irresponsibility.

"Let us suppose that . . . we were to convey a

number of infants ... from this country into distant regions, deliver them to the natives of those countries, and allow them to remain among them. Can we suppose the result to be uncertain? No: they would become, one and all, like unto those natives, whatever their character might be.

"In the same manner, were an exchange of any given number of children to be made at their birth, between the Society of Friends, ... and the loose fraternity which inhabit St. Giles's in London, the children of the former would grow up like the members of the latter, prepared for every degree of crime, while those of the latter would become the same temperate, good, moral characters as the former."

This argument is specious. The Red Indian scalps his enemy, or kills him with exquisite tortures: the civilized Roman put his slaves to the question without remorse, and after leading a captured prince in open triumph, thrust him down into a dungeon to die of cold and hunger: the Englishman of to-day, sets his captives free when a war is over, and demands no ransom; he has no slaves whom he can torture; and to exhibit even a private soldier of the enemy for the multitude to triumph over, would be an outrage disgustful to his nature. Yet which of us can doubt, that if he had been born and brought up among the Indians, he would have tortured his enemy? and that if he had been born an ancient Roman, he would have been as obdurate and cruel as his countrymen? Our superiority, then, is the result of circumstances, and is not

28

any merit of ours: it is nature and circumstances, not
our own will, which have made us what we are.

This reasoning, I say, is plausible. My reply to it
is, that though it is true as far as it goes, it is not the
whole truth. It would be absurd, no doubt, for an
Englishman to claim any credit to himself, for being
better than a Red Indian or than an ancient Roman.
But would it be absurd in you or me, to say; I am
better than Thurtell, or Rush, or Paul, or Strahan;
and I feel that part of my superiority is owing to my
exertion of resolution in resisting temptation? The
self-gratulation of the Pharisee is disgusting; but a
man need not therefore, rush into the opposite extreme
of entirely overlooking his successful struggles with
evil.

Owen's fallacy consists in treating of men by classes
instead of by individuals. The Romans generally were
severe and harsh in their manners; the modern Euro-
peans are generally mild in their manners: yet the
individual European has no right to boast over the
individual Roman. But comparing one Roman with
another, there was a great difference in character.
Cato, Cicero, Catiline, Clodius, were all cruel slave-
masters: but shall we put on the same level, the stoical
virtue of Cato and the unruly ambition of Catiline; the
vulgar debauchery of Clodius and the refined patriotism
of Cicero? So it is true. that Quaker children if
brought up in the squalor of St. Giles's, would be as
dissolute as the natives of that locality: but it is a great
mistake to suppose that one individual of St. Giles's is

not better than another. Nay, we must go farther, and remember that St. Giles's contains many honest people, while the Society of Quakers includes some reprobates. It would be an abominable injustice to imagine that the St. Giles's people generally, are half as bad as the returned convict and cold-blooded murderer, Tawell. While then, it is true that the great moral features of a particular class are determined by external circumstances, it is equally true that there is a great variety in the individuals composing that class : and I am convinced that to a considerable extent each person determines by the acts of his own will, whether he is better or worse than his neighbours.

The argument by induction therefore fails : for while we grant that comparing one community with another, the aggregate moral character will be principally determined by circumstances, we must also see that the moral character of individuals of those communities, is greatly determined by the will of each. But there is another argument, of a more abstruse character, which weighs much with reflective persons.

Granting, it is said, that I can, within certain limits, become what I please; learned or ignorant, temperate or dissolute, benevolent or malignant: granting that by the force of my will I can control myself or even urge myself forward: whence comes my will? how did I come possessed of it? what was it that made my will strong and yours weak? Whether we regard the will as a separate faculty; or whether we say with Hobbes,*

* Hobbes's *Works*, iii. 48.

28—2

that "in deliberation, the last appetite, or aversion, immediately adhering to the action, or to the omission thereof, is what we call the will; the act, not the faculty of willing;"—whatever definition we adopt, it is certain that we no more created our own will than we created our own bodily appetites or our own intellectual powers. Every event, every phenomenon, has a cause; and the will is no exception to the rule.

It is a sufficient answer to this reasoning, to appeal to the universal consent of mankind. In all ages, by all people, by the practice of those even who theoretically deny it, the freedom of man's will, the responsibility of man for his actions, the distinction between moral wrong and misfortune, the justice of rewards and punishments, are explicitly or tacitly acknowledged. These sentiments are found imbedded in every language; and those who adopt the necessitarian creed ought to form a language of their own.

But I will go a step further: I will ask my opponent; how do you know that every event, every phenomenon, has a cause? He will answer, that he is irresistibly led to this opinion: that the belief in causality is one of the first principles of the mind: that to assume the existence of anything uncaused, is just as much a contradiction as to believe that two and two make three. The savage who does not know the word philosophy, the child who cannot utter a syllable, believe that every phenomenon has a cause.

The latter part of this statement is, I think, a misrepresentation. Neither the savage, nor the child, ever forms the proposition mentioned. Both of them indeed, seeing anything happen, are irresistibly impelled to believe that some other thing, or some person, has caused the change they witness. But they are far from the maxim expressing the universality of causation.

Whether however, this be so or not, it seems to me that the freedom of the will rests on precisely the same ground with that causation by which you endeavour to prove its non-existence. We are irresistibly led to a belief in causation: we are irresistibly led to a belief in the freedom of the will: argue as we may we cannot help believing in both. You may say that the two are inconsistent with each other; and if you are a follower of Owen you may contend that this inconsistency is a proof that one of the beliefs is false, since truth is consistent with itself: but I who am no follower of Owen, am not bound by his dogma, and I maintain that with our limited faculties and imperfect knowledge, we cannot reconcile propositions which nevertheless, we know to be true.

I conclude by recalling to mind that this controversy illustrates as clearly as possible, Coleridge's favourite German distinction between the *reason* and the *understanding* : that is between truths supplied immediately by the *reason*, and truths attained by an act of *reasoning*. The truth, that the will is free, we derive at once from our reason: the alleged truth, that the will is not free, is derived from a chain of reasoning. But no chain of reasoning, no act of the understanding, can nullify a truth derived immediately from our reason. Not a hundred Owens, not a generation of metaphysicians of a thousand times Owen's power, will ever persuade the world that the will is not free.

Rash, ill-founded, absurd, as was Owen's philosophy, I cannot deny that there was much valuable truth involved in it: that the outside offensive husk contained a sweet and wholesome kernel. It is true, as Owen said, that the average character of classes of men is formed by the circumstances under which they are placed: that Quaker children distributed among the rookeries of St. Giles's will produce as many drunkards and thieves as if they had been born in the locality; that St. Giles's children adopted by Quakers, will produce as many dull, sober, demure, money-getting, citizens, as if they had sucked a Quaker breast: and the earnestness and perseverance with which this truth was urged upon all classes, produced no doubt a considerable effect. The mildness of our recent criminal laws, the institution of reformatories, the anxiety of our day to promote education, the desire to prevent crime rather than to punish it, are all of them fruits of this doctrine, so early and so laboriously insisted on by Owen.

As to the particular social reforms he proposed, it is unnecessary to say much more, because they have already been mentioned in his history. But there is one subject on which he was misunderstood or misrepresented; and with reference to which he was supposed to hold opinions, more universally offensive perhaps, than even his ravings against religion. It was said that he was an enemy to marriage and a favourer of promiscuous intercourse between the sexes. No charge could be more false.

There have been communists, and even of a recent date, who have confessed it impossible to carry out their schemes, so long as the institution of marriage subsisted: because, as they have felt, men and women who have children unquestionably their own, will necessarily prefer the welfare of their offspring to that of their community. They have declared therefore, however unwillingly, that marriage must be done away with. Ordinary people would come to a different conclusion; that communism is impossible: but these theorists prefer the sensuous advantages of communism, before the purifying and ennobling development of the affections attending on the family relation.

Owen however, had no sympathy with this fanaticism. His object was not to abolish marriage but to improve it, and render it a more effective means of promoting happiness and virtue. Yet his friends must confess that he had himself partly to blame for the odium he earned. He delivered a course of lectures in 1835, and published them under the title, *Marriages of (by) the Priesthood of the Old Immoral World.* People who saw the advertisement and nothing more, and who perceived that religion and marriage were mixed up together for censure, would run away with the notion, that as Owen was known to be an enemy to all religion, he was equally an enemy to the institution of marriage.

They would have been surprised to find that he demanded less than Milton and Luther would have granted him: that his aim was by no means " to lessen conjugal fidelity, or the permanence of marriage," but " to promote to the greatest possible extent, true purity, delicacy, virtue, and happiness, now most lamentably deficient, through the false notions of society on these subjects, and the vicious customs and institutions which have emanated from these notions."

But I will come to particulars. The first thing Owen objected to, was the compelling people to submit to a religious ceremony, in marriage: and the late Act of Parliament, legalizing the civil contract without any accompanying religious ceremony, was all he so far required.* What remained was of higher importance. He desired to see another law, " by which *divorces*, under wise arrangements, and on principles of common sense, may be obtained, equally for the poor as well as the rich," &c. The recent Divorce Act would have been some answer to this requirement: and it is only wonderful that we should have gone on so long denying to poverty what we granted to wealth.

Owen however, would have proceeded further than we have proceeded at present; further probably, than we are ever likely to go: he would have granted divorce for incompatibility; but he would have carefully guarded this arrangement, so as to prevent its being an encouragement to whim and levity. His manifesto † clearly sets out the regulations he would have adopted.

1st. If both parties desire a separation, a year after

* Manifesto, 1840, p. 6.   † Ibid. 56, 57

marriage, and not sooner, they must make a public declaration to this effect, and then live together six months longer; after which they may separate if they please.

2nd. If only one of the parties desire a separation, a year would be required to pass after a declaration to that effect, before the separation could be effected.

Such arrangements might be wise or foolish; but they certainly would be far from allowing that promiscuous mode of living supposed to be desired by communists. It must be remembered also, that these regulations were proposed for a state of society, in which the children of all would be cared for to a great extent by the community, after a Spartan fashion: an arrangement which would considerably reduce one great difficulty in divorces.

I do not think it necessary to state my reasons for condemning Owen's socialistic and communistic opinions: his desire to supersede the relation of capitalist and employer, and to arrange the world in communities instead of in families. These matters have been sufficiently discussed by a thousand authors; and in a late volume on *Social Innovators*, I expressed my sentiments at some length. The leading fallacy of Owen, as of all Socialists, is an exaggeration of the claims of the labourer, and a disregard of the claims of the capitalist. " It is a very common mistake, arising from the confusion of ideas inseparable from the present erroneous system of society, to believe that the rich provide for the poor and working classes; while, in fact, the poor and working classes create all the wealth which the rich possess." This sentence attributes all property to labour, overlooking the fact that though it is labour which originally produces, it is frugality which saves : that capital being the result of self-denial, justly confers on its possessor a right to that income which we call interest: and that it is for the advantage of society that the capitalist should be rewarded, since otherwise capital would cease to be accumulated, and society would become impoverished by a profuse and wasteful expenditure. It is worth noticing that Owen demanded a subscription of three quarters of a million sterling, to enable him to try a communistic village experiment ; and that he attributed his want of success, to the parsimony of the world which would not entrust him with such a sum. But if the social salvation of the world depended on the use of such large amounts of capital, what shall we say of the wisdom of the man, who would have denied to the frugality of those who must accumulate it, that reward which they now reap from their self-denial ?

Another of Owen's favourite fallacies was the vulgar one, that machinery supersedes labour and causes distress. That it does so in particular cases and for a time, no one will dispute : but no proposition can be plainer, none more clearly demonstrated, than the assertion that in the long run no labour is superseded by machinery, and that the working classes, considered as consumers, are benefited by all new means of cheapening the commodities they purchase.

But the grand error, as it seems to me, which Owen committed, was his entire neglect of the population question. I am myself no ardent admirer of the Malthusian doctrine: I am convinced that its author grossly exaggerated the difficulty of keeping the population down to the means of subsistence: I see clearly that he gave to vice and misery far too important a part to play on the stage of the world: I have no doubt that a well-trained labouring population will effectually keep down their numbers to the level required, just as the middle classes do now, without any necessity for vice, and without the help of misery.

But how is this to be done? By folding the hands and trusting to nature? No: but by the exertion of a vigorous resolution not to marry until there is a reasonable prospect of being able to support a family. This it is which enables the educated classes to hold their own: to keep themselves from sinking into the ranks of the destitute: to bring up their families in the same position which they themselves occupy. Remove this individual responsibility: let all the children of a society be the charge of all the members; and what is to restrain youths and maidens from marrying as soon as the inclination to do so is felt? Why should young persons deprive themselves of the sweets of virtuous love, of the comforts of a home, of the happiness of wedded life, if they have nothing to fear for the offspring that may result?

Owen was a mature man when Malthus began to write: when Dr. Price and others maintained that *depopulation* was the thing to be dreaded. It is strange that the controversy should have made so little impression on a social reformer. Malthus's aim was to show that Godwin's schemes of social regeneration were impossible; because as soon as you improve the condition of a society, there follows a rapid increase of population that can only be thinned down again by a resort to vice and misery. In this point of view Malthus's attempt may be pronounced a failure; since it is now pretty clear that vice and misery are not indispensable to an adjustment of population and subsistence. But if Malthus had written later, and had attacked Owen with his communist friends, instead of Godwin, he might have gained a cheap victory; by showing that moral restraint, which is the panacea for over-population, was exactly the thing incompatible with communism.

It is a most unfair proceeding to depreciate a man's achievements by dwelling on other things which he might have accomplished: yet it is impossible to help regretting the course which Owen pursued during the latter half of his life: for if he had persevered in his early career, and devoted himself to practicable schemes of social improvement, what might he not have accomplished! Had he abstained from wounding those religious sensibilities, which, though he did not share them, he ought to have respected: had he been content to learn by experience, that schemes of communism were so abhorrent to the spirit of the age as to be quite impracticable: had he directed his efforts to the further improvement of factories, to the extension of education, to the amendment of prison discipline, to the establishment of reformatories; to all those practical measures that spring naturally from the " doctrine of circumstances " which he preached :—had he done all this, his activity, his earnestness, his munificence, might have anticipated by twenty years the social progress we are now making.

If however, he failed to do all that was possible in his long life, yet he did far more than is accomplished by most even of those whom we regard as public benefactors. I say nothing of the men who are well satisfied with themselves, if they devote their lives to pursuing their vocation, and honestly earning a fortune for their children; and who account themselves excellent citizens because they pay their debts, and allow an occasional guinea to be extorted from them by importunity, for the maintenance of hospital or school.   Such vulgar-minded persons may hug themselves if they please, in the idea that Owen, and such as he, are objects of contempt.   Compare Owen with a higher class of men: with those who sincerely desire to benefit their kind; who volunteer their money for forwarding good works; who exhibit a real interest in the improvements going on, and set apart many of their leisure hours for promoting them: Owen did far more than these.   In early life he munificently backed the novel efforts of Bell and Lancaster: in middle life he originated important schemes of improvement, and laboured zealously to carry them out: in later life he devoted all his time, and spent a large fortune, in sincere though mistaken efforts to regenerate society.

On the whole, though I have an unpleasant remembrance of the monotonous toil of wading through Owen's tedious publications; though I sincerely vex myself when I think of the power wasted in one half of his long life; though I regret the narrowness of his mental vision, and the mistaken desire for martyrdom which urged him to deeply wound those sentiments of men, which ought to have commanded his undying respect; though I have no admiration for his very shallow philosophy, no sympathy with his crude and mischievous schemes of social innovation; I yet feel loth to part with a genial old companion: and if I cannot pronounce him a great man, I must allow his claim to be regarded as great among self-educated men.

THE END.

Printed by SMITH, ELDER & Co., Little Green Arbour Court, Old Bailey, E. C.

By the same Author.

SOCIAL INNOVATORS AND THEIR SCHEMES.

By WILLIAM LUCAS SARGANT,

Author of "The Science of Social Opulence."

Post Octavo.   Price 10s. 6d. cloth.

———————

"By exposing gigantic failures in the attempt to reorganize society, Mr. Sargant has provided a warning for enthusiastic speculators, and, by pointing out the causes of non-success, has offered encouragement to the steady and sensible reformer.   To illustrate his subject, the author has reviewed the political doctrines and career of St. Simon, Fourier, Louis Blanc, Proudhon, and Emile de Girardin, sifting carefully their various theories.   His objections to the principles laid down by these social 'innovators' are candidly stated ; and in no instance does Mr. Sargant shrink from denouncing the impolicy of the schemes, the utter impracticability of which experience has tested."—*Daily Telegraph.*

"It has the merit of going deep into the subject-matter at one of its most vital points, and it is the merit which constitutes the special value of Mr. Sargant's book.   His views are sensible and sound. They are brought forward clearly and dispassionately, with great vigour and telling illustrations.   His exposition of the various theories reviewed is executed impartially, agreeably, and with remarkable tolerance."—*Press.*

" A more judicious and valuable book than this has not been given to the public for many years.   We doubt not that its effects upon social speculators will be both powerful and permanent. . . . . Mr. Sargant writes with a calmness and moderation which gives additional force to his reasoning."—*Illustrated News of the World.*

"Mr. Sargant's work is excellent. What he seems to have arrived at, is a practical vindication of property as represented by capitalists, and of competition as a principle of industry and trade."—*Athenæum.*

"Mr. Sargant has done good service in putting upon record some of the vagaries of the pseudo-economists of the last twenty years. . . . . Mr. Sargant's views are sound and moderate on this important question."—*Guardian.*

"Mr. Sargant's style is clear and agreeable, and the reader may say that he has for once read a volume of political economy without complaining of the prolixity of the author."—*Morning Post.*

"As a text-book, Mr. Sargant's volume will take high rank, and form a valuable addition to the library of the political economist."—*Morning Chronicle.*

"Mr. Sargant has written a very useful sketch. . . . . His book is impartial, pleasantly written, and excellently arranged."—*Saturday Review.*

"Mr. Sargant has done good service in the publication of this volume."—*British Quarterly Review.*

"The whole work is stamped with the mint mark of good sense industry, and ability."—*Leader.*

LONDON: SMITH, ELDER AND CO., 65, CORNHILL.

CPSIA information can be obtained at www.ICGtesting.com
Printed in the USA
LVOW03s1913311014

411466LV00016B/508/P